Hollywood Ambitions

Wesleyan Film

A series from Wesleyan University Press
Edited by Jeanine Basinger

The new Wesleyan Film series takes a back-to-basics approach to the art of cinema. Books in the series will deal with the formal, the historical, and the cultural—putting a premium on visual analysis, close readings, and an understanding of the history of Hollywood and international cinema, both artistically and industrially. The volumes will be rigorous, critical, and accessible both to academics and to lay readers with a serious interest in film.

Series editor Jeanine Basinger, Corwin-Fuller Professor of Film Studies at Wesleyan University and Founder/Curator of the Wesleyan Cinema Archives, is the author of such landmark books as *The World War II Combat Film: Anatomy of a Genre*, *A Woman's View: How Hollywood Spoke to Women, 1930–1960*, and *Silent Stars*.

Anthony Mann
by Jeanine Basinger

The Films of Samuel Fuller:
If You Die, I'll Kill You!
by Lisa Dombrowski

Physical Evidence:
Selected Film Criticism
by Kent Jones

Action Speaks Louder:
Violence, Spectacle, and the American Action Movie
Revised and Expanded Edition
by Eric Lichtenfeld

Hollywood Ambitions:
Celebrity in the Movie Age
by Marsha Orgeron

Hollywood Ambitions

CELEBRITY IN THE MOVIE AGE

Marsha Orgeron

Wesleyan University Press | Middletown, Connecticut

Published by Wesleyan University Press, Middletown, CT 06459

© 2008 by Marsha Orgeron

All rights reserved

Printed in the United States of America

5 4 3 2 1

A version of chapter three was first published as "Rethinking Authorship: Jack London and the Motion Picture Industry" in *American Literature* 75, no. 1 (March 2003): 91–117. Copyright ©2003 by Duke University Press. A version of chapter four was first published as "Making *It* in Hollywood: Clara Bow, Fandom, and Consumer Culture," by Marsha Orgeron, from *Cinema Journal* 42:4, pp. 75–97. Copyright ©2003 by the University of Texas Press. All rights reserved.

Library of Congress Cataloging-in-Publication Data

Orgeron, Marsha.
Hollywood ambitions : celebrity in the movie age / by Marsha Orgeron.
   p. cm. — (Wesleyan film)
Includes bibliographical references and index.
ISBN-13: 978-0-8195-6864-9 (cloth : alk. paper)
ISBN-10: 0-8195-6864-3 (cloth : alk. paper)
ISBN-13: 978-0-8195-6865-6 (pbk. : alk. paper)
ISBN-10: 0-8195-6865-1 (pbk. : alk. paper)
  1. Motion pictures—United States—History. 2. Fame—Social aspects—United States. I. Title.
PN1993.5.U65O74   2008
302.23'4308621—dc22   2007037134

Contents

	List of Illustrations	vii
	Acknowledgments	ix
Introduction	Hollywood Ambitions	1
One	Celebrity in the Movie Age	17
Two	When the West Was Done: Wyatt Earp in Hollywood	31
Three	Rethinking Authorship in Jack London's Hollywood	63
Four	Making *It* in Hollywood: Clara Bow and the Cycle of the Fan Magazine	99
Five	"If We Are Ever to Be in Hollywood": Gertrude Stein's Moving Images	136
Six	Redirecting Reputation: Ida Lupino's Hollywood Fictions	170
Epilogue	Alternative Systems: Celebrity after Hollywood	204
	Notes	209
	Bibliography	241
	Index	255

Illustrations

1. Fox advertisement, *Picture-Play Magazine*, November 1919. — 24
2. William S. Hart featured in *Motion Picture Classic*, March 1916. — 51
3. Wyatt Earp photograph autographed to William S. Hart. — 59
4. Cartoon of Jack London "snapshotting" himself. — 71
5. Advertising brochure for Hobart Bosworth's *John Barleycorn* (1914) featuring Jack London. — 76
6. Jack London's image and signature in the preface to Bosworth's *Martin Eden* (1914). — 80
7. The first intertitle in Bosworth's *Martin Eden* (1914). — 81
8. Jack London "at work" in the moving image preface to *Martin Eden* (1914). — 82
9. Jack London looks at the audience in the moving image preface to *Martin Eden* (1914). — 82
10. A close-up of a posing Jack London in the moving image preface to *Martin Eden* (1914). — 83
11. Clara Bow on the cover of *Photoplay*, February 1928. — 103
12. Brewster Publications 1921 "Fame and Fortune Contest" advertisement, *Motion Picture*, January 1921. — 105
13. Contest-era, pre-star Clara Bow reproduced in *Photoplay*, February 1928. — 107
14. One of the opening shots of *It* (1927). — 113
15. Betty Lou (Clara Bow) in a lingerie-selling pose, *It* (1927). — 114
16. Betty Lou and the other salesgirls gazing at the "new boss" in *It* (1927). — 116
17. Poster image from *It* press kit. — 117
18. Betty Lou gazing at a Waltham's advertisement, *It* (1927). — 121
19. Betty Lou and Cyrus Waltham on the Social Mixer, *It* (1927). — 122
20. Betty Lou and Cyrus Waltham embrace at the end of *It* (1927). — 124

21. Cartoon of Clara Bow leaving Paramount, *The New Movie Magazine*, September 1931. 135
22. Gertrude Stein and Alice B. Toklas return to America, *Literary Digest*, 1934. 146
23. Ida Lupino in *Colliers*, 1951. 175
24. Eve (Joan Fontaine) gives a technical lecture in *The Bigamist* (1953). 185
25. Myers (William Talman) wields his gun to direct his captives in *The Hitch-Hiker* (1953). 200

Acknowledgments

Working with Wesleyan University Press on the publication of this book has been a delightful experience at every turn. My editor, Eric Levy, is exemplary on all fronts. His insights and camaraderie have made this process a real pleasure. Jeanine Basinger is a keen reader and critic, imparting criticism with both acumen and wit. This book is better because of their interventions.

A Mellon Fellowship at the Huntington Library gave me critical access to Jack London's and Stuart Lake's papers. Sue Hudson and Peter Blodgett were first-rate guides through the collection, and I thank the Huntington Library for permission to work with their Jack London holdings. Don Chaput generously shared his Wyatt Earp and Western history resources with me during this trip to California, without which chapter two would have been greatly impoverished.

A QCB Travel Grant from the Department of English at the University of Maryland, where I completed my graduate work, enabled me to make the first of several trips to the Margaret Herrick Library of the Academy of Motion Picture Arts and Sciences, where Barbara Hall ably assisted me. Two extraordinary women—Rosemary Hanes and Madeline Matz—at the Library of Congress repeatedly helped me explore the wonderful resources there.

A Faculty Research and Professional Development grant from the College of Humanities and Social Sciences at North Carolina State University allowed me to complete a final round of research in Los Angeles and Washington, D.C., during the 2004–2005 academic year. Many of the materials gathered for this book also appeared through the magic of interlibrary loan departments at the University of Maryland and at North Carolina State University. My sincere thanks to those who fulfilled those countless requests, especially to Ann Rothe at NCSU.

An early version of chapter three appeared in *American Literature* and of chapter four in *Cinema Journal*. I am grateful to these journals for publishing my work while I was writing this book, and for permission to include this material here.

I have wonderful colleagues at North Carolina State University, especially in film studies—Joe Gomez, Tom Wallis, and Andrea Mensch.

Without the encouragement and commiseration of Maria Pramaggiore at a few critical junctures in the revising and publishing process, this book may very well have been an orphan along the academic highway.

Many other good people aided me with various aspects of my research, thinking, writing, and merrymaking over the years at conferences, at my home institutions, and during my research trips, especially Jim Alchediak, Anne Baker, Zach Barocas, Laura Boyes, Jennifer Brody, Charles Caramello, Skip Elsheimer, Pat Loughney, Mike Mashon, Leila May, Anne Morey, Peggy Parsons, Brian Price, Ronnie Scheib, David Stenn, Steve Wiley, and David Wyatt.

I have extraordinary friends of considerable vintage—Laurie and Jason Spivak, Fred Arens and Jason Duguay, Hannah McCann and Jonathan Witte, Geoffrey Schramm, Heidi Glenn and Joe Easley, and Kristen Geldermann—who also happen to live in the right places for a film scholar hooked on the archives. In Raleigh, I am lucky to have found an exceptional community of people who are creative, smart, and fun. Among them, I'm especially indebted to Graham Auman, Suzy and Al Newsom, Lee Moore and David Crawford, Elizabeth Galecke and Ted Sampson, Eric and Martha Cecka, Michele Little and David Iversen, Jean and John Davis, Graham McKinney and Lou Polletta, Kay Jordan and Will Alphin, Anna Bigelow, and Julia Clarke for making life good.

My deepest gratitude goes to two of academe's finest, who have been advisors on this project from the start. Bob Kolker and Jonathan Auerbach were always available for prompt and insightful readings of chapters and for numerous other acts of mentoring, encouragement, and advice. I am fortunate to have had the opportunity of working closely with them.

I get what little EGBOK mentality I possess from my family. Norman, Nancy, and Sarah have always at least pretended to understand the strange life of the academic, and they have been generous in ways that have made getting where I am easier for me at every turn. Fred and Brenda have offered support throughout, and I'm grateful to have a second home in San Clemente.

Finally, thanks of proportions absurd and truly indescribable are due to Devin Orgeron, my perennial—and only occasionally reluctant—proofreader, collaborator, and co-conspirator in all things. May you sleep well knowing you will never *have* to read this "just one more time."

Hollywood Ambitions

Introduction

Hollywood Ambitions

Legendary frontier gunslinger Wyatt Earp spent years trying to get someone in Hollywood to make a film based upon his life story, moving semi-permanently to Los Angeles around 1906, hanging around movie sets, befriending insiders, writing letters, waiting.

*

In the nineteen-teens, naturalist author Jack London signed contracts with several motion picture companies to make films based upon his work, even agreeing to use his own image to promote these productions in an effort to remain relevant in an increasingly cinematic marketplace.

*

New York movie fan Clara Bow submitted her photograph to a movie magazine contest in the 1920s, won the contest, and found herself on a cross-country trip to Hollywood that would eventually transform her into one of the most famous, and infamous, Hollywood stars.

*

During her American lecture tour in the 1930s, expatriate modernist author Gertrude Stein was invited to lunch by the Warner brothers, went to parties with the likes of Charlie Chaplin and Mary Pickford, and spent the latter part of her career trying to write her way into a deal with Hollywood.

*

Ida Lupino came to Hollywood from England, established herself as a Paramount and then a Warner Bros. actress, and eventually tried to navigate a shift from star to independent "novelty" woman director in the 1950s.

*

These five figures, whose lives extend across the first half of the twentieth century, shared a fascination with Hollywood and its cinematic product, particularly with its potential to change the course and the nature of their lives. Hollywood has been more than just the "most talked-of city in America," as *Photoplay* editor James Quirk described it in 1922;[1] it has also served as *the* destination for those seeking to leave their mark on twentieth-century American culture, despite great odds against success in this arena. As the century progressed, cinematically derived celebrity appeared to promise a previously unimaginable degree of visibility and power, beckoning each of this book's subjects to pursue the recognition and rewards made possible by its unparalleled global reach. *Hollywood Ambitions* seeks to understand the aspirations of these people who, each in his or her own way, sought to alter, amplify, and control their identities, careers, and reputations in the new celebrity capital of Hollywood. A consideration of their diverse Hollywood pursuits provides us with a unique understanding of how and why the motion picture industry dramatically changed the stakes of public life in the twentieth century.

The characters compiled here each invested, some with more at stake than others, in the often nebulous promises of a new industry. They all fantasized—fortunately for us, often in writing—about the personal gains that might be attained by interacting with this industry, which brokered in both the material (the movies themselves; the words, images, and ancillary products that sustained the circulation of the films and stars) and the elusive (the dreams that the industry sought to manufacture). And they all took risks, of varying degrees, by undertaking pioneering Hollywood ventures, often compromising the integrity of already-established careers and prior reputations in the process.

Although all of these figures would eventually leave Hollywood empty handed, symbolically if not literally, their ambitions and, indeed, their frustrations provide insight into the ways that the very concept of success—of, quite literally, "making it"—was being altered in the new century. The idea of being *self-made*—the belief in man's ability to make something of himself no matter how humble his roots, a concept very much *en vogue* in the nineteenth century—was recast in the first half of the twentieth century partly in reaction to Hollywood and its iconography of success. The five individuals who constitute the body of this study shared a belief, some more skeptical than others, in the power of this emerging industry, which promised to "make them" in ways that they simply could not "make themselves." The motion picture industry gave the impression that it was able to circulate and sell almost anything: their images, their work, and curiously enough even their own ideas of themselves. Hollywood also seemed uniquely able to reach an audience that would, in theory, recognize them (financially and otherwise) for what they were worth (over-inflated though that might be) and, perhaps most importantly, for who they thought they were.

Certainly in the first half of the twentieth century, Hollywood appeared poised to "do something" for the aspirant with enough pluck to go out there and stake a claim. Hollywood, by which I mean both the literal and the mythic place, was being pitched in terms of exclusivity as well as possibility: With some marketable talent, optimism, determination, and a little luck, success seemed attainable. Evidence of this city's widespread allure—of its promises and its temptations—can be found in the innumerable Hollywood pilgrimages made by aspiring starlets and directors, fading legends, and literary greats alike, exemplars of which receive attention in the following pages.

*

One of the goals of *Hollywood Ambitions* is to consider the history of cinema and celebrity across disciplines to broaden the way we conceive of this highly mobile medium's impact, to acknowledge the seemingly boundless nature of the Hollywood fantasy. The following pages offer a panoramic history of a fundamental shift in twentieth century life involving the redefinition of success, celebrity, and reputation around an emerging industry that appeared capable of endowing unprecedented visibility, power, and economic reward. The lure of Hollywood is so substantial—a phenomenon so widespread—that it connects several decades of at first seemingly disparate American personalities, all of whom sought to distinguish, alter, and in some cases even to celebrate themselves in the Hollywood dreamscape.

When I first conceived of this project about the lure of Hollywood, I cast a wide net in an effort to move in patterns outside of the largely star-based thinking on the subject of celebrity. Studies of celebrity culture have provided a valuable arsenal of critical tools with which to approach my subject, but they often ignore the unprejudiced seductiveness of fame, especially when it exceeds the traditional parameters of film studies.[2] The history of celebrity is more complex and puzzling than we often imagine it to be; our expectations about who has fallen under its spell and for what reasons are repeatedly confounded once we move beyond the usual suspects. This is complicated even further by the intrusion into celebrity's history of a new medium, the motion picture, which shifted the hierarchies of fame in tangible and potent ways.

This intrusion, as I've termed it, is the real impetus for this study, which seeks to understand the implications of the mass modernization of personal renown. As my language here should indicate, *Hollywood Ambitions* owes a good deal of its intellectual framework to Leo Braudy's *The Frenzy of Renown*, which established the elaborate history and extraordinary breadth of fame throughout the ages and around the globe. My project departs from Braudy's findings by looking at a specific intervention in the history of fame—motivated by the birth of the motion picture, its evolving industry, its proliferating publicity—to discern how the ripples from that new conceptualization of renown include, but also emanate far beyond, the conventional subject of the star. "What it means to be public in Western culture," to borrow a phrase from Braudy, was radically altered by the motion picture industry and it is the reconfiguration of that concept—and its consequences for the individuals who sought to profit from this shift—that emerges throughout the chapters that follow.[3]

As I investigated those who sought to transform themselves quite literally through Hollywood, I was repeatedly surprised by the degree to which those drawn to that city and its product often failed to "fit the pattern established by leading scholars and critics," as Charles Ponce de Leon terms his own discoveries about celebrity and human interest journalism.[4] The cast of characters I assembled for this project are disciplinarily unconventional, but they reflect the wide range of temptations and motivations that I believe are central to an understanding of cinematic celebrity's stronghold on the early twentieth century. In trying to establish the concrete manifestations of Hollywood's far-reaching and apparently indiscriminate appeal, I gathered together individuals who were well-known, major cultural figures, both in their own time and now. But I also sought out those whose Hollywood engagements exceeded what already had been written about them as authors, actresses, directors, or historical figures. Each of these individuals has a substantial critical literature behind them, but none has previously been placed in the context of a truly interdisciplinary dialogue about Hollywood's far-flung impact on celebrity culture.

Hollywood's siren call appealed to an astonishing range of individuals. Wyatt Earp, Jack London, Clara Bow, Gertrude Stein, and Ida Lupino are just a sampling of those who sought to make claims for themselves in this new territory. But while it is important to acknowledge that there is a potentially endless list of other actresses, directors, authors, and historical figures who might also support the larger historical and theoretical ideas contained within this book—a fact that suggests the fundamentally compelling reason for thinking of Hollywood in the disciplinarily adventurous terms I propose here—my subjects engaged with particularly intense and well-documented struggles involving their public images. They are not the only subjects I might have chosen; however, in choosing them I hope to take the reader on a path less traveled through what might otherwise be familiar terrain, in the process illustrating the degree to which different motivations compelled this widespread desire to wrestle with reputation and identity in America's newly reconfigured celebrity culture.

The very point, then, of juxtaposing some conventional, "insider" Hollywood figures (Bow and Lupino) with unconventional, "outsider" figures (London, Earp, and Stein) is to demonstrate the unusual reach and myriad forms of the Hollywood fantasy in a progressive fashion, from the birth of cinema to the decline of the studio system. That these characters don't, at first, make sense alongside each other is precisely the point: Hollywood, I argue, became one of the great levelers of the twentieth century. To separate these disparate streams that flow toward the same central body would be to deny the boundless appeal that Hollywood possessed for the better part of the twentieth century. Instead, I hope to illustrate the fascinating congruity of these figures' ambitions and, in the process, to disrupt the disciplinary divisions that have, falsely I think, surrounded celebrity studies. Star studies has operated under certain assumptions about who neatly fits in the canon, and I deliberately sought out subjects who evinced different relationships with Hollywood in part to challenge what has been a myopic view of Hollywood's reach.

It is also important to acknowledge what may perhaps be an obvious point: that although they share Hollywood in their ambitions, my subjects are fundamentally different from one another. In uniting them here on the basis of their shared orbit around Hollywood, I do not intend to negate or neglect these truly interplanetary differences. Gertrude Stein, born of privilege, fiercely independent and savvy, commanding in presence, seems practically of another species when placed beside Clara Bow, born of poverty, perpetually dependent and naive, unable ever, it seems, to assert herself adequately. Whatever differences exist between these figures—and each of the chapters makes clear that these are individuals with markedly different stories, diverse motivations, and disparate outcomes—Hollywood seemed capable of making such differences *seem* irrelevant. What I mean by this is that part of the lure of Hollywood's brand of mythmaking was its apparently democratic ability to alter, an illusion my entire cast of characters recognized and responded to. Whether it was Wyatt Earp believing that all he had to do was to go to Hollywood and ask to get a version of himself on-screen; or Jack London perceiving that making a deal with Hollywood would ensure that his stories and image would live on, guaranteeing him immense profitability in the process; or Clara Bow thinking that she could submit a picture of herself to a contest and end up a Hollywood star; or Gertrude Stein fantasizing that if she could only get a deal to go to Hollywood then her problems with money and marginalization would disappear; or Ida Lupino deeming that she might use her star power to enter what was an exclusively male field of the industry; each of these individuals—and the many other dreamers and aspirants whose lives are not detailed here—saw in Hollywood and its celebrity culture vast possibilities.

The fundamental differences I note above might also be categorized in terms of the material relationships each of these figures had with the motion picture industry. Clara Bow and Ida Lupino had real "insider" experiences in Hollywood, where Wyatt Earp, Jack London, and Gertrude Stein remained "outsiders" despite their significant interactions with the industry. In this way, Bow might also best be understood for her typicality: She came to Hollywood and became a star, allowing us to explore the ways in which the most visible and marketable products of the studio system were made and unmade in Hollywood. Lupino's is also, at least partly, an insider's story as well; however, she took her conventional role as a star in Hollywood and made of it something atypical by using her "insider" reputation to move into a career in which she was decidedly an "outsider."

Together, these two chapters allow us to navigate rather differently what might be understood as the somewhat predictable terrain of star studies, a foundational step toward a broader understanding of the studio system's unexpected allure. By placing Bow and Lupino alongside three Hollywood "outsiders"—those who tried, in different ways, to become "insiders"—I intend to illustrate the industry's remarkable cultural reach. Uniting "insider" and "outsider" figures also enables an understanding of the complexity of Hollywood's history, for it points to the industry's efficacy in shaping the ambitions of those who make sense within the system as much as for those who seem unlikely candidates for this particular brand of cultural status. It is also Hollywood's uncanny ability to render even its supposed insiders *outsiders* that motivates an examination of Bow and Lupino, both of whom never quite fit within the system.

Uniting these disparate figures illustrates the point that, although there *may* be a generic template or master narrative for the Hollywood aspirant, there is *no* typical Hollywood experience. Anyone who claims that there is simplifies an immensely complex case. For while we may trace some elements of similarity among the subjects of these chapters and individuals outside the parameters of this study who might fit into similar categories as our figures (other actresses, directors, writers, and the like), the "Hollywood machine" produced and appealed to all manner of individuality and difference, and those who sought a relationship with the industry did so in fashions and for reasons that are related only in the broadest, categorical sense. Despite the catchy nomenclature, the "dream factory" was never the efficient and homogenizing force we sometimes casually assume it to be.

These chapters, then, do not intend to present a cookie-cutter approach to my subject, each one reinforcing, in the same way, Hollywood's impact on celebrity culture or *the* way people interacted with the industry. In these pages, I am less excited by the singularity of the celebrity experience than I am by its multiplicity, which allows this book to fork in different directions off the main branch of the Hollywood path. Reflective of a large-scale renegotiation of the terms of celebrity, the case studies assembled here do speak on behalf of analogous struggles—both literal and ideological—as they were occurring elsewhere in American culture. Cutting across geographical, educational, occupational, and class lines, the individual subjects of my chapters are nonetheless linked by the well-documented nature of their Hollywood desires—in personal and published writings, in the highly suspect but immensely useful pages of the fan magazines—some of which stands in conflict with the understanding we currently have of their careers and personalities.

Other performers, other authors, other mythmakers, other fans heeded Hollywood's call, but few left behind them such a vast and under-investigated array of artifacts testifying to their Hollywood ambitions. Those who made the final cut for this book not only left a trail documenting their struggles with the motion picture industry, but also approached these struggles from a range of perspectives that makes my task more complicated, more challenging, and more revealing. For if we can look at a fading Western legend, a vastly successful popular author, a poor girl from Brooklyn, a self-proclaimed avant-garde genius, and an actress-turned-director in a fashion that illustrates what has been an almost incomprehensible diversity of the Hollywood fantasy and the Hollywood experience, then we have gained a more realistic understanding of how Hollywood spoke to Americans in the first half of the twentieth century than currently exists. Hollywood never was a place for a single kind of talent or personality; rather, its success as an industry and as a symbol was that it was a cipher, of sorts, whose appeal cut across hierarchies and expectations. This book intends to demonstrate that these divergent experiences are part of the same fundamental phenomenon, one that has been marginalized in other, more disciplinarily constrained versions of Hollywood history.

*

All of the schemes documented in *Hollywood Ambitions* revolve around attempts to broker in or manage *reputation*, which, as John Rodden points out in his study of literary reputation, is at best an elusive concept.[5] Despite, perhaps even because of, its slipperiness, however, the concept warrants consideration in the context of Hollywood's significant influence upon it. At the most basic level, reputation denotes an individual's public image and status. Determined by the perception of others, reputation is a shifting notion, subject to the influence of political climate, personal preference, the marketplace, and, perhaps most critically, media representation. Public reputations in America have always emanated from different sources and places, circulating in varying and sometimes limited circles. Although Hollywood did not change the fact that reputations are made and unmade in a range of fashions and locales, as well as to differing degrees, the motion picture industry streamlined the mechanics of this production to capitalize most markedly on its power to *distribute* and *exhibit* public personalities in new and massively consumable ways. Hollywood did not efface other kinds of reputation-making—literary or political, for example—but it did set what we might refer to as the "gold standard" for how reputations could be constructed and circulated, and it also influenced the nature of these previously autonomous categories.

As Hollywood strengthened its hold on American cultural life, reputation became increasingly indistinguishable from the related concepts of celebrity, renown, and fame. The fact that celebrities created in Hollywood possessed such shockingly disproportionate visibility and value seems to have affected directly the way that individuals seeking even very distinct reputations—for example, literary—thought about their status as potential celebrities not unlike the Hollywood variety. In other words, as Hollywood raised the bar for celebrity in the new century, those who sought to navigate the American cultural scene often felt compelled to seek out equally potent modes of recognition. In the process, celebrity was becoming virtually analogous to reputation, and my choice of words within these pages reflects this kinship.

Hollywood Ambitions examines the history of these blurring distinctions to suggest the ways in which Hollywood was transforming celebrity culture. In many of the chapters that follow, reputations born outside of the motion picture industry were employed as a kind of speculative currency in Hollywood, with varying degrees of success. As the century wore on, a reputation made outside of Hollywood appeared to be lacking in fundamental ways that many of our cast of characters recognized and sought to remedy in the new celebrity capital. But it is not solely reputation that is at issue in the chapters that follow; indeed, many of these individuals exhibit a tension between wanting celebrity and its rewards (most of all the fortune and freedom that appeared to come with it), and seeking a more permanent and seemingly (if elusively) refined notion of reputation for doing something in particular (for example, as a heroic frontier legend or genius modernist author). Not only were these notions of celebrity and reputation converging, but the value of reputation outside of Hollywood appeared to be waning.

In his sociological study, *Difficult Reputations*, Gary Alan Fine conflates the idea of "celebrity" with the notion of "public reputations," I suspect deliberately.[6] Although it is not necessarily tied to economic reward, American culture—and Hollywood particularly—has tended to frame the idea of reputation in the context of the economic structures that nurture and, in many ways, reaffirm it. As Fine defines it, reputation can be understood as a "shorthand way of conceptualizing a person" and more generally as "a socially recognized persona."[7] I argue in these pages that to be a "socially recognized persona" in the twentieth century meant increasingly to affiliate oneself with Hollywood as it became the most seemingly efficacious avenue to success. The aspirations, then, that each of these chapters details have everything to do with a larger cultural realignment in which celebrity of the Hollywood variety appeared to trump all other forms of success, and *appeared* equally able to afford the owner of said celebrity a certain degree of control over their reputations and careers.

The enticement of Hollywood, however, was more often than not also a mirage, one that rarely produced the compensation, power, or prestige it seemed to promise. As might be expected, then, the subjects of this book did not always reap the rewards of their pioneering ventures. But as Andrew Britton reminds us in his study of Katharine Hepburn, "the importance of publicity and promotion consists in the fact that they *seek* to define an orientation to the star—not that they succeed."[8] Although this project extends well beyond the movie star, the value of public negotiation is similar for those who sought to use the medium to manipulate the trajectory of their lives in other ways through the distinct avenues offered by the motion picture industry, revealing important clues to Hollywood's escalating role in American life. The recurrent dissonance between individual intentions and results—likewise fantasy and reality—recalls Max

Horkheimer and Theodor Adorno's decidedly more sinister conclusion about the power of "The Culture Industry" in *Dialectic of Enlightenment.* Indeed, the chapters that follow attest to the insight of their declaration that "the whole world is made to pass through the filter of the culture industry."[9] This is even more the case today than when they wrote their pioneering study some sixty years ago.

While casting the specter of failure over the group assembled in these pages is somewhat misleading, for certainly each of the individuals discussed here was an exemplary success in certain contexts, the outcomes of their Hollywood endeavors suggest a different way in which to read their experiences.[10] For if, in fact, we single out only their dealings—attempted or realized—in Hollywood, these are not simply the triumphant narratives one most often associates with studies of Hollywood. Whereas nearly all critical analyses of celebrity revolve around success, however troubled, of the most extraordinary variety, this book argues that we can learn as much if not more about evolving issues of celebrity and success in American culture from the *imperfect* Hollywood encounters that are detailed in the following chapters.[11]

It is not just that these individuals all failed in Hollywood, but rather that Hollywood failed them, reneging on a promise—one never *really* made in the first place—of fame, fortune, status, and power. Nonetheless, all of the following chapters explore the attempts made by these figures to interact with the Hollywood machine for their own personal aims. All of these individuals perceived that they were not getting the success that they wanted, in quantity or type, and as a result set out to contend with a new mass media, its ingenuous modes of publicity, and its myriad cultural infiltrations, some more self-consciously than others. This tangle of emerging corporate interests and ideologies gave the impression of bestowing great things upon those who could effectively navigate the snarl, and, as the following chapters indicate, the variety as well as the intentions of those who sought to use the medium for personal advantage are often quite surprising.

My argument, then, is that the motion picture industry offered an increasingly irresistible temptation that took on many forms in the imaginations of early twentieth-century hopefuls, many of whom sought to claim ownership of their careers and reputations by diving—some more cautiously than others—into the Hollywood maelstrom. The collective frustrations represented in this book derive from the very limited ability of the individual to control the industrial infrastructure of Hollywood, suggesting the real futility, perhaps even the ludicrousness, of imagining the industry as one that might be put in the service of the individual. That some felt it was possible to do so in the first place is curious and worthy of study in and of itself. In the pages that follow, Hollywood functions as an alluring symbol, rising out of the California landscape to loom large over the imaginations of millions who charted their aspirations at least partly according to the city's spectacular products and promises.

*

Hollywood Ambitions proceeds as a series of historically progressive chapters that demonstrate how success and celebrity were redefined in relation to Hollywood, the degree to which Hollywood celebrity superceded other forms of renown, and how certain individuals attempted to use the motion picture industry to enrich, solidify, or alter their identities and their reputations. Those seeking to speculate about and in Hollywood offer us a unique window into this city's powerful mythological status, in part because those who wanted to nurture such a relationship also tended to document their desires, leaving a trail of published and unpublished, public and private material—films, letters, essays, novels, and legal documents—that shed light on the ways that Hollywood inspired widely divergent figures to seek out a life-altering relationship with the film industry.

My subjects are exemplars of this phenomenon, representing an array of motivations, goals, and professions: frontier legend; archetypal celebrity author; star-struck, impoverished Brooklyn girl; impenetrable expatriate modernist; and actress eager to explore the other side of the camera. All of these figures actively sought to *redefine themselves*, to use Hollywood to alter the course of their lives, to interact with a new kind of celebrity culture. And all of them ultimately were frustrated in their attempts to manage their reputations through Hollywood, at least in the fashion they originally envisioned. Placed alongside each other, these chapters—focused primarily in the first half of the century, the era in which cinema's impact was first felt, debated, fought, and nurtured—make a strong case for the ways in which American culture was changing in response to Hollywood and its celebrity industry.

Each of the figures explored in *Hollywood Ambitions* is well known. Less known, however, and certainly less studied, are their struggles with Hollywood's specific brand of renown. Among those examined here who imagined this specific locale as a site for making or altering their reputations are many who seem irreconcilable with the established paradigms for Hollywood dreamers: Gertrude Stein and Wyatt Earp, for example, whose forays into cinematic mythmaking failed to materialize (at least in their lifetimes), but whose efforts survive as evocative examples of this locale's promise of personal transformation. Whatever the original reason for coming—for none of these figures were natives to the movie capital, coming from places such as England, Brooklyn, and the mythic "Wild West"—Hollywood appeared to offer them opportunities for attaining cultural status that they could not find elsewhere.

One way of viewing the history of the American twentieth century is through the lens of the movie industry and its influences. Movies and their American production capital made possible the imagination of new identities for millions, both participants and spectators. Each chapter of this book traces different aspects of this transformation, demonstrating the degree to which American culture was being reoriented around the existence of Hollywood, especially toward cinematically derived conceptualizations of identity and accomplishment. Each individual studied within these pages functions as something of a barometer for how celebrity and representation were conceived of in his or her historical moment, as well as for how the film industry responded to the culture's receptiveness to their products. Although the movies did not create the need to make or control reputations, they certainly fed this desire in new and provocative ways. By considering how these figures viewed this medium through which their identities could be altered, converted, and even invented, I continue on the path Robert Sklar laid out some twenty-five years ago by demonstrating the ways that cinema has helped "to shape the character and direction of American culture as a whole."[12]

The book's central character is, in some ways, Hollywood itself, and I explore its mass appeal in ways that have often been neglected in the critical literature on the subject. *Hollywood Ambitions* seeks to fill a gap in celebrity's history precisely because the figures studied here and their conceptions of the motion picture industry allow us to map out progressive iterations of the Hollywood fantasy that both affirm and go beyond the paradigms that have already been established. Together these chapters demonstrate the ways that Hollywood—as a symbol of success, as a model of industry, and as the creator of highly visible products of both the cinematic and celebrity variety—changed the nature of representation (self- and otherwise) and the standards for success in American culture. By looking to those who explored or experienced the possibilities offered by and in Hollywood, we can better understand the manner by which the motion picture industry caused the culture at large to focus on a very specific geographic locale as the generative landscape for modern American success.

After setting the scene in chapter one for the cultural environment that encouraged individuals to set their sights on Hollywood, chapter two, "When the West Was Done: Wyatt Earp in Hollywood," examines the Hollywood pilgrimage made by the now-mythic Western lawman alongside several of his "cowboy" contemporaries who also migrated to Hollywood. Earp's reputation today owes itself almost entirely to Hollywood's retellings, but he was not successful in seeing an on-screen homage during his lifetime. However, he did perceive at an early point in Hollywood's history that making his reputation last would be facilitated by an on-screen version of his life, a kind of cinematic (auto)biography. Understanding the potential of circulating legend through burgeoning Hollywood's extensive means of distribution, Earp tried to bridge the mythmaking modes of the past with the modern media of the future, linking the nineteenth and the twentieth centuries in the pursuit of an idealized and authorized commemoration of his past. Chapter two traces Earp's commentary on the emerging importance of the moving image, but its concurrent goal is to establish a sense of cinema's early years concerning issues of representation, authenticity, ownership, and marketing that will recur throughout the chapters that follow and that will be central to our understanding of the risky nature of the Hollywood venture.

Jack London, naturalist author of narratives that often revolve around the rugged individualism of man (or animal) in nature and the autobiographically based struggle to become known, was also fascinated by the cinema's potential to distribute the image; to distribute, in fact, his own carefully crafted image. London was in many ways a practical businessman, certainly a more adept one than Earp, and his Hollywood ventures can be understood as an extension of his literary industry. London briefly worked with Hollywood producers on several motion picture projects, leaving films that testify to the relationship between the commercialism of the cinematic and the literary marketplaces. As will be demonstrated in chapter three, "Rethinking Authorship in Jack London's Hollywood," London envisioned Hollywood as a new kind of frontier territory and his failed efforts there led him back to the relative autonomy of authorship, albeit revised to accommodate the needs of the motion picture industry. His battle to amplify his marketability in these renegade teen years of Hollywood filmmaking marks an interesting moment in the cinema's evolution, one that reveals a struggle, litigious and otherwise, over the ownership of identity in the specific spheres of film production and publicity.

But his relationship with the film industry does more than just indicate the number of opportunities for representation and self-promotion created by the film industry; it also allows for an illustration of the important changes in London's literary practices that arose as a direct consequence of his Hollywood aspirations, as evidenced in his novel *Hearts of Three*.

Chapter four focuses on significant celebrity-making developments of the 1920s by addressing the confluence of cinematic and print modes of producing reputations through a figure whose career was utterly in debt to the fan magazines. "Making *It* in Hollywood: Clara Bow and the Cycle of the Fan Magazine" situates actress Clara Bow in the context of fan culture in order to analyze the growing relationship between fandom and Hollywood's peculiar brand of consumer culture. This chapter considers the ways that fans were encouraged to rethink their relationships to celebrity and to perceive themselves as both consumers and potential stars, as well as prospective players in the Hollywood market. Discovered through a Brewster Publications fan magazine contest, Bow exemplifies the propagandizing potential of the Hollywood star system and her career affords an examination of the competing forces that conspired to shape her fluctuating reputation. With a close reading of her 1927 star vehicle *It*, the chapter argues that Hollywood ambitions were being nurtured in direct and novel ways through increased interactions between fans and the Hollywood-based consumption of films, stars, and other consumer products.

Chapter five, "'If We Are Ever to Be In Hollywood': Gertrude Stein's Moving Images," assesses the unrealized plans of Gertrude Stein, a literary modern who sought out ways to profit from her literary innovations in Hollywood. While in many ways she achieved her goals of revolutionizing the literary world, Stein was unable to actualize an on-screen adaptation of her work. Stein is always acutely aware of the politics of production and publicity, and she provides unique, albeit often cryptic insights into her pursuit of a Hollywood reorientation of her career. Utilizing both her writings about cinema and her documentation of her own rising literary celebrity in works such as *Everybody's Autobiography* and *Lectures in America*, this chapter makes a case for the preeminence of Hollywood in the 1930s as the celebrity capital of the world, even for a figure as unlikely as Stein. Stein's writing suggests that the motion picture had become celebrity's defining medium, and this self-designated outsider's eagerness to "be taken in Hollywood," as she once put it, evidences the medium's far-reaching impact on the definitions of fame and success. Having one's image, one's story, or one's writing transformed into on-screen material became increasingly requisite in the perpetuation of reputation in the twentieth century, even if the nature of this reputation had little to do with Hollywood itself.

Although Stein never made it to Hollywood in the fashion she imagined, Ida Lupino experienced success as an American actress in the 1930s and 1940s. In chapter six, "Redirecting Reputation: Ida Lupino's Hollywood Fictions," I move beyond Lupino's acting career to examine her attempts to remake her reputation as Hollywood's novelty woman director. While the other figures in this book realized that Hollywood offered a way to increase their value and visibility, Lupino—working with the well-established publicity mechanisms of the industry—attempted to exploit this same capacity to alter the direction of her already Hollywood-based career. Lupino's unique value to this study lies in her very public narration of her directing career, which dramatizes how the actress used Hollywood's publicity apparatus to negotiate her reinvention, however imperfectly. For, as the chapter demonstrates, Lupino's position as director required perhaps more acting, more posing, more playing up for the cameras and pens of publicity, than had hitherto been required of her as an actress. Her position as both star and director is a confusing one, and the films she directed reflect this turmoil. In her 1953 film, *The Bigamist*, it seems appropriate that the two "criminal" characters meet on a bus tour of movie star's homes.[13] As one character explains, "Here were people going someplace, and I went along with them." Lupino's original migration to Hollywood fits with the trajectory of those seeking the movie star's fame and fortune, that "someplace" that Hollywood aspirants like Clara Bow sought out. However, her career move behind the camera is exceptional, for it at once decenters Lupino as the object of on-screen attention and reveals the complex and unfailingly spectacular politics involved in the attempt to control one's own celebrity within the Hollywood system.

Hollywood Ambitions demonstrates the ways in which certain individuals, several of whom had already established reputations without any engagement with the motion picture industry, realized that Hollywood could play a pivotal role in shaping their celebrity and their identity. As important as the details of their experiences are to both an historical and a theoretical understanding of Hollywood's influence on celebrity culture, equally important is that each evidences differing relationships to celebrity and its uses. Some of these figures aggressively worked to shape their celebrity, to actively market themselves in a particular fashion. Others were less deliberate, less careful, less self-aware. This range of authority over celebrity—from the canny to the virtually oblivious—reminds us, once again, that the Hollywood experience was kaleidoscopic in its variety.

Not everyone experienced or responded to celebrity in the same way; however, it became increasingly difficult to ignore this kind of celebrity as the cinematic century wore on.

What follows will take us from the late nineteenth-century Wild West to the post-war 1950s, in the process moving through the birth, early development, and ascension of Hollywood up through its gradual post-war decline. This book cannot hope to definitively answer the question of how the ebb of Hollywood's literal and symbolic status in the late twentieth and early twenty-first century has changed the concept of making, controlling, or revising reputations; nor do I intend to detail, beyond the suggestions I offer in the epilogue, the ways in which notions of celebrity have become—in a kind of fulfillment of Andy Warhol's well-known prophecy about the widespread but fleeting nature of fame—what they are today. I do hope, however, to lay out, in a fashion that resonates beyond the specificity of the figures I examine here, the complexity of the relationship between individuals and their specific plans for their own celebrity, between fantasy and reality as it was filtered through the lens of Hollywood.

1

Celebrity in the Movie Age

The American motion picture industry dramatically affected notions of personal identity, aspiration, representation, publicity, reputation, and celebrity, some of the key concepts that recur throughout *Hollywood Ambitions*. Central to these redefinitions was the development of the cinematic star system, which, along with related advances in mass media, escalated the exploitation of public personalities. Of course, movie stardom did not burst upon the scene unprecedented and unannounced; its models were firmly established by nineteenth-century theater and vaudeville, themselves outgrowths of eighteenth-century innovations in publicity.[1] While my primary task is not to trace either cinema's or celebrity's progress over the course of the twentieth century, which have been well documented elsewhere, this book studies the way a select group contended with the cinematic medium and its modes of publicity to make a particular name for themselves in the first half of the twentieth century.[2] This chapter lays the groundwork.

The emergent mass media of the nineteenth century—what Daniel Boorstin terms the "Graphic Revolution"—changed the way individuals perceived themselves and the world in which they lived.[3] By providing an array of new lenses through which to view things, mass media, in its various manifestations, facilitated the creation of communal sources of information and culture; events, places, and people became more accessible, even familiar. By 1850, as Richard Ohmann observes, the modern sense of celebrity—someone who attracts attention because of who they are as much as for anything they have done or continue to do—was already in place.[4] The public's knowledge of celebrities was by the turn of the century a kind of "cultural capital" resulting "in a storehouse of shared knowledge about individuals who had attained standing as cynosures, or were on the way to it."[5] The modern iteration of celebrity culture relied heavily upon visual representation, which was becoming pivotal not just in relation to the famous but also in everyday life. Leo Braudy provides numerous testaments to this shift in his influential tome, *The Frenzy of Renown*.

For example, Braudy notes the mid-nineteenth-century proliferation of daguerreotype studios in New York City, which provided "ordinary customers" with a way to preserve and disseminate their own images while also creating a precursor for the eventual mass distribution of celebrity likenesses.[6] The proliferation of photography at the turn of the twentieth century enabled individuals with recognizable names to become even more familiar through the distribution of their images.

Publicity was also streamlined at the turn of the twentieth century when so many of the factors facilitating renown coalesced. Although celebrity's status as a mass phenomenon in the middle of the nineteenth century was made possible by a host of new technologies, certain ones, such as the telegraph and rotary press, allowed information to be transported particularly quickly and affordably.[7] The turn of the century also saw an increase in the institutionalization of many of the organizations facilitating fame in American culture: *Who's Who* was founded in 1898; the first "Hall of Fame" began in 1900; and the first publicity firm opened its doors in 1900.[8] Through the business of aiding wealthy individuals with their public interactions, publicity firms allowed cultural figures, such as industrialists like John D. Rockefeller, to alter their images dramatically.[9] Realizing that one's reputation could be changed through the creation and distribution of new images, people began to go about the business of enhancing and molding their public status through the available public media.

With the growing popularity of the press—attributable in part to decreasing prices and national syndication—alongside an increase in photographic reproduction, which began in 1880 and was common by 1900, individuals began to link names to faces and thus to have new perceptions of public figures.[10] In *Self-Exposure*, Charles Ponce de Leon argues that the mass-circulation press was the industry "most responsive to the growing interest in exposure" and that celebrity journalism and the mass-circulation press matured concurrently at the end of the nineteenth century.[11] Although the film industry might pose a challenge to Ponce de Leon's hierarchy, his assertion that "media visibility was the distinguishing feature of celebrity" is apt;[12] it is also the conclusion arrived at collectively by the cast of characters assembled within these pages who sought this visibility at its apparent source. Cinematic celebrity ultimately would trump what could be achieved on the written page, as Campbell MacCulloch points out in a 1928 *Photoplay* article, because actors "work before hundreds of thousands each day all over the world, and they are actually *seen* instead of being heard or read about."[13] Mechanical reproduction had its most tangible rewards.[14]

Such shifts in publicity, image making, and celebrity did not go unnoticed as they were transpiring. Authors of novels, articles, medical journals, political tracts, and so on, remarked upon the changing status of fame in the first half of the twentieth century. Attentive to such developments in the realm of renown, Theodore Dreiser, in *Sister Carrie* (1900), details a young woman's developing consciousness concerning the need for media attention in relation to the public role of the "personality." Dreiser, an important cultural documentarian of the last turn-of-the-century's obsessions and mores, created a text rich with, and archly ironic about, America's growing reliance upon "recognition" in the modern city, which, as he painted it, was a sea of anonymity. For Carrie, the novel's protagonist, being indistinguishable in the chorus line is nearly as bad as being a cog in the assembly line at the shoe factory; neither position offers any hope of breaking out from the dreaded anonymity of the crowd and into public prominence. Although the audience's favorable reaction to Carrie's first impromptu comment on the theatrical stage—"I am yours truly"—is thrilling to her, more thrilling is seeing her name in print in her first review.

Although writing specifically about the theater, Dreiser anticipates the kind of publicity mania induced by the cinema. Carrie's entry into the realm of the press is an initiation into the public discourse of personalities—it is her first step to being "talked about," that all-important component of becoming cultural capital. With media recognition, Carrie also learns a valuable lesson about the market value of reputation when a hotel manager approaches her because her name is a commodity worth the price of her rent. This encounter provides a concrete example of something that the narrator has already stated about Carrie's performance: "She was capital." The double valence of "capital" suggests that the more that Carrie gains media attention the more value she comes to represent in the culture at large, a premise that the Hollywood studios adhered to with regard to both their on- and off-screen commodities. For those who recognize her in the press—Hurstwood, Mrs. Vance, even the jilted Drouet—Carrie's presence in its pages speaks to her cultural status, her fame, her seemingly limitless success, all things suggestive of the external appearances assumed to be the foundation of Carrie's happiness. The very "point" of celebrity, after all, is that it should be admired and desired by all who come into contact with it, a position aptly demonstrated with Dreiser's Carrie. For Carrie, the media creates a mechanism for personal reinvention, a means of facilitating and validating success, and a way to elevate and disseminate her reputation. So too for the non-fictional personalities discussed within these pages, many who came to understand and then to try to utilize the seemingly boundless influence of media attention made possible by cinema's incredible cultural reach.

Carrie's celebrity consciousness, her unembarrassed pleasure in being talked about, hints at the flourishing of such desires in other arenas of the culture. Being talked about became important for any public figure who wished to remain public in the twentieth century. As the cultural shift from nineteenth-century "hero" (implying an individual who invented, created, labored for the greater good, etc.) to the twentieth-century "celebrity" (implying less substance, more image) transpired, keeping oneself in the minds of the public took on escalating magnitude for those individuals whose livelihoods became dependent on making and perpetuating their reputations. As Daniel Boorstin puts it, "the hero was a big man; the celebrity is a big name," implying the shallowness often associated with celebrity as well as the allegedly ephemeral nature of the category.[15] "The passage of time, which creates and establishes the hero," Boorstin asserts, "destroys the celebrity. One is made, the other unmade, by repetition."[16]

*

Another case in point for the confluence of celebrity and an increasingly visual image-centric culture at the turn of the century is *Celebrities Monthly*, which began publication in April of 1895.[17] The magazine had an exceptional premise: Not just reproducing photographs of various celebrities on newsprint or magazine stock, it included, as the first issue's "announcement" explains it, "ten actual photographs of prominent persons."[18] Indeed, these issues contain photographs affixed to almost every page, including the cover. Claiming to bear "the stamp of originality," the magazine sold itself primarily as a monthly photo album, suggesting that readers might become more intimate with select celebrities by looking at *actual* photographs of them alongside brief biographical notes. In fact, the cover highlights this through dramatic graphics that emphasize "Actual Photographs of Prominent Personages with Biographical Sketches." The value of such a publication, according to its own prefatory information contained in the September 1895 issue, was that it enabled subscribers to create "an album which it is practically impossible to acquire in any other way."[19] It also allowed—and perhaps encouraged—subscribers to make celebrity images their own. Although these images were, of course, still images, they could be removed, rearranged, or traded, making them potentially mobile—unwedded from their original source—and yet, unlike regular magazine photographs, retaining a patina of authenticity.

Even in the age of mechanical reproduction, *Celebrities Monthly* strove to gain readers based upon the authenticity of its photographic images. The periodical was betting on its audiences' perception that the reproduction of *actual* photographs would have a distinct advantage over print versions of the same; in other words, that these photographs possessed a more proximate aura of the person pictured than could be reproduced otherwise and that their value was transmitted more effectively in photographic form. This was so much the case that the second issue, dated May 1895, included a statement explaining the patented and "*entirely new*" process by which the photographs were printed "direct from photographic negatives by artificial light on sensitized paper in a continuous roll" with "the most careful precaution and scientific supervision" to guarantee "the *finest of bromide prints* of *absolute uniformity*."

The magazine also uses this logic to insist on reproducing primarily images of living celebrities, since the process of reproduction necessitated using original negatives. Touting the process that provided "this most beautiful and effective means of illustration," *Celebrities Monthly* asserts in its third issue that these photographic portraits were not only more real but also more *valuable* than other modes of photographic reproduction. The periodical thus attempted to cater to their perception of the public's desire for "personal" access to celebrities, a desire that had yet to be linked to the emergent motion picture industry.

Who was eligible as a celebrity in the 1895 issues? People the likes of Elizabeth Cady Stanton, Mark Twain, pre-presidential Theodore Roosevelt, Harriet Beecher Stowe, Thomas Edison (whose invention of the kinetoscope is noted with the same degree of regard as his invention of the phonograph), and a spate of theatrical performers, singers, artists, newspaper editors, reformers, inventors, ladies of society, and clergymen. These men and women of achievement stand in marked contrast to the cinematic celebrities *du jour* of twenty—and especially of one hundred—years later. But *Celebrities Monthly* is every bit a precursor to the fan magazine and its modes of publicity. Like the fan magazines that encouraged their readers' involvement through letters, contests, and the like, as we shall see in chapter four, *Celebrities Monthly* also possessed an inherent component of audience participation. From its second issue onward, the magazine asked its readers to "send in the names of celebrated persons whom they would like to see photographed in its pages," thereby encouraging the public to aid in the canonization of celebrities, or at least endowing the appearance of such agency to its subscribers.

The publication also included advertisements from its second issue onward. Some of them, like the May 1895 advertisement for body and brain strengthener "Vin Mariani," promised to send any inquirers "75 Portraits and Autographs of Celebrities Testifying to the Uniform Excellence" of their product. With images of men like Emile Zola attesting to the product's promise of "vigor, health and energy," the advertisements predict the kind of movie (and to a lesser degree literary) star endorsements made popular in the era of the fan magazine, which in turn supported the logic of identification and mimicry that became the linchpin of fandom. By the October 1895 issue, one advertiser, Dr. Jaeger, maker of "sanitary" underwear for adults and children, would go so far as to include a real photograph in his advertisement, hoping no doubt that, following *Celebrities Monthly*'s logic, a photograph would compel readers to buy his underwear more than would a conventionally reproduced magazine image.

As the content of *Celebrities Monthly* would indicate, by the turn of the twentieth century, even the relatively new photographic mode of representation was employed as a strategy to increase the supply and demand for images. It was being readily observed that people wanted, and would pay, to *see* more things, more frequently—daily, bi-daily, hourly, minute to minute. This hunger for information worked in tandem with the progression of other technologies, specifically technologies of mobility, including the cinema. Trains, streetcars, and automobiles quickened the pace of everyday life, coinciding with the desire for an equally responsive mode of representation. The movies were simultaneously mobile and, unlike print culture, managed to capture mobility for a society that was itself increasingly on the move. In this way, the motion picture industry could offer what *Celebrities Monthly* couldn't, though the magazine's attempt to unite the principles of biography and photography are a notable testament to this broader tendency. Since so much of celebrity culture relies upon the visual, all of these technological developments contributed to the mass redefinition of fame.

*

Of course, mass media and fame existed well before the invention of photography and filmmaking. Raymond Williams has demonstrated that the rise of a "large new middle-class reading public" during the eighteenth century in England triggered a shift from a system of literary patronage into modern-day commercial publishing, allowing the novel to become a commodity and its author to become an important, if controversial figure in the marketplace.[20] The "broad social and technological changes which ushered in the beginnings of a middle class" also facilitated a more tangible relationship between the producers of culture—such as authors and theatrical performers—and their audiences.[21] Celebrity and commodification became entwined with the communications technology of the day, expanding exponentially over the course of the eighteenth and nineteenth centuries.

The impulse toward fame was aided by technology—the photograph, the telegraph, the printing press—which eased the path to renown. But the impulse to live life in the public eye was equally nurtured by ideology. Emphasizing the growing importance of success in the marketplace, Braudy asserts that "by the latter eighteenth century, men ... could proudly say that their greatest goal was 'literary fame.'"[22] As Braudy indicates, the popularization and visualization of heroes and artists during the late eighteenth and early nineteenth century caused success itself to become conflated with visibility, an association that would solidify over the course of the twentieth century, in no small part thanks to the motion picture industry.[23] Modern mass publicity was, then, already in some nascent form by at least the early nineteenth century, setting the stage for what would become an unprecedented convergence of media and personality in the twentieth.

By the late nineteenth century in America, touring theatrical companies had famous players who attracted audiences by virtue of their reputations; the theater, however, had neither the means of mass distribution nor the popular mechanisms of publicity that its cinematic counterparts could boast of just a few decades later.[24] Motion pictures could not only be distributed globally, but Hollywood also ardently supplemented their product with an array of fortifying devices ranging from publicity agents to well-fed fan magazines. Newsreel films, too, helped spread images of reputation-making athletes, politicians, authors, and actors—all a part of the afternoon or evening's fare. However, cultural events like the theater of the nineteenth century prepared Americans for the mass cultural phenomenon of cinema in the twentieth century; as Ohmann notes, Americans of the nineteenth century "learned to pay for amusement, learned to expect that it would be provided by professionals (and strangers), learned to accept publicity as the forerunner and framer of a major event, learned that they *must* have certain experiences—or at least know about them—to feel adroit in the medium of the social."[25] This cultural conditioning paved the way for the motion picture industry, which quickly learned to exploit the most commercially advantageous of these earlier techniques while also inventing new approaches to publicity and commerce.

The motion picture industry offered a new kind of product to Americans,

FIGURE 1: Although this November 1919 Fox advertisement differentiates between "great stars" and "great authors," it also places them alongside each other in this constellation of talent. *Picture-Play Magazine.* Collection of the author.

one that by the second decade of the twentieth century was emerging primarily from a more centralized locale than its itinerant entertainment predecessors. During the winter of 1910–1911, production companies flocked to California, many not planning to make it their permanent home.[26] Kevin Starr concisely explains that "by 1915 Hollywood was an established fact; by 1926 it was the United States' fifth largest industry, grossing $1.5 billion a year and accounting for 90 percent of the world's films."[27] Poet and early theorist of the cinema Vachel Lindsay put it more tentatively in his 1915 work, *The Art of the Moving Picture*: "Will this land [California] furthest west be the first to capture the inner spirit of this newest and most curious of the arts? . . . Some of us view with a peculiar thrill the prospect that Los Angeles may become the Boston of the photoplay."[28] Lindsay's gesture is significant not only because he remains uncertain about Hollywood's permanence and dominance, but also because he places cinema and literature on potential par with each other, a pretty radical statement for 1915, albeit one that was also being pondered by Jack London, among others. Indeed, Hollywood would come to displace both Boston and New York as the nation's hotly contested center of cultural capital, at least of a certain sort.

As Lindsay intimates, during the nineteen-teens, the standoff between literary and cinematic status—east versus west—came to a head, as the film industry, which was establishing its production base more firmly in California, began to exploit well-known authors and literary properties as marketing devices. In so doing, a curious intersection of film and literary renown was born, as is evidenced in a Fox Entertainments advertisement from the November 1919 *Picture-Play Magazine*, which equates the status of authorship with that of on-screen celebrity by including images of actress Pearl White alongside Mark Twain; Henry Wadsworth Longfellow alongside Tom Mix (see figure 1).[29] Cinema was changing the face, the tastes, and the relative values of American life and letters.

But unlike the printed word, films were perceived as universally accessible, both economically and intellectually, something Jack London noted with particular interest. The motion picture industry was also offering increasingly palpable rewards to those involved in its productions, creating a new class of elite and a new kind of celebrity. Kevin Starr surmises that "There was literally no precedent in American history for the capacity of Hollywood stars to speak directly to the dream life of the masses."[30] Movies appealed not only to "the masses" as leisure-time occupations, but also to those seeking the wider dissemination of their own images and products. The public figures who occupy the pages of this study stand as distinct examples of Hollywood's impact not only on these newly directed dream lives, but also on the newly directed real lives of those who sought to profit from this influential industry's workings.

More so than its literary or theatrical predecessors, so much of cinema's success relied upon the savvy and relentless deployment of publicity. Although the advertising strategies employed by Hollywood and its studios did not originate with the cinematic product, those selling movie star images to the public virtually perfected them. Stars were the most effective way for studios to brand their products, and this concept of product differentiation mirrored commercial manufacturers' attempts to establish reputations for their brand names at the turn of the century.[31] Over the course of the past hundred years, the discursive web surrounding cinematic practice—fan magazines, studio publicity, even mainstream print media—has focused increasingly on biographical star-based information, partly as a means of enhancing the public's willingness to pay the price of admission to see these people in action as actors and actresses. Hollywood also became adept at creating the kinds of personalities that lent themselves to biographical exploration and exploitation, urging the culture to desire information about their lives, their homes, and their marriages. As Gertrude Stein would astutely observe about the culture of celebrity, "Now, you see, even the cinema doesn't do it for them. A few actors or actresses do, but not the characters they portray."[32]

*

In response to the public's desire to see more of the stars off-screen, in February of 1911 the *New York Telegraph* added a motion picture section to its Sunday editions that included portraits of movie players;[33] this is also the date of publication for the first movie fan magazine, *Moving Picture Story Magazine*, which became a fan-oriented publication in response to readers' pressures for it to move beyond its initial film promotional (versus star promotional) role.[34] The fan magazine emerged out of the public's growing curiosity about personalities, not new but newly invigorated. But it equally evolved out of film producers' need to increase the discourse on stars as a means of achieving product differentiation, an economic necessity in an increasingly competitive field. The early teens were contentious years for cinematic star identity, with many players' names being withheld from the public for a variety of economic, professional, and cultural reasons. Before 1907, Richard deCordova argues, no discourse existed on specific film actors; instead, audiences focused on the apparatus itself, on its ability to magically reproduce the "real."[35] Coming to see actualities, early cinema spectators were lured by the medium's ability to capture and transport different places, people, and events.

Tom Gunning has theorized these early years in terms of a cinema of attractions, suggesting that early movie-goers sought precisely to view events, novelties, spectacles, things that would excite their curiosity along the lines of what they might see at a fairground.[36] Without intending this notion of a cinema of attractions to be applied beyond the early years of cinema or outside of the scope of early film images, Gunning has provided an interesting framework for thinking about the allure of screen stardom. Since, as he puts it, the term signifies early cinema's "foregrounding of the act of display," we might consider the degree to which the logic of stardom relies upon the relationship between audiences and the presentation of stars as spectacular attractions of another sort.[37] As Gunning points out, the notion of attractions is not negated by the onset of narrative cinema since "attractions are not abolished by the classical paradigm they simply find their place within it"; their newfound situation might, in fact, be understood as stardom itself.[38]

After 1907, cinematic spectators began developing more tangible affinities for on-screen actors, who were previously anonymous components of the film product. It took several more years before the film industry began to reveal the identities of their stars—and before stars were entirely willing to be identified with this novel medium—and yet another decade before stars regularly became distinct from their on-screen roles. As testament to these shifts, a January 5, 1910 article in *Moving Picture World* notes "a new method of lobby advertising" by the Kalem company that includes photographs of "principal actors" for "lobby display."[39] The article claims that acting "professionals" frequently tried to "shield their identity" fearing "that their artistic reputations would suffer." Ten months later, the same magazine would acknowledge that the "better known moving picture actors and actresses are known to the public at large," but that "the rank and file, however, are not," using this lack to make a plea for "each picture or reel [to] be preceded by the full cast of characters . . . with the names of actors and actresses playing the parts."[40]

By the 1910s, autographed photos, publicity tours, and print media continued to feed the growing cinematic culture market as the relationships between popularity and profitability were firmly established.[41] By 1913, stars were receiving top billing that rivaled the brand names of the companies that produced them. As picture performers took on more importance for film audiences, the picture personality or movie star became a distinct entity and the film product began to revolve around the treatment of this particular attraction. Speaking precisely to this tendency, *Photoplay* writer Campbell MacCulloch explained in 1928 that the star remained the anchor of moviemaking because "you and your family and your friends and most of the rest of the population scan the lights and the billboards to see *who* is showing at the Palace, rather than *what* is being exhibited there."[42] Stars brought audiences and audiences brought revenue and revenue kept the system going.

Such attraction relied increasingly upon not only on-screen appearances but also on other means by which the public could consume images of and knowledge about the stars. By the late teens, stars were not just highly visible and recognizable, they were almost familiar. As deCordova notes, the concept of the star began to involve the player's existence outside of his or her work in film; private lives emerged as a new site of knowledge that took on increasing importance, sometimes to the point that this knowledge overshadowed the players' roles in the films themselves.[43] This burgeoning culture of personality also prevailed through a series of commercial, ideological, and moral transactions. Scott Sandage observes that "by the 1920s, character traits (honesty and thrift, for example) gave way to personality traits (style and assertiveness, say) as tickets to success."[44] But this is more than just an act of substitution; these traits were competing impulses that created their own set of challenges for those attempting to attain success in the culture as well as for those evaluating the strivers.

*

As the movies matured in the early twentieth century, so too did notions of Hollywood-based reputation that made certain industry workers—especially actresses and actors—into public commodities with often staggering economic value and cultural visibility. Their status raised the bar for achievement in America, and the following chapters suggest the degree to which attaining validation for one's work—even outside of Hollywood—often translated into striking an analogous lode of attention and money, something attainable only in Hollywood. Sandage argues that "with few exceptions, the only identity deemed legitimate in America is a capitalist identity"; when wealth is endowed with the patina of success, acquisition becomes a necessary rung on the ladder of achievement.[45] Hollywood appears to have confused these notions even further, and the tensions among the desire for wealth, success, celebrity, and reputation are discernable in each of the chapters that follow. Hollywood's ascension helped to endow the very notion of reputation with the burden of the marketplace and with pressure to attain comparably staggering proportions of recognition. Scandals and moral concerns aside, the first decades of the twentieth century witnessed a widespread belief that contact with the motion picture industry marked one as exceptional.

As described in the chapters that follow, reputation could function as a form of currency, although not always as effectively as individuals imagined it could. But herein lies the fascinating uncertainty of reputation's value and meaning in the age of Hollywood. Hollywood celebrity greatly affected the aims and strategies of those who sought to act as "reputational entrepreneurs," which Gary Fine defines as those who work to create their own reputations.[46] By framing this book in the context of both reputation and celebrity, and also by linking these concepts to the intimately related issues of success, fame, and financial reward, I hope to suggest the degree to which Hollywood's particular brand of renown was exerting its somewhat disorienting influence on a range of ambitions that were envisioned and enacted in this specific geographic locale.

Reputational value, which Gladys and Kurt Lang perceive as encroaching upon the designations of celebrity and renown, increases based upon the circumference of an individual's status.[47] As they acknowledge, value and publicity are inseparable from reputation, are in fact the foundation for it. But these concepts also transform reputation into celebrity, or perhaps simply render the two indistinct from one another. The motion picture industry, I argue here, facilitated precisely this blurring of status, recognition, and reward as it also initiated a shift in the curiosity and leisure time of a populace who wanted increasingly to know—and were willing to pay for—the details of the Hollywood lifestyle, making Hollywood players appear both familiar and extraordinary. The press, both industry-generated and not, fostered a representation of Hollywood as an exceptional city, detailing the simultaneous glamour and immorality, freedom and paralysis of the movie star lifestyle. *Photoplay* warned its readers about the hazards of stardom in a March 1929 article, "Don't Envy the Stars," one of a genre of cautionary pieces of this era: "A star is in the public's payroll. It is his duty to be a good fellow at whatever cost. And the cost is tremendous! . . . You can't blame the public for demanding the idols it has bought and paid for and you can't blame the star for wanting a private life."[48] Despite such discouragements for both star and fan, made in part to help stem the westward flow of aspiring stars and starlets (and perhaps even star-gazers), the dreamers kept dreaming and the more ambitious continued to embark on their pilgrimages to tinseltown.

Hollywood will serve as the figurative epicenter of this book. The city has a virtually unique symbolic weight in American culture; it is inseparable from its industry and its aftershocks: wealth, lifestyle, publicity. For the figures examined here, Hollywood is a place of unparalleled mythic significance, invested with many of our culture's collective fantasies. Their understandings of Hollywood, which are not always as romantic as one might anticipate, are indicative of its status in the culture at large as a creator and captor of American dreams. The allure of the possibilities afforded by the American motion picture industry is simply unmatched in twentieth-century American life. How else to explain the transformation of Wyatt Earp from a fading frontier legend into an eager observer on the constructed sets of Western movies; Jack London from a successful writer to a frustrated and exploited literary commodity; Clara Bow from a fan to a star receiving more fan mail than any of her contemporaries; Gertrude Stein from under-read modernist icon to aspiring Hollywood sellout; or Ida Lupino from star to director? By thinking about the ways that the movies and their publicity were, in fact, used by a host of aspirants, my hope is to offer a new lens through which to view the impact of the film industry as *the* medium for defining success, American style, even in the face of almost inevitable frustration. These chapters offer a chronological sampling of the wide-ranging appeal of Hollywood, filling in part of the picture of early twentieth-century American life with regard to the fantasy of celebrity and the drive for reputation that remain doggedly with us today.

2

When the West Was Done

WYATT EARP IN HOLLYWOOD

In the mid-ninteen-teens, Jack London and Wyatt Earp reportedly turned up together at a Hollywood set asking for director Raoul Walsh. How Jack London and Wyatt Earp came to know each other before this visit or if the two ever saw each other again are undocumented in the writings by or about London or Earp. However, Walsh was impressed enough by his meeting with the literary giant and the frontier marshal (as Earp would later be labeled) that he describes it in some detail in his notoriously creative autobiography, *Each Man in His Time: The Life Story of a Director*. Walsh explains why the two men decided to seek him out that day: They wanted to hear about Walsh's meeting with the Mexican revolutionary Pancho Villa. As Walsh narrates it,

I gave them a short rundown on what had happened between Juarez and Mexico City. When I had finished, London looked at Earp. "How do you like that? Here we've been trying to live up to our reputations and this guy comes out of nowhere and rides with the man who thumbed his nose at President Wilson." He turned back to me. "Great stuff. I envy you."[1]

Though Earp's was a posthumous celebrity created by later cinematic retellings, he was known to some of his contemporaries for the widely and wildly debated "shootout" at the O.K. Corral that took place on October 26, 1881; London, however, was by the time of this alleged meeting a world-renowned author who was himself involved with the motion picture industry. That these two men—symbols of masculine adventure and heroism, readily associated with notions of a wilderness rapidly disappearing in "civilized" America—were compelled to seek a first-hand account of another legend is intriguing in itself. According to Walsh's narration, London and Earp were fascinated by the notorious Villa and wanted to find out what he was *really* like, to get at the man behind the image by seeking a first-hand account from Walsh, whose *The Life of General Villa* (1914) cast Villa as himself (shot in Mexico) with Walsh playing the younger Villa (shot in California). London's commentary on his own and Earp's struggles to live up to their reputations introduces us to the focus of this chapter and to this project as a whole: the way that personal aspiration and public representation quite literally met on the Hollywood movie set.

Walsh reports that he "tried to draw both men out about their own doings. Neither wanted to talk about himself, but I did manage to get a few good details from Earp about the Clanton family and the famous shootout at the O.K. Corral. London reminisced about Klondike days and the circumstances that spurred him to write *The Call of the Wild*."[2] Walsh's report suggests the degree to which both London and Earp experienced renown by recycling adventures and tales of the past: from life, to literature, to film. London and Earp both made names for themselves outside of the motion picture industry while also seeking to utilize the medium to rearticulate these past experiences in cinematic form. Their goals in this regard were multiple: to enhance their renown and their pocketbooks, while also ensuring their status in the culture's collective memory. Drawn to a man whose current film was semi-documentary in nature, and whose subject was still living to see his image on screen, it is reasoned speculation to suppose, based upon their future engagements with the medium, that Earp and London were interested in exploring similarly conceived cinematic versions of themselves and their "works," ones that might be of use to them both during their lifetimes and after.

But there is another way to read this story. This anecdote has been told and retold since the publication of Walsh's autobiography in the 1970s without question, despite the fact that this encounter likely never happened; in fact, this meeting is as difficult to prove as it is to disprove.[3] Such a statement will not surprise anyone familiar with the mythology surrounding both of these men, whose lives were littered with imposters and fabrications, and whose after-lives have been similarly plagued with fictionalizations and unsubstantiated claims that get recycled in article after article, book after book. The only evidence we have of this meeting resides in Walsh's words, published a good sixty years after the original event. One man's whimsical recollection has become history.

Walsh's is certainly an appealing scenario: these mythic figures on the same stage together, if only for an afternoon; it is seductive as all myths are, which explains why it is cited so frequently and perhaps why no one has questioned its veracity, at least in print. It is also a reminder of the degree to which so much of what is circulated about public figures—particularly those who enter the sphere of Hollywood publicity with its penchant for exaggeration, fictionalization, and misremembering—is oftentimes questionable, at best.

This much is arguable: Earp and London were drawn to Hollywood in part to document their previous adventures in that myth-laden space of the West, both literal and, in the case of London, also literary. Wyatt Earp's twenty-first-century reputation, his current status as a household name, owes itself almost entirely to Hollywood's posthumous retellings, reliant though they are upon the literary biography he settled upon during his lifetime. Working in the territories between Kansas and California (and, later, Alaska), Earp allegedly spent time as a stagecoach driver, buffalo hunter, marshal, gambler, boxing referee, real estate investor, and proprietor of various saloons. After his tenure in the "Wild West" Earp made his way to Hollywood, hanging around movie sets and befriending such newly minted Hollywood Western movie luminaries as William S. Hart and Tom Mix. Earp tried to initiate a cinematic version of his life, in large part to correct what he perceived as a violent misunderstanding of his role in the West.

This chapter examines Earp's desire to have his life documented cinematically, in part by considering his goals of autobiographical representation and his investment in cinema as a vehicle for ensuring his place in American history. What follows is closely connected to chapter three, which investigates the Hollywood leg of Jack London's career; both men's approaches to the industry also allow for a discussion of important changes occurring in the culture of representation during the early decades of the twentieth century. Why did Earp strive so vehemently for a specifically cinematic corrective to the various versions of his life? Was cinema already perceived as more permanent or powerful than literary biography? This chapter seeks to answer such questions and to better understand Earp's ambitions in the context of cinema's early years, to which Earp was witness. Earp was also more than a witness: He participated in an era that was in the process of defining what movies might be used for in American culture.

While this chapter builds on existing Earp scholarship, these writings do little to further an understanding of Earp's relationship to cinematic representation, in large part because there are so few tangible materials with which to work.[4] Existing Earp scholarship also fails to account for the complexity of the film culture that surrounded him, much as it neglects the significance of Earp's cinematic goals in relation to the status of publicity and representation in the early twentieth century. Like Gertrude Stein years later, Earp failed to see his life recast through the lens of the motion picture industry during his lifetime; however, his efforts reveal cinema's curious potential as a personal mythmaking vehicle at a point fairly early in Hollywood's history. Earp was seduced by something happening to the nature of representation in the culture at large. His actions suggest that he believed in the redemptive powers of cinematic imagery and that his own belief in Hollywood's mythmaking potential relied on a faith in the cinema's legendary and legend-making capacities.

For Earp and several of his "cowboy" contemporaries, like Charles Siringo and Emmett Dalton, Hollywood seemed able to effectively make history of a very personal variety. While Earp is the titular subject of this chapter, debates over cinematic authenticity and realism, and discussions of other significant contemporary figures such as Dalton, will play a prominent role in the chapter's secondary goal of establishing the status of cinematic representation during the industry's early years. Understanding this context for Earp's Hollywood speculation is key, for it offers evidence of the way that Hollywood film functioned more broadly in the contemporary imagination. Film producers were employing ideas of authenticity and simulation to create and market their films, and these notions directly affected how Earp went about his reputational pursuits. Earp's representational dilemmas remind us that he was situated firmly at a crossroads between nineteenth- and twentieth-century modes of mythmaking, publicity, and representation. Earp's interest in the motion picture industry—and Jack London's for that matter—occurred at an important historical juncture, virtually at the birth of Hollywood as the center of American image making. Earp witnessed the medium's transition from the nickelodeons of the early 1900s to the motion picture palaces of the 1920s; from one-reel films to features; from working-class to middle-class entertainment.[5]

While Earp was known to some degree for his exploits by the turn of the twentieth century, he was not a household name until the movies made him one posthumously. Paul Hutton explains that "Earp was certainly well-known in his time, especially in the mining camps and on the gambling circuit, and the October 26, 1881, gunfight at the O.K. Corral was widely reported in the national press. But Earp was never remotely as famous as Jesse James, Wild Bill Hickok, or Buffalo Bill Cody," men whose deeds were already being mythologized by the movies.[6] Earp was aware of his own marginalization and, despite numerous press accounts of the infamous shootout, he in no way lived the life of a celebrity, Western or otherwise. In fact, Earp was better known by many of his contemporaries as the controversial referee for the 1896 Fitzsimmons-Sharkey fight, one of the most publicized sporting events of the 1890s.

The "facts" surrounding Earp's jobs—lawman, motion picture consultant, referee—remain murky, even questionable. According to his associate John P. Clum, he "played an important and strenuous part in shaping the orderly stride of Empire on its westward course," the very narrative that many Western movies repeatedly mythologized.[7] But Earp's life appears today as a chain of factual uncertainties: the details of the shootout at the O.K. Corral have been debated virtually since its occurrence; no paperwork survives to prove that Earp served as a paid movie consultant or ever appeared in a movie; and Earp was accused by his contemporaries of illicitly profiting from the hotly debated victory he bestowed upon Sharkey at the aforementioned fight. Had the match been captured on film, audiences might have later perceived the truth for themselves as they did with future filmed sporting events, and certainly as they do now with instant replay. In fact, Charles Musser demonstrates that publicity for filmed fights "emphasized that spectators could decide for themselves whether the referee's decision was just"; a blurb in the August 8, 1913, *Variety*, "Picturing Horse Race," suggests this same possibility with regard to a complaint leveled against a judge's decision that was validated by "a moving picture of the event" that proved the blue ribbon winner had not "been ridden according to the rules."[8] It is precisely this logic of witnessing, judging, and remembering that piqued Earp's interest in Hollywood and the motion picture industry.

When Earp arrived there in the early 1900s, Hollywood was in many ways the last frontier, a new mythic territory for those willing to wrangle with and attempt to harness the nascent medium. One of the earliest film genres, the Western, aligned itself with ideas of expansionism, masculinity, realism, and frontier nostalgia, particularly during its formative years. Selig and Essanay sent their companies west in the first decade of the century for outdoor location shooting with real cowboys who were experienced with horses and cattle. As Bowser describes it, "the Western film genre was a rediscovery of the wide open spaces, of the days of freedom and adventure, not very long before the time of these films, when the American people opened up a wilderness."[9] While Bowser's description here is infused with a certain degree of romanticism, this was precisely the appeal of the Westerns, which hearkened back to a past that, as Richard Slotkin has argued, never existed.[10]

Westerns took advantage of outdoor locations, which many early spectators understood as a testament to the films' realness, their "actuality," as one advertisement put it in 1912.[11] This mise-en-scène served as a backdrop for the visual celebration of male movement and adventure as it supplemented—some would say supplanted—a culture's memory of its frontier past. These films and the discourse elicited by them commemorate heroism, aggressiveness, and virility during an era in which many men were faced with the diminishing importance of these traits in their increasingly urbanized, industrialized lives. Consequently, the Western is one of the first film genres to establish cinema's interest in the exploration of spaces that are almost exclusively populated by men. The movies also visually captured the mythological West with all of its attending associations in a fashion no other medium could rival. Earp's recognition of this fact was hardly unique, though it will serve as the basis for our understanding of why Hollywood became such an important site for imagining the making or remaking of reputations. Earp's failure to achieve this during his lifetime attests to the fantastic difficulty facing those who hoped to shape their on-screen image; however, his posthumous cinematic status also reminds us of the potential power of the movies in the making of reputations.

Representational Frontiers: From Buffalo Bill to Boxing Films

Wyatt Earp was not the only Western figure to run head first into the brick wall of modernity, trying to figure out how to live and profit from an increasingly archaic if romanticized past in the evolving media landscape of the twentieth century. William F. Cody, better known as Buffalo Bill, was also renowned for his Western adventures, particularly his scouting and killing of both Indians and buffalo; he too sought new modes of adventure, representation, and earning a livelihood in a post-frontier America. Jane Tomkins concisely narrates his post-frontier career:

> He wrote dime novels about himself and an autobiography by the age of thirty-four, by which time he was already famous; and he then began another set of careers, first as an actor, performing on the urban stage in wintertime melodramatic representations of what he actually earned a living at in the summer (scouting and leading hunting expeditions), and finally becoming the impresario of his great Wild West show, a form of entertainment he invented and carried on as actor, director, and all-around idea man for thirty years.[12]

Buffalo Bill's Wild West show began in the 1880s and lasted through the 1920s, outliving Cody, who Joy Kasson describes as "the most recognizable celebrity of his day."[13] As Buffalo Bill's Wild West faded in popularity, Cody tried various gimmicks to regain its previous success, such as restaging train robberies. Unfortunately for Cody, train robberies already had been "staged" more successfully on celluloid with Edison and Porter's *The Great Train Robbery* (1903), one of the films we might consider as setting the precedent for the American cinema's Western genre. It seems audiences were less impressed with live reenactment after the advent of such novel cinematic technology. In a 1913 article, "Movies Bust Bill Show," *Variety* affirms cinema's deleterious effect upon Cody's Wild West, noting that the mass of "movie programs . . . have satiated the juvenile and adult followers of the wild west life, and destroyed the following that the early seasons of the Bill exhibition could invariably command."[14] Cody had once made a living as a Western hero, but he was now "tamed by Writer-Promoter Ned Buntline" and reduced to circus appearances, as *Time* magazine put it in their analysis of his career in 1959.[15]

Film technology made it possible for people in the early twentieth century to witness representations of events for the first time, not just recreations or reenactments. While this is not to suggest that any representation can be unmediated, the accuracy with which events could be captured and replayed through motion picture technology lent to the medium a degree of perceived authenticity, despite its equal potential to manipulate reality. Buffalo Bill's Wild West remains a curiously self-reflexive bit of recreated reality, one that was both subjective and interpretive. But it is also testament to one man's attempt to etch himself in the culture's memory and to profit from his unique experiences by selling himself as frontier manhood incarnate. Kasson understands the Wild West show as "memory showmanship": "Buffalo Bill's Wild West became America's Wild West."[16]

Cody's Wild West resonates with the way that Wyatt Earp sought to memorialize his own tales of the "Wild West" through the movies, which appeared able to create a vivid corrective to what Earp perceived was historical inaccuracy, in the process allowing him to stake his own (presumably profitable) place in the culture's collective memory. Earp claimed to want to show America the deeds of the "real" Wyatt Earp, just as Buffalo Bill sought to align himself with the spectacle of his own heroic West. Although there is no doubt in the case of either man that these would be rather colorful interpretations of the real, there appeared in the culture at this time a tendency to accept certain signifiers as authentic in a fashion that privileged performance over history. Frank Norris noted in 1902 that,

We may keep alive for many years yet the idea of a Wild West, but the hired cowboys and paid rough riders of Mr. William Cody are more like "the real thing" than can be found today in Arizona, Mexico or Idaho. Only the imitation cowboys, the college-bred fellows who "go out on a ranch" carry the revolver or wear the concho. The Frontier has become conscious of itself, acts the part for the Eastern visitor; and this self-consciousness is a sign, surer than all others, of the decadence of a type, the passing of an epoch.[17]

Norris insightfully invokes the issues of authenticity and simulation that inform this chapter's discussion of Wyatt Earp, as well as the next chapter's consideration of Jack London. Pointing to the "consciousness" of the frontier as an indication that what was left of it was only a simulation of its former self, Norris implies that what remained was a re-creation, perhaps *as* authentic as any other surviving form of the frontier. In fact, Norris implies that a geographically removed simulation in the form of Buffalo Bill's Wild West—a self-contained frontier reenactment—had become more real than the places and people that his show represented.

Although Cody opted for his reenactment show as a means to celebrate himself and turn a profit, he also dabbled in the celluloid craze that was sweeping the country.[18] In the early twentieth century, Buffalo Bill anteceded three of his annual tours with a self-produced documentary film, *Buffalo Bill Bids You Goodbye*.[19] Bowser also notes that, "inspired by the success of the Johnson-Jeffries fight film [Pliny P.] Craft convinced Buffalo Bill to let the Wild West Show be recorded on film and then found backing for a three-reel feature."[20] While little documentation exists to indicate exactly how Cody used these films, Anderson's description suggests that Cody essentially endowed his own "theater" with exclusive rights to his image. Using the boxing film as inspiration, Buffalo Bill's three-reel feature is aligned with a genre of films that were attempting to capture and replay "real" events, events that would have taken place with or without the camera's presence. But like the movie Western, which created the imaginative iconography with which we are familiar today, repeated representational fictions often come to signify authenticity, eventually inheriting the patina of historical reality. However much Cody staged his West in a contained arena of cowboys and Indians turned *actors*, the point is precisely that made by Norris: that it was as much a reproduction of reality as it was reality itself.[21] Cody's film was a representation of a re-creation, removing film audiences at least thrice from the "real" that Cody tried to depict.

Like Cody, Wyatt Earp turned to the motion picture industry with an eye toward the future of his reputation, but with little effect during his lifetime. Moving semipermanently to Los Angeles around 1906, Earp maintained mining interests, often traveling to Arizona via railroad while spending summers in the temperate climate and mining financial capital of Southern California.[22] Earp perceived at a fairly early moment in the medium's history that he might be able to use film to represent, correct, and perpetuate his own legend. A venture of this nature would have been an act of personal re-appropriation, for Earp's past had already been caught up in the machine of public discourse.

Earp claimed that he despised his own notoriety but had not "put forth any effort to check the tales that have been published, in recent years, of the exploits in which my brothers and I are supposed to have been the principal participants" despite the fact that he claimed, "Not one of them is correct."[23] But this was not an entirely accurate representation of his own involvement: Earp had already been actively pursuing Hollywood representation for some years, even claiming to have hired someone to write a movie script in 1925.[24] As early as 1900, Earp had first penned an "account of his adventures" that he shared with George Parsons while in Nome, Alaska; as with so many Earp-related documents, no copy of this manuscript survives.[25]

What does survive are letters, primarily between Earp and either actor William S. Hart or biographer Stuart Lake, many concerning Earp's autobiographical and cinematic intentions. Earp's speculative relationship to Hollywood touches on issues central to the earliest years of film; the very idea, after all, that an individual could tell his story through a film radically revises the concept of autobiography, which has been (and still remains) a traditionally written event. The films of cinema's formative years testify to the multiplicity of uses for the medium—as fiction, as spectacle, as documentary, as reenactment. In fact, before turning specifically to Earp's story, it is worth considering how the culture created by the motion picture industry at the turn of the century might have helped to shape Earp's Hollywood ambitions.

*

The issues surrounding the making and reception of early documentary and reenactment fight films help to illuminate Earp's desires for self-representation, in part because of Earp's own role as a boxing referee. In the fight films, we witness masculinity conceived strictly in terms of violence, the male body scrutinized and celebrated as spectacle. Like much frontier mythology (Buffalo Bill's Wild West, for example), in the boxing ring men acted out a kind of nostalgic performance of behavioral traits that were perceived by many as rapidly fading away. The Corbett-Fitzsimmons fight also initiated important debates over representation and reality in early cinema that are pertinent to an understanding of Earp's Hollywood efforts. This is particularly the case because the celebrity names of boxers "attracted publicity and facilitated advertising" for these films, forecasting the kind of "authentic appearances" in Western movies by famous men of the West such as Emmett Dalton and Al Jennings in the late nineteen-teens and early twenties, as will be discussed momentarily.[26]

On March 17, 1897, Robert Fitzsimmons and James Corbett fought it out in front of a crowd *and* in front of the cameras in Carson City, Nevada. Musser reports that "the battery of cameras, grouped together in a wooden shed, were given the best seats in the house while paying customers were forced to look into the sun."[27] Among those looking into the sun was Wyatt Earp, who was there as "a special reporter for the *New York World*."[28] Earp's attendance at the fight is significant, for it suggests his awareness, as early as 1897, of the motion picture industry's ability to capture and record history in the making. There is little possibility that Earp missed the media attention concerning the filming of the match or the big wooden stand from which the fight was filmed, visible as it is in surviving photographs of the event. The fight is thus one of the many probable sources for Earp's thinking about cinematic representation.

At the Corbett-Fitzsimmons fight, Earp attended not as a referee but as a reporter. *The New York World*'s March 18, 1897, front-page coverage of the fight notes Earp's presence virtually at the beginning of its story, describing him as "the famous referee of the Fitzsimmons-Sharkey fight"; no mention is made of the shootout at the O.K. Corral. *The World* reported that no fight was "ever reported as fully as diversily [sic], as graphically as is this one in The World to-day," and the newspaper's coverage included a series of visual representations of the boxers, showing the location of each of the "362 blows struck during the fourteen rounds."[29] This layout suggests that the paper was responding to their perception of their one million plus readers' (per the newspaper's circulation byline) demand for visual representation. *The World* further reported that they had "two official stenographers (for the first time in the history of reporting) taking down the words of [reporter John L.] Sullivan and of *The World*'s technical reporter as the fight progressed, and reporting blow for blow and every movement for *The World*'s minute technical report."[30] In their self-promotion, *The World* reminds us of exactly what they perceived as valuable to a turn-of-the-century audience: visual representation, detailed commentary, and near simultaneity of reporting.

So while the Kinetograph captured the Corbett-Fitzsimmons fight on film, newspapers, telegraphs, and theatrical reenactments (another way to dramatize a fight from afar) sent *representations* of the event across the country.[31] The Veriscope (meaning "truth-viewer") Company debuted its "heavily promoted" film of the actual fight to a packed house on May 22, 1897, a full two months after the actual fight had transpired. As Musser describes it, "Theater seats became seats at ringside as patrons saw this ritualized sport unfold from a single camera perspective in realistic time."[32] Viewers could now watch the event that they had previously only had access to via print and live reenactment; here was reality replayed for anyone who wished—and was willing to pay—to experience the event *with their own eyes*.

This film presented to audiences one of the exciting possibilities for cinematic documentation; however, it also spawned a significant variation in the hands of Sigmund Lubin, who "took advantage of the reenactment tradition to produce his own fight films 'in imitation of Corbett and Fitzsimmons.'"[33] With actors "made up to look like the champions" on a rooftop stage, Lubin "advertised his REPRODUCTION OF THE CORBETT AND FITZSIMMONS FIGHT a week before the Veriscope's premier and sent several exhibition units on the road."[34] Musser documents a range of audience reactions to this reproduction ranging from acceptance, to incredulity, to outrage over being duped into witnessing a fake representation. This latter reaction suggests the degree to which audiences sought a discernable truth from their representations in situations that lent themselves to realist expectations, particularly those, it seems, for which images were already in circulation through other media. Audiences wanted to see the actual Fitzsimmons in the actual fight, not a Fitzsimmons look-alike and not even Fitzsimmons himself reenacting the fight (another method used when the event itself could not be recorded). Musser describes one audience that collectively demanded a refund after learning what "facsimile" meant, reinforcing the degree to which perceived authenticity could reign over these nonfictional narratives.

Although boxing films present just one kind of cinematic event, they also indicate the extent to which the industry and its consumers were in the process of defining each other. The newspapers and the moving pictures vied for the public's money, in part by touting their respective abilities to capture the real. Earp's presence at this match is only one probable source for his awareness of such issues concerning the early movie industry, its growing status in American culture, and the debates over representation and recreation as they would pertain directly to his own cinematic pursuits. Not long after this filmed fight, Earp began expressing the idea of cinematically recreating his past, evidenced in part by his pleas to established cowboy actor William S. Hart to re-enact them on his behalf.

What's Wrong with a Cowboy in Hollywood?

By the early 1920s, Earp found himself discouraged by his failure to inspire a cinematic version of his story, so much so that he spent significant time and energy working to initiate the production of this moving record. With his efforts frustrated at every turn, he decided to allow his friend, John Flood, an unfortunately incompetent writer, to pen his story, still with the hopes that the book or its serialization would initiate a film deal. Flood finished the manuscript in 1926 and William S. Hart tried unsuccessfully to help the men shop it around. In 1927, Stuart Lake approached the frustrated Earp and eventually took over the botched writing job, successfully, though posthumously, reinventing Earp in his *Wyatt Earp: Frontier Marshal* (1931), published two years after Earp's death.

Lake's biography presents a romantic portrait of Earp as a heroic upholder of frontier justice. This highly fictionalized rendering of Earp's life, particularly the showdown at the O.K. Corral, became the basis for virtually every film that has dealt with his life since the movie rights were first sold to Fox in 1932.[35] As Paul Andrew Hutton asserts, "no frontier legend owes more to Hollywood, and less to contemporary historical fame, than does the story of Wyatt Earp."[36] In "Celluloid Lawman," Hutton is even more explicit, avowing that "Earp's reputation—now almost a national myth—was essentially invented," and furthermore that Lake was a "literary godfather who through the power of his pen elevated this itinerant gambler and sometime lawman into a towering frontier legend."[37] Certainly in 1920s Hollywood, Earp could hardly claim the kind of fame that he would garner after posthumously becoming a character in Western films, in large part precisely because Earp's attempts to have his story filmed during his lifetime were consistently thwarted.

Robert Anderson traces the Western's roots as an American genre, discussing the degree to which "increasingly, from 1907–1909, American manufacturers cinematized the legendary domain of Buffalo Bill with its six-shooters, stagecoaches, cowboys and Indians."[38] By 1910, 20 percent of all motion pictures produced by American manufacturers were Westerns; these figures held through the 1920s.[39] This significant body of film shaped America's envisioning of the West. As Andre Bazin observed, "Without the cinema the conquest of the West would have left behind, in the shape of the Western story, only a minor literature."[40] Bazin's statement recalls Earp's attempts not to be left behind by trying to re-make himself in Hollywood during this transitional period. Earp appears to have done everything in his power to this end, even claiming to have commissioned a script to facilitate his story's transition into film. In a July 3, 1925, letter to William S. Hart, Earp writes: "I have just received word that the script which I am having written will be ready in a short time. As soon as I receive the same, I will immediately forward it to you as I am very anxious to get your judgment on it . . . I am in hopes that the material in the script will be available for your use."[41] While Earp is not explicit about the subject matter of the script in the letter, his discussion of it is sandwiched between complaints about his misrepresentation in the press and a plea for Hart to make a movie of Earp's life, suggesting that the script Earp refers to was likely autobiographical in nature. Hollywood had already established cinematic Western heroes; Earp was doing everything in his power, and eliciting Hart to do the same, in order to add himself to this growing roster of Western legends.

James McQuade's 1910 article, "Famous Cowboys in Motion Pictures," similarly acknowledges the role that motion pictures eventually would play in establishing Western legends like Earp. McQuade begins his piece by bemoaning the death of the "real" cowboy, lamenting that "he, too, will soon become a memory that will be revived only in song and story."[42] This contemporary account at first ignores the motion picture industry, but McQuade eventually corrects himself, noting that he "had overlooked the potency of the motion picture and the wonderful part it will play in handing down to future generations not only a memory of these 19th and 20th century centaurs, but accurate duplicates of the living, acting men themselves."[43]

McQuade's account is one of the earliest recorded discussions of the cowboy that takes into account cinema's potential to record—to duplicate, as he terms it—history and historical figures.[44] Acknowledging the degree to which movies might function as cultural memory, McQuade predicts the role that the motion picture industry did, in fact, play in recreating the West on film, particularly during the teens and twenties, and again during the Western genre's resurgence in the 1950s. But McQuade also seems to suggest something more than just representation when he refers to "accurate duplicates of the living, acting men themselves"; in fact, he seems to be hoping that films might not just tell stories of the West involving mythic figures of the past, but that it might record these "living, acting men themselves."

And, as we shall see, it did. Wyatt Earp was far from the only cowboy to make his way to Hollywood; numerous working cowboys lived in, perhaps even flocked to Hollywood during this period as well.[45] Men like Earp were faced with life *after* the frontier and making movies as cowboys offered one of the few lifestyles that did not require a rejection of that increasingly outmoded identity, just one of the reasons that Hollywood was an appealing destination for the displaced Westerner. The early years of cinema drew on a multiplicity of talent from a variety of walks of life: vaudeville, theater, opera, and the like. But the cowboy was certainly one of the most often utilized "non-actors" for the early motion picture, bringing with him a sense of authenticity that directors and audiences perceived as essential to the success of the genre.

Like the many cowboys who sought to make livings for themselves by reproducing Western adventure for the motion picture industry, Earp came to Hollywood and spent time hanging around movie sets. Over the years, Earp made his way through various Hollywood social circles, garnering behind-the-scenes interactions with both major and minor industry players. Like so many other Hollywood hopefuls, Earp viewed Hollywood as a potentially profitable place, but particularly so because he felt that he already possessed a reputation that could translate into something cinematically valuable. Earp's curious failure to garner cinematic self-representation in Hollywood occurred during a period in which the West was actively being redefined on-screen, particularly by Earp's Hollywood associates William S. Hart and Tom Mix. But while Hart and Mix were actors by profession, a number of Western figures, many of whom were not as well known by their contemporaries as Earp, already had managed to finagle their way into the industry. These are the men Earp would have been watching during the teens and twenties, for many of their successes with the motion picture industry supported his contention that there was a role for a man like him in Hollywood, even if he was too old to play the part himself.[46] Emmett Dalton, Al Jennings, and Charles Siringo are just three of these Western figures. Not surprisingly, their much-publicized value within the industry resided in their "authenticity" and their ability to connote "realism," terms that were used repeatedly to describe them, much as they also were being applied to Jack London and the films made of his works, some of which were concurrent with these productions.

Dalton is a case in point. A March 27, 1920, *Motion Picture World* discussion of his *Beyond the Law* (1918) notes first and foremost the film's popularity, which was "smashing house records at every performance after the opening, when the waiting lines reached half a block in both directions from the Symphony entrance."⁴⁷ The film beat box office records at the Symphony theater previously shared by a Tom Mix film and Lew Cody's *The Beloved Cheater*, which employed what *Moving Picture World* called an "exploitation 'stunt'" in which a contest winner won a role in Cody's next picture. So what did *Beyond the Law* have that might have impelled it beyond the success of Mix's and Cody's films? *Moving Picture World* commended Dalton for not exploiting his picture through cheap stunts and, more importantly, for making a film that they described as "mainly historical": "It is said to be built wholly on facts and to be a true history of the exploits of the famous Dalton gang."⁴⁸ Despite the tentative language used here—"it is said to"; language likely borrowed from the film's own publicity—the success of this picture clearly resided in its perceived authenticity, its reenactment of the historical past through the stories of a group of men whose reputations, like Earp's, preceded them.

This emphasis on historical authenticity was also used for an earlier Dalton film, *The Last Stand of the Dalton Boys* (1912), which claimed that "every scene [was] an actuality."⁴⁹ While "actuality" was the term widely used to refer to non-acted, nonfiction films around the turn of the century, here it is used to connote reality. The advertisement uses other terms associated with the industry's earliest descriptions of its products, language that had been replaced by 1918 when *Beyond the Law* was released: "Pictures Posed by People That Actually Took Part in the Raid." Acting had replaced the idea of posing for pictures by the late teens, but this 1912 production emphasizes the same kind of authenticity that was still at issue in Dalton's later performance. In fact, the publicity for the 1912 film makes certain promises to its readers about the realistic content of the film: "You will see Emmet [*sic*] Dalton, the last of the Dalton Gang . . . The actual cave . . . The actual store where they purchased ammunition." One of the film's primary functions, then, was to present visually to its audiences as many of the people, places, and objects associated with the "actual" events of the past. While obviously not a documentary in the sense that the Corbett-Fitzsimmons fight film might be, the filmmakers in charge of this publicity operate on the assumption that conveying a connection to the original events would increase the value of their (re)production.

The advertising campaign for the latter Dalton film takes these issues to their logical extreme in a way that directly mirrors Earp's concurrent and later attempts for his own cinematic representation. A *Moving Picture World* advertisement appearing in the November 30, 1918, issue proclaims that, "Unlike other pictures, it offers the live showman a rare opportunity to give the people something different, by featuring EMMETT DALTON one of the characters of the original story."[50] This is a commercially ingenuous advertising strategy, seducing audiences based upon a direct appeal to the desires fostered by a culture of personality. It is also an attempt to rehabilitate the idea of aura, to use Walter Benjamin's term for this concept, or to establish a different kind of "cinema of attractions," to borrow from Tom Gunning, since the film purports to present a real Western figure, not just a representation of a Western figure. This idea had roots in the late-nineteenth-century boxing films already discussed. As a crucial marketing strategy, such logic is also closely aligned with ideas that were helping to link celebrities with commercial value.

A September 14, 1918, advertisement makes further gestures toward the importance of Dalton's presence in the film when it describes him as, "The Only Survivor of the World's Most Noted Outlaws, THE 'DALTON GANG.'"[51] The advertisement appeals to a very important logic that privileges authenticity, a logic that did not dissolve with the advent of mechanical reproduction; it was, as Dalton would indicate, merely transformed. So that, while *Moving Picture World* claimed that Dalton did not employ any "stunts" to gain popularity for his film, a *Los Angeles Times* advertisement suggests otherwise when it promises that "Emmett Dalton personally will appear before every showing of his six reel picture *Beyond the Law*."[52] Dalton was himself a relic of America's outlaw frontier past; his presence was meant to ensure the success of his film.

Dalton's existing reputation therefore functioned as a cinematic commodity. This is reinforced by the film's content, which departs somewhat from the earlier film, which took its spectator to real locations in order to convey a sense of history. The advertisement for the 1918 film, however, does emphasize the degree to which this film would function as autobiography: "A true story with Original Characters—Hear of his Beautiful Love—Mothers devotion and Brothers help—Why he held up trains and robbed banks."[53] The exhibition of the film thus promised several related things through its advertising campaign: imagistic and historical authenticity gained from Dalton as an actor; insight into the sensational life and psychology of a real outlaw gained from the film's depiction of the outlaw's "true story"; and a guarantee of the above based upon and exceeded by Dalton's actual presence at the screening.

Beyond the Law also demonstrates the degree to which the first twenty or so years of film production established irregular patterns of source material: Much as films were often derived from literature, some literature was being derived from films, as the following chapter will investigate more thoroughly. Wyatt Earp and Jack London were both caught up in the flux of these battles over resources: the former unsure of how to best parlay his story into the cinematic realm and the latter who would eventually write *Hearts of Three*, a novel based upon a movie serial. Dalton's *Beyond the Law* advertising campaign also leads with an acknowledgment of the film's evolution that details the iterations that one particular story could generate with the help of the new medium: "A Big Super Feature Production. The story which ran for five months in the Wide World Magazine, and which will soon be serialized and issued in book form, so tremendous has been its success with the public."[54] These are the layers of Dalton's mythological origins, the many ways in which he was able to insinuate himself into American popular culture: as a member of the notorious gang, as the subject of a written story, as a film star, and as a character in a novel. The production of these strata mirrors Wyatt Earp's ambitions for a similarly layered, multimedia, post-frontier legacy.

Dalton appears to have achieved by the 1920s precisely what had eluded Earp, and fellow cowboy Charles Siringo was mining similar territory. Just four years after the shootout at the O.K. Corral that would in later years establish Earp as a frontier legend, Charles Siringo, according to William Luhr, wrote the first cowboy autobiography, *A Texas Cowboy, or, Fifteen Years on the Hurricane Deck of a Spanish Pony* (1885). Like Earp, Siringo came to Hollywood, although much later, in the early 1920s:

A favorite hangout for aspiring cowboy movie stars was the Water Hole Saloon, only a few blocks away, at the corner of Cahuenga Avenue and Hollywood Boulevard. It was there that assistant film directors could usually round up cowboys whenever they were needed, and drivers would customarily stop to give them a ride to Universal or the Lasky ranch. Siringo often walked to the Water Hole, as he liked to see the movie cowboys and cowgirls with their silver-mounted spurs and high Stetson hats. Although such costumes evoked memories of his cowboy days, he confessed that "such high hats and girls wearing pants were not seen on the early-day ranges."[55]

The presence of an established hangout for "aspiring cowboy movie stars" evidences the degree to which the Western figure was a viable commodity in early Hollywood. What was authentically Western—as Norris pointed out in relationship to Buffalo Bill—is a bit murkier.

Like Siringo, Earp came closest to success through his ongoing relationship with William S. Hart. Hart considered himself an advocate for "real cowboys," who he viewed as unquestionably heroic and troublingly neglected, by his industry in particular. Siringo also corresponded with Hart, writing in a letter that "it looks as though I might get into the play

[Metro Goldwyn Mayer Studio's production of *Billy the Kid*] as technical advisor."[56] Although not as successful as Dalton, Siringo did maintain visibility during these years in Hollywood. He received his first part as a movie extra in *Nine Scars Make a Man* (1924), but Siringo struggled to sustain himself on motion picture work when Hart hired him as a consultant for his immensely successful comeback vehicle *Tumbleweeds* (1925), probably out of pity for Siringo's poverty.[57] Why Siringo won this honor over Earp is unclear, but Hart clearly desired cowboy authenticity as much as many of the cowboys needed his Hollywood clout.

Around the same time of Dalton's and Siringo's flirtations with the industry, Al and Frank Jennings, the sometimes bumbling bandits of the West, were also receiving praise for their outlaw film, *The Lady of the Dugout* (1918), which *Moving Picture World* described as "based on true incidents of their outlaw days."[58] This had become a veritable subgenre of the period: the Western film starring and based on the "authentic" Western outlaw. The 1921 *Motion Picture Studio Directory* in fact describes Al Jennings as making films "based upon personal experiences."[59] These autobiographical renderings changed the stakes of reputation by making on-screen celebrity function as an extension of history. The Jennings' film was thus praised by *Moving Picture World* for its "naturalness" and "historical value," terms that are echoed in the praises leveled at Emmett Dalton's film. Concepts of history and reality were valuable commodities in the vocabulary of the industry, and like Dalton, Jennings relied upon himself to entice spectators to his films. *Moving Picture World* also noted that "Al Jennings appears in person at the evening performance and delivers an address that is as much of an attraction as the picture." This recognition acknowledges the degree to which both the "real" Jennings and the "reel" Jennings, to borrow language used by William S. Hart, were considered marketable and valuable.

Reel Representation

James McQuade, whose 1910 article expresses concern about the cowboy legacy, was far from the only one to articulate an urgent need to recognize and record Western legends of the nineteenth century with the technology that was defining the twentieth. Earp's friend and de facto literary agent, William S. Hart, played a significant role in trying to preserve Earp's reputation. He also created a cinematic West that millions of Americans experienced during the silent era. While Horace Greeley's suggestion to "go West" was intended literally, for many city-bound men and boys the closest they got was the movie theater, where they saw the West on-screen, often watching an actor like Hart live out adventures that were increasingly removed from the realities of city living. Boxing matches functioned similarly, as Jack London explained in his coverage of the 1910 Johnson-Jeffries fight for the *New York Herald*: Men "want to see fights because of the old red blood of Adam in them that will not down."[60] Earp expresses a similar reaction in a letter to Hart about an upcoming Dempsey-Tunney fight: The very thought of it "starts my blood to flowing again and makes me want to be at the ringside too."[61]

Westerns, too, sought to foster a sense of real, rugged, and invigorating adventure for their audiences. As a *Pictures and Picturegoer* correspondent notes, "To spend a day with Bill [S. Hart] and his company up in the mountains or out on the deserts is to lose that strange sense of 'unrealness' that haunts you more or less on the 'sets' of the big moving picture studios . . . never for a moment did I lose the feeling that I was living a vital bit of the life as it used to be in the great golden West."[62] Reinforcing the myth of the "great golden West," the article understands location-shot Westerns as possessing an authentic backdrop for the vital, typically masculine roles being depicted within them. The Western, the piece implies, exists on the "real" side of the Hollywood spectrum.

The realness of cinematic simulation was also echoed in discussions of the status of the actor versus the status of the fading real hero of the West. In a wonderfully self-reflexive article written for the *Morning Telegraph* in 1921, "Bill Hart Introduces a Real—Not Reel—Hero," Hart, in the words of the article's subtitle, "explains that there are living two men who did the daring deeds he tries to do on screen": Bat Masterson and Wyatt Earp.[63] Already pointing to the difference between actual and represented deeds, Hart further delineates what he perceives as a vast difference between performing the role of Western frontiersman and living it:

Now, I am just an actor—a mere player seeking to reproduce the lives of those great gunmen who molded a new country for us to live in and enjoy peace and prosperity. And we have to-day in America two of these men with us in the flesh. . . . They are the last of the greatest band of gunfighters—upholders of law and order—that ever lived.

Diminishing his own role as actor, Hart implicitly values the role of experience in his celebration of frontier heroism. Though he remembered traveling through the American West as a child, Hart had a theatrical background and was not a "cowboy," per se. Earp and Masterson had therefore "been there" in a way that Hart had not.

Hart's attempt to challenge audiences' acceptance of his cowboy characters implied that these men—the real cowboys—held the key to the memory of the West. Although Hart prided himself on lending his films a kind of authenticity that other Westerns lacked, he could not provide audiences with anything more than a secondhand account of the West—an account of an account. Earp, like Cody, might have had the firsthand experience Hart lacked, but Hart's suggestion that Earp's West might be more authentic is rather curious given the fact that any cinematic representation of the West is just that. Within the context of this era's representational conventions, as exemplified by Dalton and Al Jennings, such thinking was the norm, which suggests why Earp may have considered himself such a marketable commodity in the face of so much seeming simulation and inauthenticity.

Hart continues in this self-deprecating vein, restating that "we still have these two giant figures with us—not imitations like myself—but the real men." In many ways mirroring the representational issues raised in the Corbett-Fitzsimmons fight, Hart tries to reverse what was, by the 1920s, an unqualified acceptance of certain representational fictions. But Hart was complicit in this self-perpetuated delusion, this attempt to recreate his own frontier—at his Newhall ranch, buffalo and all—while men like Earp traded in life on the ranch for cheap Hollywood bungalows. And despite his purported efforts to let Earp "do the talking," Hart signified the West as much, if not more, than Earp; his visibility in the culture guaranteed this. On one occasion, Earp asked Hart if he would tell Earp's story to a reporter for him. Hart replied, "I will be damned if I'd ever have the nerve to substitute for Wyatt Earp in talking of the frontier. No, my friend, I would not attempt it for a million dollars."[64] Ironically, of course, Hart was, in a sense, doing just that every time he made a film.

However complicit Hart may have been in the "reel" overtaking the "real," he also seemed intent on encouraging audiences to question their adulation of him by reinforcing Earp's and Masterson's authentic value, even resorting to sentimental appeals: "Gentle-voiced and almost sad-faced, these men are to-day uncheered, while I, the imitator, the portrayer, am accorded the affection of those millions who love the West." Like the fan magazines that both criticized and valorized the Hollywood lifestyle, Hart's conflicted sentiments about his own status as Western icon suggest imposture without sacrificing its rewards. The West that Hart points to here is, of course, not the West of Earp's youth but the West of cinema's

THE MAN WHO KNOWS HIS WEST

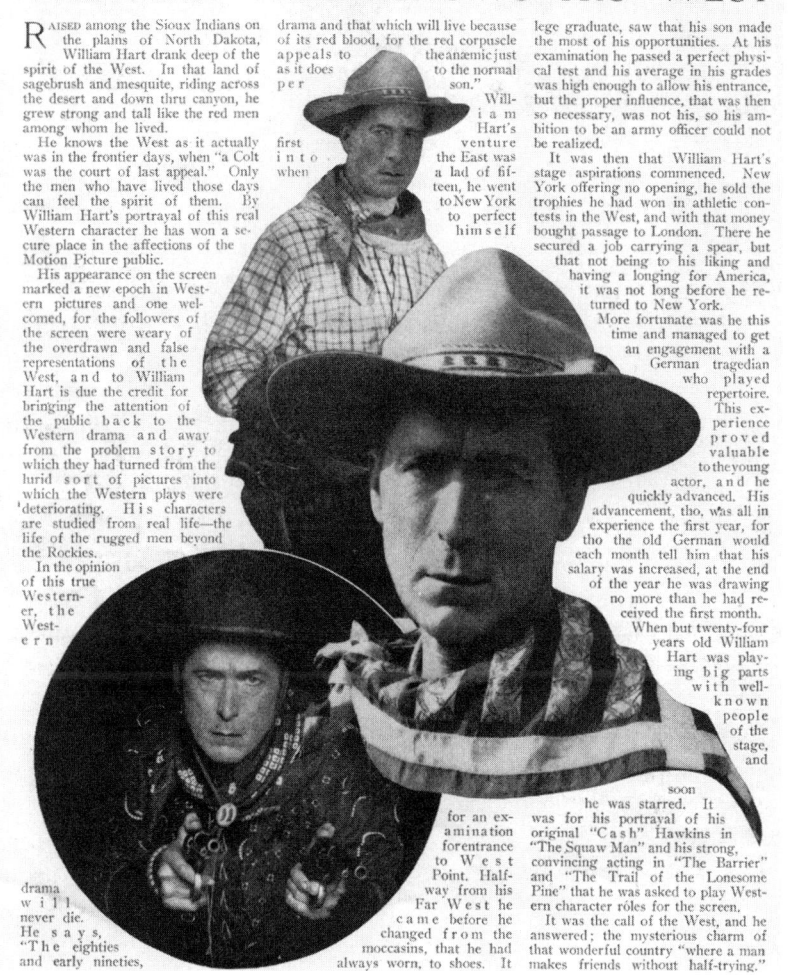

RAISED among the Sioux Indians on the plains of North Dakota, William Hart drank deep of the spirit of the West. In that land of sagebrush and mesquite, riding across the desert and down thru canyon, he grew strong and tall like the red men among whom he lived.

He knows the West as it actually was in the frontier days, when "a Colt was the court of last appeal." Only the men who have lived those days can feel the spirit of them. By William Hart's portrayal of this real Western character he has won a secure place in the affections of the Motion Picture public.

His appearance on the screen marked a new epoch in Western pictures and one welcomed, for the followers of the screen were weary of the overdrawn and false representations of the West, and to William Hart is due the credit for bringing the attention of the public back to the Western drama and away from the problem story to which they had turned from the lurid sort of pictures into which the Western plays were deteriorating. His characters are studied from real life—the life of the rugged men beyond the Rockies.

In the opinion of this true Westerner, the Western drama will never die. He says, "The eighties and early nineties, drama and that which will live because of its red blood, for the red corpuscle appeals to the anæmic just as it does to the normal per son."

William Hart's first venture into the East was when a lad of fifteen, he went to New York to perfect himself for an examination fore ntrance to West Point. Halfway from his Far West he came before he changed from the moccasins, that he had always worn, to shoes. It lege graduate, saw that his son made the most of his opportunities. At his examination he passed a perfect physical test and his average in his grades was high enough to allow his entrance, but the proper influence, that was then so necessary, was not his, so his ambition to be an army officer could not be realized.

It was then that William Hart's stage aspirations commenced. New York offering no opening, he sold the trophies he had won in athletic contests in the West, and with that money bought passage to London. There he secured a job carrying a spear, but that not being to his liking and having a longing for America, it was not long before he returned to New York.

More fortunate was he this time and managed to get an engagement with a German tragedian who played repertoire.

This experience proved valuable to the young actor, and he quickly advanced. His advancement, tho, was all in experience the first year, for tho the old German would each month tell him that his salary was increased, at the end of the year he was drawing no more than he had received the first month.

When but twenty-four years old William Hart was playing big parts with well-known people of the stage, and soon he was starred. It was for his portrayal of his original "Cash" Hawkins in "The Squaw Man" and his strong, convincing acting in "The Barrier" and "The Trail of the Lonesome Pine" that he was asked to play Western character rôles for the screen.

It was the call of the West, and he answered; the mysterious charm of that wonderful country "where a man makes friends without half-trying."

FIGURE 2: William S. Hart repeatedly engaged with the process of credentialing himself, especially in comparison to "real" Western heroes. "The Man Who Knows His West," from March 1916, argues for his authenticity, something Hart himself would question in other contexts. *Motion Picture Classic. Courtesy Laura Boyes.*

youth. While Hart appears condemnatory of his own role as imitator and portrayer, he also misses making a point that he seems on the verge of acknowledging: that "those millions" in his audience in fact had no real love for the West, but rather a love for the medium that provided a mythic reinterpretation of the idea of the West to them. Hart's predominant message in the piece at hand, implied in the word play of his title, is that the public should not "pass up those real men—those real figures—who did so much for us in bygone days." Hart makes a pitch here for Earp and Masterson as scarce resources through which to preserve an authentic American past, as McQuade implied was possible to do through cinema.

This concept is echoed by the *Oklahoma City News* in its October 20, 1919, photo-article, "Which of 'Em Looks Most Dangerous? Outlaws, Real and Mimic, in Films." Below the headline are two large pictures, one of Al Jennings and the other of William S. Hart. The pictures rhyme: both men wear hats and gaze off in the general direction of the camera; Jennings holds a gun while Hart does not. The caption points to some of the debates being rehearsed here: "Al Jennings is the one with the revolver. The other is W. S. Hart. Jennings once was a real outlaw. Now he's in the movies, as pictured above. Note the expression in the two portraits and answer this question: Is Hart imitating Jennings, or is Jennings imitating Hart?" A good question, particularly given Hart's preeminence as the cowboy star and Jennings'—along with Siringo's, Dalton's, and Earp's—desire for on-screen, legendary status. The article cleverly points to a blurring of these distinctions, to the erasure of difference between manufacturing and preserving. The best case might be made, in fact, for the loss of the divisions between "real" and "mimic" here. After all, this seems increasingly a scenario in which Hart was every bit the real cowboy Jennings was, and vice versa.

Hart probably would have disagreed, as the plea in his article would indicate. This is particularly the case because his entreaty can be further contextualized through his many efforts to get cinematic or literary recognition for Earp, attempts that are well documented—in a way that few things in Earp's life are—in the two men's correspondence. Hart campaigned for many years on Earp's behalf, trying to get publishers to print Earp's story as a logical first step toward cinematic representation. Hart wrote dozens of letters to papers and publishers such as the *Saturday Evening Post*, the Thomas Y. Crowell Company, Houghton Mifflin, and the Bobbs Merrill Company of Indianapolis, with no success in getting Earp's story published. In a letter to the editor of the *Saturday Evening Post*, George Horace Latimer, Hart organizes his argument for the publication of Earp's memoirs around a plea for factual historical representation, much as he does in the newspaper article just discussed. Making a case "for the furtherance of the true American history," Hart stresses the need for Earp's autobiography to reach "world-wide circulation [so that] the rising generation may know the real from the unreal."[65] This plea echoes Hart's argument in the *Morning Telegraph*, and reflects the degree to which he perceived that the public was being distracted by *reproductions* of reality instead of attending to reality itself.

Hart appears to have latched on to Earp as a means of correcting the misstep of history by providing the culture with one of the West's last surviving legendary figures. Ironically, Earp was quite a mythmaker in his own right, and researchers (including myself) have been checking and double-checking the veracity of his tales in a fashion that affirms the degree to which he perpetuated his own inaccuracies. Regardless, Hart's statement is made in a preservationist vein, and he continues his argument to Latimer with a personal plea:

I love the west. I was brought up in it until the age of fifteen years. Through my memory of those boyhood days, through the memory of my father and all the fine western men he knew, and through the fact that I have made in the neighborhood of one hundred western pictures, I have gained considerable knowledge of these frontier days, and I know that Wyatt Earp is the last![66]

Hart's case revolves around a conception of Earp as the sole living relic of the West. Testifying to his value as a symbol of historical truth, Hart fails to recognize that the John Flood manuscript that he was trying to peddle was as mythic as any other circulating account of Earp's frontier days. While Earp claimed that "all the fiction has been ruled out in the MS," there is little to suggest that his was an historically accurate account.[67] Hart's faith in the value of Earp's personal story is conveyed repeatedly to Latimer in the terms of authenticity that he used to distinguish the "real" from the "reel": "Should this marvelous first-hand true history be lost?" But Hart's naiveté on this subject of Earp's historical accuracy is less interesting than the degree to which he firmly believed that Earp deserved a place in cinematic Western history, both for his own sake and for generations to come. As he wrote to Earp in a 1925 letter, "Posterity needs such authentic documents."[68]

Reports about Earp's actual involvement in the motion picture industry vary, as is the case with everything else he occupied himself with. The *Los Angeles Times* obituary published on January 15, 1929, claimed that "frequently he was called on by motion-picture directors to aid in the work of adding color to Western pictures, but he never took an actual part in any of the productions."[69] The *Seattle Times* suggested that he served, along with Bat Masterson, as a consultant on the set of *Wild Bill Hickcok*; other rumors spread that he was actually in Hart's film. There is no evidence to support the latter claim, though this is one of the many pursuits repeated in the literature about Earp. If Earp did serve as a consultant for Hart, his labors went unpaid, for there is no documentation of payment in Hart's meticulous financial records. Mrs. Josephine Earp did write to Hart in a 1928 letter: "Just a line to congratulate you upon your new picture 'Wild Bill Hickok.' I saw it twice with several friends and each time the house was packed. When you appeared upon the screen, the applause was wonderful."[70] There is no mention of anything concerning Earp's participation in the filming or production in this or other letters.

Earp initially had tried to angle his story and his image into Hart's cinematically able hands. Often implying that Hart might have a role in the film version of his story, Earp wrote to him that he might be able to take his finished book manuscript—a compromise from his original cinematic goal—and parlay it into a motion picture: "There are the questions of copyright and the royalty and the separation of the story rights from the picture, if you think it would be something worth while now, to have filmed."[71] While Earp is far from forceful here, he effectively transfers responsibility to Hart with regard to this production. Furthermore, he invokes issues of copyright that became a preoccupation for him in the 1920s, much as they were the decade before for Jack London. Earp is even more explicit in a July 7, 1923, letter to Hart, anticipating a battle he would become engaged in over photographic copyright five years later:

During the past few years, many wrong impressions of the early days of Tombstone and myself have been created by writers who are not informed correctly, and this has caused me a concern which I feel deeply. You know, I realize that I am not going to live to the age of Methuselah, and any wrong impression, I just want made right before I go away. The screen could do all this, I know, with yourself as the master mind. Not that I want to obligate you because of our friendship but I know that I can come to you with this and other things and not feel hurt at anything you may wish to say. Could the story be published in the Examiner? . . . Perhaps there are other events of the early days, in connection with your pictures, that have grown dim; old memories that need polishing. Maybe I can help. I hope you will ask me and I am sure you will.[72]

Here Earp acknowledges what lurked beneath many of Hart's urgings: that he would not live on, but that his image of himself could survive if captured on film. This is not just a matter of wanting to achieve celebrity, although it may be that as well; it is, more importantly, a deeply felt desire to control his own cinematic representation. Earp also expresses a real hope that a movie could right the wrongs of historical inaccuracy. In so doing, Earp lends to the screen that same belief in reality or actuality that he likely learned by observing the treatment of the Western genre.

In fact, much as Gertrude Stein in the following decade would be taken with the fanciful idea of playing herself in a Hollywood version of *The Autobiography of Alice B. Toklas*, Earp had very specific ideas about who would best represent him on the silver screen. In a letter to Hart regarding some changes Hart made to his manuscript, Earp asks: "I wonder whether you still would be inclined to film the production. If it goes on the screen at all, I would not want anyone but you to play the role and to put it there."[73] While no doubt flattering Hart with the hopes of ingratiating him to his cause, Earp is also responding to the cultural perception of Hart as the heroic and gentlemanly Western figure that he wished to be remembered as. Earp, in fact, reiterates the sentiment: "I am sure that if the story were exploited on the screen by you, it would do much toward setting me right before a public, which has always been fed up on lies about me."[74] Wanting to correct his reputation, Earp seemed equally invested in the idea of cinema as history-producing.

It is worth keeping in mind that Earp, by this point, was banking on the mythic value of events that had transpired *over forty years* previous. Kevin Brownlow quotes Allan Dwan's less-than-heroic description of Earp when he met him in the 1920s, which speaks to the urgency Earp felt of reinventing himself on screen: "When I knew him, he was no longer a marshal, and there was no longer a West, and he couldn't be the symbol that he'd been."[75] Displaced from the mise-en-scène in which he envisioned his mythic value, Earp tried to recontextualize himself in Hollywood and on-screen, much as Buffalo Bill did in the context of his Wild West. Earp had witnessed similar transformations of image in the medium's infancy, as in the instances of the Corbett-Fitzsimmons fight and the successes of those "lesser" Western outlaws, including the degree of attention that filming their lives had created.

Earp sought an autobiographical narrative that would ensure his place in American frontier history, both to change the record and to endow it with the kind of realism that would persuade the public into believing the truth *as he saw it*. He wrote to John Hays Hammond on May 21, 1925, in reference to a fallacious article published in *Scribners* that "notoriety has been the bane of my life . . . My friends have urged that I make this known on printed sheet. Perhaps I shall; it will correct many mythic tales."[76] Earp appears reconciled in this letter to a noncinematic corrective, no doubt a result of the lack of interest shown toward his movie ideas. Having witnessed history being redefined through cinema's visual register, Earp knew that film had a power to persuade and authenticate that made the "printed sheet" a lesser alternative.

It is, in fact, cinema's retellings of the Earp myth that have created the reputation Earp currently possesses. Not surprisingly, the majority of these films show little if any investment in historical accuracy. Earp is most often depicted on-screen as the epitome of mythic Western masculinity: authoritative, strong, and in control of those around him.[77] Earp's quest for cinematic representation also raises questions concerning how reputation translates from one venue to another. On July 21, 1883, the *National Police Gazette* referred to Earp as "the celebrity who about two years ago went on the warpath at Tombstone, Arizona"; on May 15, 1883, the *Kansas City Journal* termed Earp "famous in the cheerful business of depopulating the country."[78] While the hyperbolic rendering of Earp here is typical of the distortion of his deeds, it is worth noting that he already had achieved the linguistic transition from gunfighter to celebrity.

As has already been discussed, Earp's interest in cinematic representation had largely to do with what he perceived as egregious misrepresentation in the popular press. A case in point was J. M. Scanland's 1922 article in the *Los Angeles Times*, the piece of journalism that most outraged Earp. Its most glaring error comes midway through the piece, when Scanland states that "Wyatt Earp located at Colton, where he was killed."[79] Reading of his own death in the morning paper, Earp fumed, particularly because it was printed in the paper that all of his Hollywood associates were likely reading. Such claims only reinforced the degree to which Earp was not in control of his own reputation. While I am not interested in rehashing the other factual errors that Scanland may have made in his account, particularly since Scanland later wrote a retraction to the piece after Earp confronted him, I am interested in the way that Scanland represents issues relevant to this chapter of Earp's story.[80] Opening with a statement that "Bandits change their methods with the times and improved facilities," and further detailing the transitions between repeating rifles, dynamite, and revolvers, Scanland elides from his list the method to which several ex-frontier legends had swayed: the movies. For even in his own description of Earp and his gang as "of the swaggering kind now seen on the movie stage," Scanland acknowledges the medium that managed to capture the spirit of the West and that had, arguably, supplanted it. In response to the grave errors of the Scanland piece, Earp complained to Hart that, "It does beat the band how the truth will be warped and misstated over a period of years . . . Thus it goes when a man is not present to defend himself."[81] Couched in the language of the frontier battle, Earp appropriately implies that the struggle over representation was equally rigorous and that the defense of his image would be mounted most efficaciously on the silver screen.

In the end, Earp was right about the rigors of representation, as he learned during a series of copyright battles in the 1920s. Hart was aware of these same hazards, no doubt because of his involvement in the film industry; London had similar troubles with rights to his own stories, as will be discussed in the following chapter. Hart warned Earp to, "Please be very, very careful into whose hands this story falls."[82] This was, after all, a legend that had been circulating in the public for over forty years; to maintain any sense of proprietary rights, Earp had to keep an eye out for those who might infringe upon his autobiographical territory. Accordingly, Earp kept copyright issues in the forefront, writing to Hart in a December 14, 1925, letter in anticipation of a book deal that might facilitate a motion picture: "Would the Houghton Mifflin Company appreciate a distinction between the copyright for a book and the copyright for a motion picture? This question occurred to me at the moment I read the copy of your letter addressed to them. That, however, is something, I suppose, that is arranged later."[83] By the 1920s, copyright issues had been well-tread within the motion picture industry. In the first decades of filmmaking, producers had a reckless relationship to crediting sources—or compensating authors—until narrative cinema and the widespread need for good stories and credible authors forced the issue. It was not until 1909 that moving pictures were covered by copyright law, a decision upheld by the Supreme Court in 1911; by 1918, publishing houses had film rights departments to negotiate contracts.[84]

Earp had several battles involving copyright during his lifetime, but the first was only symbolic. Walter Noble Burns's 1927 *Tombstone*, Earp feared, would rob him of his one valuable commodity: his story. He wrote to Doubleday to object to the publication of the book, clearly with a sense of proprietary rights that extended beyond just himself to include the place and the events with which he was associated. He expressed that his mandate was "that the story of Wyatt Earp be not published." "I am thus left, of course," he continued, "to take whatever steps may be necessary for my own protection."[85] While Earp had no rights to such a public legend, particularly when it was researched and written by someone else, he managed to scare executives with his repeated protestations. A telegram sent to

Burns, which Earp presumably never caught wind of, reflects Doubleday's initial willingness to concede to Earp's right to his own story: "WILLING TO GIVE EARP TWENTY-FIVE PER CENT OF MOVIE RIGHTS STOP WILLING TO GIVE HIM ONE THOUSAND DOLLARS OF SATURDAY POST MONEY STOP MUST BE MADE PLAIN TO HIM THAT THIS IS PURELY FOR PURPOSE OF AVOIDING TROUBLE WITH HIM."[86] The assumption of a motion picture deal confirms Earp's suspicion that getting into print was a means to a cinematic end. Though Earp appears never to have received any compensation for Burns's book, the issues of value and rights that he raises are crucial: Earp's reputation, after all, was compromised in someone else's hands. As Tefertiller puts it, "All that remained of value was his life story. Now that was being taken away."[87]

Perhaps the greatest copyright battle occurred not just with regard to "his story" (a questionable notion given Earp's murky relationship to the 1881 events he became famous for and the number of other people involved), but with regard to his image. The issue arose while Earp worked with Stuart Lake on a version of his autobiography. As Lake put it in a letter to William S. Hart after Earp's death, "When Mr. Earp and I planned this biography, he quite definitely disposed of any first-person form of telling the story; no autobiography for him; I was to shoulder all responsibility of authorship and a third-person form of narrative was to be produced."[88] This is an interesting strategy on Earp's part, for it has the effect of appearing to be an unbiased history rather than a subjective autobiographical account. Perhaps this is why Earp also wanted Hart to play him, to lend the story a kind of authenticity that might be compromised by his presence despite the clear value of first-person stories such as Dalton's. But although Earp had settled on Lake as a biographer when film prospects looked dim and after Flood's original bungled attempt, he tried to attend to the integrity of his image in part because he still hoped to garner cinematic representation.

Although this may seem like an unusual concern, Earp had real reasons to fear that his image, like his story, might be effectively stolen from him. Lake wrote to Earp in 1928 regarding the publication of William Breakenridge's *Helldorado* (1928), which not only represented Earp in a negative light but also contained a photograph of the frontier marshal that apparently was copyrighted by a man named Newton, making it impossible for Lake to use it in his "authorized" biography. This conflict points to the increasing importance of visual representation, which was requisite for the modern celebrity. Earp's image had now been quite literally stolen from him.

FIGURE 3: Wyatt Earp autographed this photo for his *de facto* agent, William S. Hart, a mark of their friendship as well as a reminder of the sometimes risky nature of the early twentieth-century autographing craze. *Courtesy Seaver Center for Western History Research, Los Angeles County Museum of Natural History.*

As Lake explains in his letter to Earp dated November 2, 1928, by copyrighting the image, "it spoils the chance of my using it, unless the matter can be straightened out in some way."[89] Earp responded to Lake in a handwritten and obviously anxious letter:

Your letter came yesterday and it sure was a surprise for me to hear that the man by the name of Newton [would?] take the liberty to have my picture copyrighted. *He can never get away* with it. I have lived a great many years, and in all of my life have I never heard of such a nerve.... Mr. Lake you go right ahead and use the photograph you have of me as I have told you I have never given Mr. Breakenridge any of mine ... I am not able to go and pose for another picture and why should I be a damn fool and stand back and let these people try to do [me?].[90]

Earp is exasperated here, having been confronted with the reality that he had little control over his image. Lake's November 7, 1928, reply to Earp refers him to the Author's League of America for assistance, a resource crucial to Jack London's battle with the motion picture industry regarding rights to his works. These issues of ownership were up for grabs, even as late as the 1920s, following over a decade of legal battles that seemed unable to restore stability to those who sought to protect themselves. Earp was especially frustrated by his cinematic failures in large part because his opportunity to take control of his life and legend, of securing for himself a place in the culture's cinematic-historical register, seemed increasingly hopeless.

Earp is adamant here about not submitting to the whims of copyright law, but something must have changed his mind because he wrote again to Lake a week later: "I am sending you today the proofs I had taken of myself. Mrs. Earp and I like the one with my arms crossed, but the hand looks bad. They told Mrs. Earp that they could touch it up so it would look better. We will leave it to you whichever [?] will like best for the book."[91] Earp is obviously concerned with the status of his image here, both in terms of his self-representation and in terms of how others were disseminating it. This was so much the case that Earp reluctantly decided to legally pursue the purloiners of his image. In a letter to Lake written from Los Angeles on November 9, 1928, Earp writes that, "You know I am not much of a hand to get mixed up in litigations. But in this case I know something must be done as they have gone a little too far.... all a pack of lies ... Well your book I know is going to be something different and you will have to find a good title, and that I know you will do.... I wish to get away from here."[92] In another letter to Lake written January 7, 1929, Earp writes "I have been wondering what progress you have been making with the story, and if you have done anything towards copyrighting the portrait of myself."[93] This is the copyright lesson learned, however late.

While Earp was no diarist and, in comparison to Jack London or Gertrude Stein, was hardly a dedicated correspondent, he was clearly aware in what little he did write of the degree to which myth and reputation could be transformed by the film industry. The fantasy of William S. Hart as Wyatt Earp suggests the degree to which Earp was invested in an illusion that was not merely his own, but was symptomatic of the beliefs concerning representation, cultural memory, and publicity that were circulating in his historical moment. A notable nod to this effect issued from the pen of renowned fan magazine author and "friend to the stars," Adela Rogers St. Johns in "I Knew Wyatt Earp." St. Johns writes about coming over to the Earps' when Wyatt was reading *Hamlet* one day. Apparently Earp and Tom Mix had decided to tackle Shakespeare for the first time: "Both of us admired education and one day we got to wondering how Mr. Shakespeare would stand up if you could uncondition yourself to his reputation and renown. You always got to take into consideration that a man's reputation will most usually influence your judgment of him."[94] This may be too neat a conclusion for a man about whom so little that is reported is true. But St. Johns's report is a cogent summation of Earp's representational dilemmas, primarily because Earp wanted very much to avoid the "unconditioning" of his reputation.

At the end of his life, familiarity with Earp as a public figure was fairly specific to the Western United States: Tombstone, Los Angeles, San Diego, and San Francisco in particular. The reasons for this had largely to do with press attention, both good and bad, most of which appeared in these cities. Charles Ponce de Leon argues that media visibility became the "distinguishing feature of celebrity," and, indeed, without it—in print, on screen—Earp seemed certain of his own disappearance.[95] However, Earp was not entirely exempt from the kind of adoration bestowed upon the country's movie stars, however much to a lesser degree: He received an occasional autograph and photograph request, and answered some of them, with serious consequences in the case of Newton, who had acquired the infamous copyrighted image in this fashion.[96] But this was hardly the kind of widespread recognition and attention that might have been facilitated through a cinematic rendering.

Had Hart made the motion picture Earp wanted him to, it is impossible to know if Earp would have felt adequately satisfied, compensated, or represented. But a film most definitely would have changed his reputation, perhaps no more or less during his life than it did after. Earp's Hollywood ambitions remind us of the often-overlooked autobiographical and history-making tendencies of the motion picture in its earliest decades, the degree to which that industry changed what it meant—to return to Leo Braudy's words—"to be public in Western culture." The following discussion of Jack London, whose reputation was precisely the currency that paved his way to Hollywood, will afford another perspective on the ways that cinematic representation appeared capable of altering and affecting the course of an individual's life and afterlife.

3

Rethinking Authorship in Jack London's Hollywood

A person in New York City in the middle of June 1913 wanting to see a moving picture "installation" or "exhibit," as they were often referred to at the time, would have had several choices: the eight-reel Italian spectacle *Quo Vadis?* at the Astor Theatre, Thomas Ince's five-reel *The Battle of Gettysburg* at the Grand Opera House, or *Jack London's Adventures in the South Sea Islands* at the Criterion, a Broadway playhouse.[1] Having just read the news in April that London had signed an agreement with H. M. Horkheimer and Sidney Ayres—the Balboa Amusement Company—for a series of novel-based moving pictures in which the author might even star himself (not knowing, of course, that the latter claim would prove essentially untrue), and having in the past followed press reports of London's exciting travels, one might have been drawn to the "London film."[2] The desire to see London at work, both as "author" and as American adventurer, materialized over the course of the early 1900s. But while photographs of the famous author were disseminated widely, this was the first time audiences could see the famous author seemingly "in person," moving about the screen as large as life.

A person opting to go to the Criterion for one of its twice-daily screenings (one in the afternoon and one in the evening) of the London film would have seen, as the title promised, exotic views of the South Sea Islands while listening to Martin Johnson, who accompanied London on his journey and was credited with making the film, provide a descriptive lecture to accompany the images. According to press accounts of the day, it would have been an exciting, worthwhile moviegoing experience. This despite the fact that while London's name, itself a valuable commodity by 1913, might have persuaded some to pay admission to the theatre, the author appears to have played no significant part in the final product. In fact, not only does a detailed contemporary synopsis of the film note London's on-screen presence on only *one* occasion, but Johnson appears to have taken the majority of his footage during the additional time (between one and two years) that he traveled after London and his wife, Charmian, had already returned home.[3] Would this have been a disappointing realization for a paying spectator? Not according to the press coverage, in which there is not a single discussion of London in relation to the film's content; nor is there any mention of his absence.

In fact, what most impressed reporters were the film's realism and its uncanny verification of the "strange" rituals and appearances of the unfamiliar, noncivilized world. The *Morning Telegraph* reports in its June 16, 1913, coverage that spectators would see "scenes from Polynesia, Melanesia, The Solomon Islands, New Guinea, New Zealand, Borneo, Sulu, Sumatra and Java," many of them "handsomely colored."[4] Spectators also would have been entertained by Mr. Johnson's "highly amusing" and "instructive" lecture, no doubt including anecdotes relating to the renowned author to enhance the images.[5] For even if Jack London was not centrally figured within the moving picture itself, he was a central though invisible attraction nonetheless. As Johnson writes in the preface to his 1913 book, *Through the South Seas with Jack London* (yet another instance of the famous author's name recycled as a commodity), "The *Snark* alone was enough to compel attention, but the *Snark* sailed by Jack London, a writer of world-wide celebrity, was irresistible."[6] London's celebrity had effectively been transferred from page to screen.

The *New York City Call* further explains the film's contents in its June 25, 1913, coverage:

Johnson, the lecturer at the Criterion, took the pictures himself; pictures of the people and the glories of nature that they encountered, and explains them as they are thrown on the screen.... The pictures of Jack London's cruise and Martin Johnson's perilous efforts bring to the close, crowded and pampered city that which is of earlier civilization and thousands of miles away. He who dreams of the tropic land, the blue ocean and isles of coral that stud the sea like gems of nature, can best realize his desire by viewing these, the pictures of the dusky children of the South Sea Islands as recorded by the never failing eye of the cinematograph.[7]

The late 1890s travel program typically consisted of a lecturer whose talk was punctuated by moving images; the concept appears little changed twenty years hence, except that the moving images are here punctuated by the narration, which serves to enhance the sights instead of vice versa.

The article reminds us of the ways that perceptions were being reordered by cinematic representation through its assertion that viewing this film is the "best" way to see such sights. Jack London himself made claims about not needing "to go to the North Pole or the heart of Africa to take risks any longer. Just join a moving picture company and take a trip with them about San Francisco Bay."[8] Here "the never failing eye of the cinematograph" purports, in essence, to perceive in a fashion that at least approximates human sight and experience, allowing contemporary city dwellers the chance to travel to exotic places without having to leave the bounds of the "pampered" city. Like the Westerns that were lauded for their actuality, lent in part from their exploitation of real Western outlaws, the *New York City Sun* writer notes in his June 22, 1913, coverage that the London views "are altogether real."

In the context of cinema's teen years, several implications arise from such a claim. Unlike staged dramas filmed on sets, this movie promised and delivered views taken in the real world of real things and real people, not actors. London's association with the film also granted it a special kind of authenticity. Indeed, despite Johnson's conspicuous presence at the screenings and in spite of London's apparent diegetic absence, *The Evening World*'s June 16, 1913, coverage credits London entirely for the production: "Jack London did the verifying last night when his wonderful moving pictures of life in the South Sea Islands . . . were shown at the Criterion Theatre and explained by Martin Johnson." Although London appears to have had nothing to do with the making of the film beyond the fact that he was responsible for the existence of the *Snark* and its highly publicized voyage, his name was both easily identifiable and highly marketable. London is granted authorship by association here, a connection made because the London name and, as we shall see, image possessed a cultural value that successfully (or so it seemed at the time) translated into the cinematic arena. Jack London had become a one-man cultural industry.

London's first important film venture, in which he is neither star, director, nor author, provides a window onto the interrelated notions of authorship, stardom, commercial value, publicity, and representation that were being redefined during the early 1900s in response to the motion picture industry. Jack London's transition from literary to cinematic production can be traced by examining his fascination with the cinema's potential to distribute images, including his own, which led him to actively seek a relationship with the Hollywood film industry. London was concerned with the value of his name and the status of his image, but his interactions with Hollywood suggest that current accounts of his relationship to film production, which emphasize financial motivations, overlook other important factors at play in this shift in London's ambitions, including the influence of cinema on his literary production. Moving images made London rethink the concept of authorship, particularly once he began writing with the ultimate goal of cinematic production in mind. But it was not just London who was forced to redefine what it meant to be an author in these rapidly changing times; rather, London's career illuminates a moment of widespread cultural redefinition in which notions of authorship and literary success were being challenged and reinvented in response to the motion picture industry.

According to Tony Williams, almost a dozen films based upon London's literary works were produced during the author's lifetime.[9] This is a substantial number to emerge from one author's cache during the nineteen-teens, when filmmakers were seeking out stories produced by established authors for credibility and for quality script material in an effort to improve, extend, and differentiate their products. Tony Williams and Robert Birchard have done the diligent work of describing London's relationship to films that were based upon his works, authorized or not.[10] However, their work is almost purely historical in nature, detailing dates, names, and other production information, often neglecting the greater cultural significance of London's relationship to the advent of the motion picture. Williams has written so detailed a narrative of London's encounters with the motion picture industry that I will avoid replicating all but the most important details of it here. Instead, what follows is an analysis of London's interactions with the medium that seeks an understanding of both the stakes of London's Hollywood involvement and the degree to which his decision to participate in the development of this nascent medium reflects the status of the cinema as a reputation-making and circulating vehicle in America during the early decades of the twentieth century.

London became interested in participating in the motion picture industry by the early teens; at the time of his death, he was preoccupied by the business of the motion picture. This interest is not altogether surprising, particularly given London's consistent awareness of the power of his personality and the value of his name and image. Jonathan Auerbach argues that London understood that his success as an author "depended on symbolic capital—mass marketing, self-promotion, and the projection of an exciting name" to "keep readers interested by offering himself as the ever present, energetic subject of his writing."[11] But while Auerbach contends that "the single occupation that London from early on most cared about—in fact the only calling that allowed him to make sense of himself—was that of professional writing," I suggest in the pages that follow the ways that the motion picture industry offered London an alternative market for his personality and his works, one that he at least initially understood as both more effective and as potentially more valuable than literature. To a certain degree, cinema interrupted the status quo of representation, with moving images radically revising established modes of narration and illustration in a progressively visually oriented American culture. For if, as Auerbach suggests, "success in the market means personal validation, the 'stamp' of approval conferred during the process of getting into print," then motion pictures presented an entirely new territory of conquest, of which London was acutely aware.[12]

Accounts to date also would have us believe that London had purely financial motivations in his interactions with the nascent motion picture industry. Loren Glass claims that London was trying to "write himself out of debt" during the last decade of his life, making it seem likely that any deals enacted during this period were made to remedy this dilemma.[13] Robert Birchard explains that London "looked to the movies to provide a much-needed source of steady income," as a means of combating said debt.[14] Even Hobart Bosworth, who would direct and star in many a London film, is reported to have said that "London will reap a fortune from the production of his stories in moving picture form," however inaccurate a prediction this ultimately would prove.[15]

While not dismissing such claims altogether, particularly since so much of London's career was based upon the practical economics of the literary marketplace, I want to explore the ways that London's decision to allow his works and his persona this secondary life in cinema emerged out of more than just economic necessity. London's financial motivations need to be understood in conjunction with his realization that the stakes of representation and reputation were undergoing a tremendous change. London recognized that cinema was a new language that could convert his product and himself into something with a different value, both economic and cultural. The ongoing transition into a popular culture dominated by moving images also greatly affected who could cash in on an existing literary reputation. London's story stands as a telling example of how a writer went about building an identity marketable in relation to celebrity of the cinematic variety, however ultimately failed London's speculations in this arena would prove to be.

Cinematic Language and the Value of Authorial Celebrity

In a 1915 essay, "The Message of Motion Pictures," London espouses an understanding of cinema as a new language with the potential to educate the masses and distribute "knowledge in a language that all may understand."[16] Conceiving of moving images as a conduit for ideas previously written, he argues that film is an ideal medium for "universal education." London also identifies a more self-serving motivation for his interest in the movies: "The motion picture spreads . . . [literature] . . . on the screen where all can read and understand—and enjoy."[17] Motion pictures, London believed, might provide a significant advantage in the cultural marketplace. Like Vachel Lindsay, who in 1915 prophesized that cinema was a "new weapon of men," London no doubt had political intentions in regarding cinema as a universal language.[18] But he also had personal ambitions, and movies appeared especially able to transmit his kind of writing onto the screen for a wide audience. London's further observation that the motion picture "will teach by visualization" is particularly noteworthy considering that his own image eventually would become part of that education: His contract with Bosworth Incorporated stipulated that footage of London precede all of the films based upon his works. Virtually every article written in reaction to the London-Bosworth Inc. agreement notes this fact with interest and anticipation.

London elaborated upon these ideas in a 1914 interview with W. Stephen Bush for the *Moving Picture World*: "I want to make this dry mass of things live and flash the ideas into the minds of all. There, of course, the motion picture would be my most valuable ally. Ninety-nine per cent of mankind remembers by eye; we recollect the passage in a book by its position as it remains in our recollection."[19] London confers his faith in the potency of writing upon the motion picture, inferring that the potential power and influence of the cinema derives from the authority and effectiveness of the visual image in a fashion reminiscent of "the never failing eye of the cinematograph." London also appears deliberate about the way he plans to use the motion picture to influence the public, suggesting that he had, in fact, been considering the way that motion pictures could be used precisely in the terms he uses: as a "valuable ally." But as an ally for what?

London acknowledges the superiority of motion pictures as a mode of representation, outdoing the written word, perhaps even ultimately replacing it: "In the portrayal of action, which often is [a] fight, the motion picture is supreme as a medium of expression and it carries the underlying motive, perhaps, better than the alphabet could."[20] London seems aware that cinema might surpass literature in the transmission of ideas and certainly in the transmission of images, particularly of the "action" variety that London's writing epitomized. Motion pictures could serve as a personal ally, allowing London to stay a central player in the marketplace. He further envisioned his work's transition onto the screen as a way for him to transfer information more efficiently from himself to an audience, literate or not. Cinema's potential derived largely from its ability to show, not tell (one of London's own literary dictums), and to do so on a large scale. London's goal, after all, was "to get the images living in my brains into the brains of others," a notion he forecast several years earlier in his autobiographical novel, *Martin Eden* (1909).[21]

Such conceptualizations indicate the degree to which London wanted to align himself with this innovation in communication and entertainment, so much so that he appears to credit cinema with a potential superiority to literature from the outset. In part, London was recognizing that film opened the doors to a vast new audience. Bush's 1914 article repeatedly refers to London as "the famous writer," asserting that "the motion picture will add to his fame." But Bush also describes London as "barely forty years old, with a fame as wide as the *printed page* can diffuse it."[22] While the emphasis that Bush places on London's fame is important because it indicates the degree to which London's name and image could carry a motion picture to success, it is notable that Bush marks the limits of London's fame with the "printed page." This is a significant observation because it acknowledges a border that cinema promised to transcend, pushing the boundaries of fame and reputation beyond literary and journalistic limits, however much these categories ultimately relied upon and supplemented each other. Film was thus a way to "diffuse" (to borrow Bush's phrase) London's literary product and, by implication, himself.

London's entrée into the motion picture industry occurred at a crucial moment, when films were becoming longer and when audiences and commentators alike began to concur that they were more than just a passing fad, so that theaters were being built specifically for the projection of moving images for the first time. Although optimistic about the representational potential of film, London did not immediately concede to this vision of cinema's enduring or unquestionably reputable qualities, writing to Hobart Bosworth on September 12, 1913, that "If you insist upon using JOHN BARLEYCORN right away in the 'movies,' why go ahead. It means a possible decent loss to me from the chance of staging it as a *legitimate* production."[23] That which is deemed "legitimate," the theater, still possessed a degree of respectability and reliability that the motion picture industry had yet to achieve, but London appears willing to gamble, despite his skepticism, on the emerging industry's potential long-term benefits for his career.

Authorial celebrity of London's variety had been facilitated almost entirely by the press at the turn of the century, which helped foster and perpetuate London's charismatic and virile image. In 1905, the Macmillan Company produced a slender, self-promotional volume entitled *Jack London: A Sketch of His Life and Work with Portrait*.[24] The title of this volume points to the growing importance of the visual image of the author in relation to his literary celebrity. Inside the front cover, a portrait shows London in what had become his traditional shirt-and-tie pose, looking off to his right with a cigarette in hand. This glimpse of London in the frontispiece is a photographic precursor to the cinematic prologue of a strikingly similarly posed London in Bosworth Incorporated films. As with the moving version of this preface, the still photograph makes a kind of static argument about the author and his value as an image. In the films these images also suggest, however incorrectly, not just conceptual but cinematic authorship; London's image, seated at his desk in a performative work-like pose, appears not only as "bearer of the valuable image" but as creator of the images to follow.

Henry Meade Bland's 1904 essay echoes Macmillan's publicity for its star author, reprinting two photographs of London and describing him at length: "In personal appearance London is not especially striking. He has light curly hair, blue eyes, square face, firm-set chin, and rather prominent cheek bones. He is of medium height, and now weighs about one hundred and sixty pounds. He is agile and strong."[25] If Bland purports to find London "not especially striking," his narration suggests otherwise; or it perhaps suggests that Bland, despite his dismissal of London's appearance, was aware that readers anticipated or desired further interaction with the London's image. London's success, here and elsewhere, appears implicitly linked to his appearance, both the way he looked and the fact of his being pictured (see figure 4). The author was not just an anonymous producer of great literary works, he was a recognizable literary star. Bland's decision to describe London in such detail after presenting two photographs of him reminds us of the degree to which literary production was becoming linked to personality and image, and that the producers of language were attempting to approximate and do justice to the visual.

In fact, much as this era was being redefined by cinema as a new form of mass entertainment, authorship was being reconceived in terms of mass

FIGURE 4: The author's enthusiasm for the new celebrity image culture is invoked in this gently mocking cartoon of unknown origin, which shows Jack London "snapshotting" himself with a still camera, placing its likely publication date before his involvement with motion pictures. The circle around London's image was drawn by either his clipping bureau, his wife Charmian London, or London himself. *This item is reproduced by permission of* The Huntington Library, San Marino, California *(Jack London Collection, JLE 2356).*

cultural celebrity. Loren Glass has demonstrated that "signatures of famous American authors became a hot commodity during the second half of the nineteenth century... and an authorial star system emerged in the wake of the international copyright bill of 1891."[26] One need only browse through the collection of Jack London ephemera at the Huntington Library in San Marino, California, to realize that the author received autograph requests throughout his career from individuals wanting to "complete" collections of signatures of great men, great authors, and great Americans.[27] As Glass points out, London was unusually aware of the degree to which his name functioned as a kind of cultural currency that could enhance the value of his work. His savvy self-publicity climaxed with his decision to allow the "currency of his name" and, perhaps more important, of his image, into the arena of the motion picture industry. In so doing, London was speculating on the potential of this new medium to translate both literature and personality into something new and, it may be inferred, newly valuable.

Although not the first, London was among those writers on the cutting edge of this transitional phenomenon of selling stories to the industry. As producers struggled to create more complex stories in their films, they looked to literature for source material. In 1908, Kalem was borrowing from Shakespeare and Essanay from Dickens.[28] Furthermore, the motion picture industry sought established writers "for the uplift of the industry."[29] The Huntington Library's Jack London scrapbooks for 1913 and 1914 contain numerous articles that address the translation of literary works into movies.[30] The *Spokane Washington Review*'s "Literary and Dramatic Ability Mark New Motion Picture Era," published on August 4, 1914, is subtitled: "Tendencies are Toward Legitimate Actors in Standard Productions of Established Writers."[31] The article notes that there are "two decided tendencies in the moving pictures today": the use of established writers and "legitimate" players. New pictures, it explains, are being released with "several angles": "There is the feature by a popular playwright or novelist; the feature with the legitimate star in its stellar role or roles; and the feature by the popular novelist with the legitimate stars in its cast. The latter seems to be the last word in feature productions." London's relationship to the film industry complicates this division between "stars" (albeit not of the stage) and "established authors" because London was both; this double identity was, after all, what made him such a valuable commodity to the many film producers who sought association with him. London's cultural status—the value that he brought to the industry—offered a double dose of symbolic capital (to borrow the term Auerbach uses to suggest London's cultural value) to his cinematic ventures.

This much is clear: Something in the culture of authorship was changing, and the shift was at least partly a reaction to the motion picture industry. London's participation in this shift marks an important step in the evolution of print and visual culture, which were becoming increasingly interrelated, and not always successfully so. In fact, the question of how this transition in authorship would change the status of the profession was being debated widely. As the *Los Angeles Express* noted in its April 25, 1913, piece, "Jack London Here on Business; Hints 'Movies' Want Him": "Jack London, one of the most picturesque characters identified with present-day literature, is in danger of being grasped by the moving picture octopus."[32] The *Express* voices a significant concern here that London's involvement with Hollywood might be ensnaring or otherwise debasing; that it might somehow compromise his literary talents, leaving him tangled in its vividly imagined tentacles. The *Herald Times* echoed the sentiment in the title of its article, "Another Great Author Succumbs to the Movies," just a few months later.[33] This anxiety over the divisions between high and low art, between literature and commercial writing, were not, as Auerbach points out, London's concerns: "London's significance was to see from the start of his career how these oppositions were beginning to lose their distinct definitions in the new century."[34] The motion picture industry is merely the best example of *how* and *where* these distinctions were being blurred.

Not all of the press coverage about London's entrée into the motion picture business emphasized the risks involved, suggesting that not everyone feared the degradation of high culture with the infiltration of popular culture. The *Fresno Republican*, in fact, curiously reframed London's film work by collapsing autobiography, authorship, action, and the motion picture industry: "It is not often that a man has an opportunity to direct the films that depict the doings of his own life. Many have written their autobiographies, but this is the first case on record of any man picking out actors and locations (the authentic ones of the original occurrences) who were to reproduce the history of his own life."[35] However wrong the reporter's facts are, the point is that this is precisely the fantasy of self-representation that the cinema seemed able to perpetuate; think of Wyatt Earp, whose own version of this fantasy fits into a larger picture of Western legends who used moving pictures to autobiographical ends.

In a related move, the *Batania New York News* dubbed London's motion picture deal "Something New," writing that London's:

idea is not only to dramatize his thrilling tales of adventure, but to moving picturize them, appearing himself as his leading character. To read a story is one thing, to hear it read by the author is another, to have its characters temporarily come to life and act out their parts on the stage is still another, but to have the author go through the whole business in pantomime on the screen is the very acme of realism, and there is no one who can do this better than London. . . . Jack London is the pioneer. He has done or is about to do something entirely new and unique, but as the labels on the patent medicine bottles say, "beware of imitations."[36]

Through his narration, the author of this piece has nicely addressed not only the mass of myths and debates surrounding London's entrée into the moving picture business but more generally the status of movies in the culture at large. The article holds motion pictures up as a sign of progress, illustrating just how far modern forms of representation have evolved. While evincing the false but enticing belief that London would "pantomine" his own leading character, it turns out that London's brief appearances on screen during his productions were, indeed, considered as marking his films with the "very acme of realism." The author's final warning, "beware of imitations," also speaks to problems that plagued these years of London's life: Not only was London subject to continuous impersonations of his person, which he dealt with in a rather congenial if irritated fashion, but the motion picture industry presented him with the most frustrating and damaging imitations of his prized literary output, which he fought against vehemently across almost the entire decade of the nineteen-teens.

The Business of the Motion Picture

To approach London's cinematic business ventures, we might begin with the first rupture: London broke his initial April 29, 1913, contract for exclusive motion picture rights with the Balboa Amusement Company when they failed to produce the number of films they had initially promised, initiating years of legal battles between the two. London's new partnership was with moving picture businessman Frank Garbutt and actor Hobart Bosworth. It is hard to imagine a more focused and reciprocal business relationship: London gave Bosworth Incorporated exclusive rights to his works, and Bosworth Incorporated was formed to produce only films based upon Jack London's work. During the teens in America, there was a sense that motion pictures were about to fulfill their promise of offering superior entertainment that would engage, educate, and thrill audiences. Bosworth Incorporated's first London film, the seven-reel adaptation of *The Sea-Wolf* (1913), was intended to be an exemplar of this brand of superior filmmaking.

Coming on the heels of London's first unsuccessful moving picture contract with Balboa, the July 26, 1913, agreement signed by Jack London and Frank Garbutt regarding the Bosworth Incorporated productions included a series of notable stipulations. The contract provided for the filming of London at his Glen Ellen ranch in a fashion that would require "no acting part in the moving pictures per se," the hiring of "a competent professional scenario writer to transform" London's works, and London's consequent "right to inspect all such scenarios."[37] These aspects of the contract were highly publicized, leading to claims—made both by the filmmakers and, no doubt as a result of their publicity, by the press—concerning the value of these film productions based precisely on London's involvement. The *Los Angeles Times*, for example, published an article concerning the Bosworth Incorporated contract, opining that "the celebrated author himself helped make them, picking out the players who most nearly conformed with his conception of the characters he created. London also acted as judge and jury for the picture after it was completed and it comes to Tally's today with his personal O.K. on the work."[38] The details of London's contract—more so than his actual involvement in the production (which, from all indications, was minimal)—confers upon the final product a commercially motivated London stamp of approval that seems particularly important with regard to the first film of their partnership.

Bosworth Incorporated's first London production, *The Sea Wolf*, was released in 1913 (as was the Balboa Company's three-reel production of the same). One of the most remarkable aspects of seeing his work translated on screen, according to London, was the supplanting of Bosworth's vision of his characters for his own. London saw this as an enhancement, not as a territorial infraction: "After I saw Mr. Bosworth's representation of the part my own vision disappeared and was merged in the personification of Bosworth."[39] On the one hand, this statement is reminiscent of authorial testimonials for literary adaptations that intend to encourage the adaptation's financial success. But in London's commentary on Bosworth's visual translation of his work, he seems fascinated by the way that visual images supercede (quite naturally, according to the author) written ones, thereby implying, as he did elsewhere, that moving pictures were ultimately superior conduits of narrative. In other words, Bosworth had improved London's novel for even the author himself.

By exploiting London's reputation as a celebrity author, Bosworth Inc. was following the tradition of those early Westerns that used famous outlaws to draw curious audiences into the theaters. London's name and signature were widely known to the public and were made even more so

FIGURE 5: The front page of this advertising brochure for Bosworth's *John Barleycorn* (1914) relies upon the already-established value of London's image, which was now being developed and exploited on-screen as well as through this kind of print marketing. *Collection of the author.*

Rethinking Authorship in Jack London's Hollywood 77

through the marketing of Bosworth Incorporated's productions, in effect transmitting London's authorial celebrity into the new cinematic market and thereby expanding the life of his literary product. Hobart Bosworth's scrapbook contains a page from an unidentified periodical with an image of London in white shirt and tie, pen poised over paper and surrounded by the tools of his trade with the label "Jack London" appearing beneath him.[40] The caption at the bottom of the page reads, "A Word from Jack London in His Own Hand Writing." The text of this advertisement is, in fact, reproduced in London's own handwriting, a likely attempt to transmit the aura of London, to borrow the term Walter Benjamin used to connote what was lost in the age of mechanical reproduction: that which is tied to a person or thing's presence in space and time.

The text reaffirms London's position with regard to the cinematic adaptation of his works:

When I wrote the "Sea Wolf" the physical image of Larsen that took shape in my mind was more or less vague in outline and detail. Nevertheless, it was there, in my mind, and I carried it with me for years, until it was almost real to me. But it fled like a ghost at day-break when I saw, on the screen, Mr. Hobart Bosworth, the real, three-dimension, flesh-and-blood Sea Wolf. Until I die the image of the Sea Wolf will be Mr. Bosworth as I saw him on the screen.

This message is followed by a reproduction of London's autograph. The advertisement signifies triply. First, it uses London's image as a visual hook, meant to lure readers into the text and, implicitly, the film. This is a version of the product testimonial, which movie celebrities became involved with when manufacturers realized that stars could sell more than just motion pictures, and which London did during this era as well. Second, the decision to print the piece in London's own handwriting suggests that the value of the author might be transmitted through a refusal to submit to the anonymity of typescript, to the mass reproduction of the written word that robbed it of its individuality. This is a variation on the logic of the autograph. It is also precisely the logic that leads to London's image being used in Bosworth's film productions as a reminder of the literary figure behind the cinematic product, as a reminder of the "three dimension, flesh-and-blood" author.

Third, London testifies to the value of cinematic interpretation, again articulating a kind of cinematic superiority over his own literary work. In fact, London's interview with Bush, discussed earlier, is probably a reiteration of the publicity already prepared for this advertisement by those in charge of the film's publicity, complete with London rehearsing agreed-upon selling points of the film. Although getting somewhat carried away with himself in his invocation of a three-dimensional Wolf Larsen, his suggestion is that the moving image possessed an unparalleled representational realism. London thus gives Bosworth's cinematic production a triple stamp of approval with the hopes of ensuring its success; conversely, the success of the film would confer value upon the author in another arena of representation and distribution. Such carefully constructed, commercially oriented, and repeatedly reproduced statements also signify beyond mere publicity to suggest the potential impact of cinema on the future of representation.

In fact, the publicity campaigns surrounding Bosworth Incorporated's London productions were reliant upon the value and authenticity lent by London's already-existing reputation. In a 1913 *New York Dramatic Mirror* advertisement for *The Sea Wolf*, Jack London's name is central: "Bosworth presents The Sea Wolf by Jack London."[41] Authorship is redoubled here, with the film and novel represented as virtually synonymous creations. It is interesting that Bosworth's image, as Wolf Larsen, graces the top of this advertisement and not (for a change) London's. This is particularly the case because advertisements for the films of *Martin Eden* and *John Barleycorn* played up the autobiographical nature of the texts, almost always using London's image and autograph instead of images of the actor or director to encourage readers to make the connection between the author, the character in the book, and the character in the film.

The *Dramatic Mirror* advertisement for *The Sea Wolf* takes a different slant on the production by reinforcing Bosworth's rights to London's literary properties, asserting that "We are the exclusive producers in motion pictures of all Jack London's works, past, present and future." Because London and Bosworth were concerned, and rightly so, with copyright infringement of their properties, it is also worth noting that the lower third of the page of this advertisement is a direct plea from London, titled in bold "**Jack London to His Friends**":

I have made a contract under which Bosworth, Inc., has the rights to make moving pictures of all my works. Bosworth, Inc., has made a fine seven-reel picture of "The Sea Wolf," **authenticated** over my signature with twenty-five feet of moving pictures of myself writing at my desk. All other films made by BOSWORTH, INC., will be similarly **authenticated**. Unauthorized persons are raiding my copyrights and are attempting to sell to exhibitors moving pictures of my novels and stories, including a three-reel picture of The Sea Wolf. It is necessary, in order for me to protect my rights by suits for injunctions and damages, to know immediately in whatever city these unauthorized films may be exhibited. Wherefore I ask all my friends to notify me immediately whenever such unauthenticated films are exhibited or advertised to be exhibited.[42]

This advertisement uses the now-familiar genre of the testimonial to prepare audiences to distinguish a "real" Jack London picture from an illegitimate one, more specifically from the one produced by Balboa. Using the logic of product advertising—in which brand names signal the authenticity and quality of the product—the campaign reinforces the cultural value of London's name, image, and signature. His is the brand name, his image the product trademark, under which the "real" filmic product circulates in the market. Copyright and "authentication" mattered precisely because the author's reputation and subsequent value were at stake.

London's authorship is central to virtually all of Bosworth Incorporated's advertising for *The Sea Wolf*, which uses his name and image to authenticate the film production. While also emphasizing that the film is "universally copyrighted" and "fully protected," any ambiguity over the status of *The Sea Wolf* would be answered by the initial images of London that served to introduce the picture, or so went the logic of Bosworth Inc. An August 23, 1913, *Moving Picture World* blurb notes the London visual trademark attached to each Bosworth film: "As a further identification of each London subject a twenty-foot view of Mr. London will be prefixed, typifying as nearly as possible the local color of the story."[43]

London's presence conveyed much more than "local color." Three reels of Bosworth's 1914 version of *Martin Eden* survive at the Library of Congress and the first reel preserves the crucial images of the author discussed above.[44] These few seconds of film served as the trademark for every Bosworth Incorporated production. *Martin Eden*'s prefatory images are punctuated with a portrait of Jack London wearing his customary white shirt and tie, with his signature underneath, replicating the familiar autographed inscription on celluloid (see figure 6). The image and signature convey the author's stamp of legitimacy, appealing to the authenticating logic behind the autograph craze of the late nineteenth century. This static image leads into the first title of the film: "PREPARATION—Forced by necessity to gain an education in the University of Life" (see figure 7). Our expectation that this intertitle, which refers to the titular character of the novel-turned-film, will be followed by the film's opening moving images are not disappointed. But these moving images are not of the characters but of London himself, an appropriate slippage given the book's explicitly autobiographical nature.

FIGURE 6: The opening image from *Martin Eden* affirms the iconographic value of star-author Jack London, including his autograph as an authenticating device. Bosworth Incorporated, 1914. *Courtesy Library of Congress Moving Image Section.*

The two shots that precede the narrative but follow the film's apparent beginning are worth describing in some detail because they are unexplored in the vast criticism concerning London's career. The first medium shot is about six seconds in duration. London's whole body fills the frame as he sits, legs crossed, outside of his Glen Ellen estate in a wooden chair, smoking and reading a book (see figure 8). The table next to him has half a dozen or so books, but the author is not engaged in the performative task of writing to demonstrate "the author at work," although this is the supposed premise of the opening image, at least according to later press reports. Rather, he is looking directly into the camera as he holds out his cigarette and flicks it, thus ending the shot (see figure 9). The second shot lasts for about ten seconds and begins with a close-up of London, creating more of an intimate relationship with the famed author than in the first shot (see figure 10). But a gaze of outward regard has replaced the direct stare of the author, as London looks on a diagonal line toward the lower right bottom of the screen. London is smiling slightly but holding very still, obviously in the act of posing as if for a stationary camera, as opposed to the first shot in which he moves. In fact, the only real movement in this longer, second shot is performed by the trees in the background as the image slowly fades out.

> PREPARATION
>
> Forced by necessity to gain an education in the University of the World

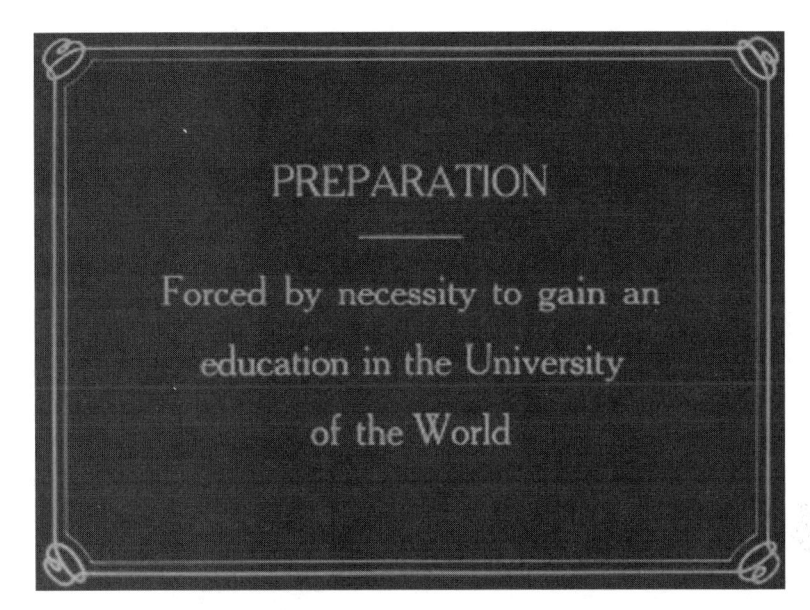

FIGURE 7: Following credits, which list the cast, director Hobart Bosworth, cinematographer George Will, but not author or scenarist, *Martin Eden*'s first intertitle suggests that the film is about to begin. Bosworth Incorporated, 1914. *Courtesy Library of Congress Moving Image Section.*

These sixteen seconds of film are crucial to an understanding of London's engagement with the medium as well as to a sense of how the medium changed the ways that individuals could negotiate their reputations. These shots invite a series of questions, most obviously, *what is their purpose?* And why do they come after what appears to be the beginning of the film? It is clear that London's image functions as a visual signature, endowing the film with a stamp of authenticity. The image marks the film as a legitimate and legally sanctioned London product in order to steer audiences clear of "imitators." London is the maker of the book and thus the first in the creative chain that culminates in this cinematic product; he is implicitly the maker of the film as well. But the placement of the images also results in a more thorough collapse of the author's identity with the semifictional Martin Eden, for certainly London's appearance after the first intertitle suggests that it was London himself who sought to "gain an education in the University of the World," a conclusion supported even further by London's relentless use of autobiographical materials in his writings. These images also reveal their maker's twin assumptions: that Jack London would be a recognizable figure and that audiences would value his appearance *as part of the film*. Part of building a reputation compatible with

FIGURE 8: Instead of proceeding with the narrative of *Martin Eden*, the film spends more time authenticating itself and celebrating its star author, first by appearing to stumble upon London "at work" . . . Bosworth Incorporated, 1914. *Courtesy Library of Congress Moving Image Section.*

FIGURE 9: . . . and then through London's direct gaze at the camera/audience. Bosworth Incorporated, 1914. *Courtesy Library of Congress Moving Image Section.*

FIGURE 10: The second shot of London at his ranch develops the audience's relationship to the author through an intimate close-up. Bosworth Incorporated, 1914. *Courtesy Library of Congress Moving Image Section.*

cinematic celebrity meant literally becoming a part of the visual register of the cinema.

This pre-film appearance also represents a technological advancement over those films being made and screened by Westerners like Emmett Dalton, as discussed in chapter two, who physically attended screenings in order to provide the same kind of authoritative stamp, albeit with obvious quantitative limits. Bosworth Incorporated's concept is an innovation, a cinematic extension of the concept Auerbach notes: "If the writer's 'self' is a detachable logo, marked again and again in the material act of writing for a public, then the primary task is to market it as your own."[45] The incorporation of the authorial image within the film itself, an incorporation so carefully attended to that London himself quoted the number of feet of film exposed to capture his image, moves well beyond the realm of cinematic narration (as employed by Martin Johnson) or personal appearances (as in the case of someone like Dalton); it would, in fact, suggest both the antiquity of such extra-cinematic devices, which hearken back to the emblematic shot contained in Edison and Porter's *The Great Train Robbery*, as well as their evolution and continuing effectiveness, evidenced by the forward-thinking innovation of the mechanically reproduced London appearance.

Here, reputation becomes narration and speaks, quite eloquently, on behalf of the film. Authenticity is once again explained, but cinematically and synecdochically: Moving images of London speak on behalf of a catalogue of other images and associations. These images also suggest a certain degree of faith on the part of their producers, who banked on the impossibility that London's image could be reproduced illicitly. His stories might circulate in disguise, but without this preface, they would be quickly recognized as "forgeries." Furthermore, while Tony Williams contends that "London's appearance also parallels Hitchcock's cameo 'walk-on' performances in his films," it more accurate to say that it *predicts* these appearances, hinting at the escalating value of authorial image and personality.[46]

There is a circularity here: from author, to text, to film, to author. London's image was being distributed widely and his texts were being reinvented in this other venue, thereby extending their cultural lives. The author offers up both himself and his products for a chain of consumption that keeps his name and image in the public's eye, largely through "that dreadful single eye of the camera," as he once referred to it in a published Christmas letter;[47] in other words, he was getting the most out of the products of his labor and, perhaps most importantly, trying to protect them and his reputation through the virtual trademark afforded by his own image. Trademark and copyright were of central importance in this era during which legislation was being put into place concerning both authors' and motion picture makers' rights. Although the practice began much earlier, by 1909 trademarks were required in all films by article seven of the Motion Picture Patents Company; this was the case until around 1912.[48] Trademark was, of course, so important because of what London would experience as the pirating of his works in the industry, partly a consequence of the vagueness of contemporary copyright law. As he put it to Garbutt in a September 11, 1913, telegram, "PLEASE REMEMBER THAT COPYRIGHT LAW AT PRESENT IS CHAOTIC AND NEEDS SPECIALISTS."[49] The attempt to create a personal trademark, in this case in the form of London's signature and image, was only the first step in the process of reclaiming proprietary rights and mitigating against the potentially damaging mismanagement of his image and literary property in the hectic realm of the moving image.

London's copyright case with Balboa Amusement was very much a test case for American authors. The Author's League of America, to whom Earp and associates turned for help with the illegitimate copyright of his photographic image during the 1920s, became involved with the litigation.

As the *New York City Journal* reported in its piece that details London's case, "Authors to War for Copyright Against 'Movies'": "Most authors and publishers believe that the present copyright law, passed before the dramatization of novels became important, and before the rise of the moving picture, is awkward and hazy in its application to modern conditions. It has never been fully tested."[50] Around the same time, Jack London wrote to Arthur Train of the Author's League that "it seems that the time has come for all authors, magazine publishers, and book publishers, to get together and make a fight for themselves. I am now being attacked by a pirate raid."[51] Using the language of adventure that he would employ a few years later in *Hearts of Three*, a novel based upon movie scenarios that was itself about the hunt for buried treasure, London acknowledges his pioneering role as a defender of authorial rights. In fact, his "Introduction" to *Hearts of Three* can be understood as an historical essay on the status of authorship in relation to the industry, in which he vituperatively notes that, "Thousands of scenario writers—literally tens of thousands, for no man, nor woman, nor child was too mean not to write scenarios—tens of thousands of scenario writers pirated through all literature (copyright or otherwise), and snatched the magazines hot from the press to steal any new scene or plot or story hit upon by their writing brethren."[52] London became so embroiled with the legal details of copyright and trademark that he devoted much of his time to studying the law and corresponding with his lawyers and business partners regarding its intricacies.

Copyright sought to enable authors to retain the financial rewards earned by their works, but an author's reputation was also at stake when copyright failed to protect the source material, particularly when dealing with the immensely distributable and yet hard-to-track-down motion picture. London and his associates were often only made aware of pirated versions of his films, such as Balboa's *A Piece of Steak*, by seeing advertisements for these films in the trades. As London telegrammed Bosworth, "MOVING PICTURE WORLD OF AUGUST THIRTY SAYS PIECE OF STEAK IS RELEASED IS THIS SO WHAT ABOUT IT WHAT IS BEING DONE BY US IF OTHER MAN SUCCESSFULLY RELEASE ONE FILM HE PROVE TO THE FILM EXCHANGES THAT THEY CAN RELEASE ANY AND ALL OF HIS FILM."[53] London paid close attention to what the film industry was producing and distributing because he rightly feared that a precedent would be set through which he would lose the rights to all of his works. This came to a head during his battle with Balboa Amusement Company after the severing of their contractual relationship. Frank Garbutt, financial backer of Bosworth's production company, wrote to London about the concurrent release of the Balboa

Amusement Company's production of *The Sea Wolf*, noting that "The most serious criticisms that I have heard are that the Horkheimer production will damage your reputation all over the country, wherever shown, and I am inclined to concur in this belief."[54] Living in the public eye had its consequences, not the least of which was the sense that the author no longer had exclusive rights to his reputation once it had entered the public sphere, as will be evidenced throughout this book. But this is particularly the case with these battles London fought over copyright, during which his literature and his identity, like Wyatt Earp's story and image, could be purloined and exploited in a fashion over which he had limited control.

The other question that plagued London during this era involved precisely how to understand the value of his name, image, and writing. This was of particular concern because London had not seen significant income from his motion picture endeavors despite promises to the contrary. In his copyright infringement trial against the Balboa Amusement Company, London's legal representative, Donald Barker, attempted to describe the *value* of the motion pictures based upon London's previously published materials, writing "That the said films when so produced have great value; that the said works of the plaintiff Jack London have had a large sale and distribution throughout the United States; that the author thereof is well known and plaintiffs are informed and believe and therefore allege that a large demand now exists and will exist for such moving pictures dramatizing and illustrating said stories."[55] These ambiguous terms—large, great—suggest the degree to which all parties involved were unable to really determine the economic worth of a film amidst all of the changes taking place. How could the value of these films be predicted?

London was similarly frustrated in his attempts to define the value of films based upon his work. He believed that there was a window of opportunity during this decade, and that his reputation had been tarnished by his public battles with the industry and the less than satisfactory authorized translations of some of his works by Bosworth Incorporated. Writing to Garbutt in an October 14, 1915, telegram after Bosworth Incorporated ceased producing his works, the author expresses an urgency with regard to the cinematic marketplace: "NOW IS THE TIME YOU CAN HELP ME THE VALUE OF MOVING PICTURE RIGHTS IN MY WORK HAS NOT ONLY STEADILY BUT RAPIDLY DECLINED IN LAST TWO YEARS IF I AM GOING TO GET ANYTHING FOR WHAT YOU DID NOT USE I MUST GET IT."[56] London uses language that might be mistaken for discussion of stock value here, a form of economic speculation and an appropriate linguistic connection given his treatment of the subject in *Hearts of Three*. The analogy is also apt given

London's experiences: He had little control over the value of his "stock" in the marketplace and seems at this point interested in selling out to recoup his losses. This is all, to one degree or another, about commercial speculation, since there was no way to gauge what might happen in the cinematic marketplace. As London had written to Garbutt several months earlier: "I have a feeling that you do not comprehend the value of my asset which you have in your possession by contract, the value of which may be perishing from day to day."[57]

Although *The Sea Wolf* was acknowledged by many as a superior example of motion picture art, as a whole the Bosworth Productions did not succeed, leading to what London feared was a further devaluation of his literary assets in the cinematic marketplace. Toward the end of their business relationship, Garbutt explained to London: "The strongest criticisms which we have had from most of our exhibitors in the East is that the endings of our stories are not suitable for motion picture audiences; also that our interest runs more to dialogue and not enough to plot."[58] London, too, made critical observations about what made a good film and what was wrong with some of Bosworth Incorporated's decisions. Writing to Garbutt, London opines:

If you will remember, from the first I voluntarily advised both you and Bosworth to take all the liberty in the world with my text. To follow my text literally, I deemed would not make [it] popular, from [a] moving-picture standpoint. Another thing you will remember I always insisted upon, that sitting in the audience I could not see my films getting across because they did not have enough of the legends or printed explanations thrown on the screen in the midst of the pictures.[59]

Most interesting in this series of observations is London's decision to renege upon his formerly noted belief in the superiority of the cinematic image. Here he falls back upon a logic that relies on the written word to convey meaning, particularly with regard to those things that are difficult to convey visually: motivation, the internal states of characters, and the like.

Much as he studied up on copyright when he needed to, London gave the industry almost scientific attention and his literary output began to reflect these observations: "Now I have become hugely interested in the motion pictures, I am getting the habit, I am beginning to study them and learning to tell the difference between the good and the bad. Yes, I thought that the screen was all right for landscapes, events, etc., but of its real might I had no idea."[60] This was so much the case that London's writing, that labor with which he had so proudly made himself a great man by, was fundamentally changed during these cinematically engaged years. At least at one point during these years, London deemed motion pictures as potentially all-encompassing, stating that "every thing with the possible exception of demonstrations in political economy will eventually go through the hands of the filmer."[61] It is no wonder that moving pictures and the culture surrounding them would enter so forcefully into the world of London's literature.

Writing for the Screen

It is my contention that, at least in the latter part of his life, London began to write with the motion pictures and their attendant publicity in mind. This became part of London's strategy to keep up with the changing literary marketplace in the face of the motion picture industry, to some extent by trying to anticipate its future needs. Although his involvement with the industry resulted in cumbersome legal troubles and only moderate success, London never gave up hope for his future with the medium. In fact, he actively participated in one well-documented, if critically neglected, foray into authorship that revolved entirely around the motion picture industry: *Hearts of Three*. My consideration of the circumstances from which this text evolved, along with an analysis of the text, will illustrate the degree to which London had revised his ideas of authorship to anticipate and accommodate cinematic production, suggesting the extent to which London tried to remain valuable in the new cinematic economy.

Hearts of Three was first printed as a book in England in 1918; the *New York Evening Journal* and *Oakland Tribune* serialized it in 1919; Macmillan published the United States edition in 1920.[62] London completed the manuscript well before his death in 1916, through a deal facilitated by Edward Grant Sisson, editor of *Cosmopolitan*, the magazine that had contractual rights to all of London's fiction. As Alex Kershaw notes, this book-writing deal was a financial boon for London. For writing *Hearts of Three*, he would be paid $25,000, "ten times the advance he had received from Century two years earlier for *John Barleycorn*."[63] Charles Goddard, a Hearst employee and photoplay writer, provided London with installments of motion picture scenarios as he completed them for what was conceived of as a weekly moving picture serial; London followed Goddard's plots to produce a novel of the screenplay, which would then be made into a weekly serialized film that would be accompanied by the publication of London's novel, serialized and in book form.

This collaboration may seem like an unusual way to approach the business of novel writing, but serializations were a central part of this decade's filmmaking practices. Kalem and Biograph were making serials in 1909, based largely on nineteenth-century Victorian novels; by the nineteen-teens they had become a popular commodity, with certain tropes such as the suspenseful weekly endings already in place.[64] The relationship between the moving picture serial and the literary serial was also taking shape, as films were produced on the heels of a story's weekly or monthly magazine or newspaper publication. This is an interesting reciprocal relationship: The newspapers and motion picture producers both profited from the venture, one gaining readers and the other spectators. As a business venture, it also represents yet another provocative instance of the merging of print and visual culture. London knew all too well that the motion picture producers were hungry for source materials and needed the print industry. It was, perhaps, only slightly unusual that an author of London's status would undertake a project that might be considered so overtly derivative.

London appears to have found this new kind of literary production arrangement rather agreeable. On January 25, 1916, London wrote to Sisson about his next project: "Either let me lay off for six months and do some non-fiction work that I am very anxious to do . . . or give me another job of serialization of scenarios in collaboration with Goddard, like the one I am at present doing."[65] Seven months later, on August 5, 1916, London repeated the sentiment when asking Sisson to "please keep me in mind for some future serialization like the HEARTS OF THREE."[66] Writing was a business for London, and Goddard's scenarios made the industry of writing more efficient and as a result more profitable, since London was always calculating the cost of his labors in relation to his returns. Furthermore, London had partnered with someone who had achieved success in similar ventures: Goddard had already written *The Perils of Pauline* and *The Exploits of Elaine*, both successful Pathé serials in 1914.

London's *Hearts of Three* can be understood as an embellishment of Goddard's photoplay, appearing at first glance to rely on elaboration more than invention.[67] Notable for its frantic pace and unbelievable plot twists, *Hearts of Three* reflects the conventions of the movie serial, which kept audiences hanging on the proverbial edge of their seats in anticipation of the next episode. The side-by-side crescendos and climaxes in *Hearts of Three*, as a novel, seem a bit preposterous; but to the movie spectator of the teens, who would have had a full week in between each cliff-hanging moment (to use a term whose origins reside in the moving picture serials), these events would have appeared less contrived and, as the genre established itself, more in line with the conventions associated with this kind of unfolding drama.[68]

For precisely this reason, the novel's plot is difficult to convey without replicating the confusion of the novel itself. *Hearts of Three* tells the story of Francis Morgan, a wealthy young college man living on Riverside Drive who decides, in good Rooseveltian fashion, to take two weeks in the woods because he feels he's "growing soft."[69] But first he encounters Alvarez Torres, who claims he can lead the young man to find a treasure buried by his father, Sir Henry Morgan. Many sensational events transpire over the course of the novel's 373 pages: Francis goes to the Mosquito Coast and runs into unknown descendants of his father, including his half brother Henry who looks almost identical to him (spare the difference in moustache); Francis meets and falls in love with a mysterious wild woman, Leoncia, whom he marries at novel's end after an incestuous marriage almost takes place between Henry and Leoncia, who are siblings, and after Francis' brief pagan marriage to the Lady Who Dreams, queen of a world of ancients and sun gods where explorers find Mayan treasure worth hundreds of millions of dollars, which is eventually brought back to New York to save Francis from losing everything in the stock market. (His financial plight is caused by the evil machinations of someone he took to be his father's dearest friend, Regan.) It will not surprise anyone that in the process of making it through such a fantastic series of events, there are several ambushes, imprisonments, forestalled executions, mistaken identities, gun battles, assorted wild goose chases through the Panamanian wilds, and even a giant spider. London describes the plot in the introduction to the novel: "And action! I have written some novels of adventure in my time, but never, in all of the many of them, have I perpetrated a totality of action equal to what is contained in 'Hearts of Three.'"[70]

More than any other piece of London's writing, the novel's "Introduction" contends with issues of literary and cinematic production central to this chapter. As London explains the process of reinventing his authorial self in relation to cinematic production, he considers the status of the writer in early Hollywood:

With the rise of moving pictures into the overwhelmingly most popular form of amusement in the entire world, the stock of plots and stories in the world's fiction fund began rapidly to be exhausted. In a year a single producing company, with a score of directors, is capable of filming the entire literary output of the entire lives of Shakespeare, Balzac, Dickens, Scott, Zola, Tolstoy, and of dozens of less voluminous writers. And since there are hundreds of moving picture producing companies, it can be readily grasped how quickly they found themselves face to face with a shortage of the raw material of which moving pictures are fashioned.[71]

This statement is a striking articulation of the competing anxieties of the decade cast in terms of production and consumption, supply and demand. By describing this relationship in economic terms, pointing to the limited "fiction fund" that existed to serve these markets, London implies a kind of rabid capitalistic consumption, with the motion picture producers madly ingesting the world's great literary works. As star author London was particularly subject, however willingly, to such consumption. His acknowledgment of an industrial conceptualization of the relationship between the moving picture producers and the literary market reminds us of the degree to which he understood his own image as requisite for survival in the new cinematic economy.

Part of London's behind-the-scenes explication of *Hearts of Three* involves the formal arrangements of the text and its analogous life on celluloid:

On the Ranch, in the Valley of the Moon, he wrote his first several episodes. But he wrote faster than I, and was done with his fifteen episodes weeks ahead of me. Do not be misled by the word "episode." The first episode covers three thousand feet of film. The succeeding fourteen episodes cover each two thousand feet of film. And each episode contains about ninety scenes, which makes a total of some thirteen hundred scenes. Nevertheless, we worked simultaneously at our respective tasks. I could not build for what was going to happen next or a dozen chapters away, because I did not know. Neither did Mr. Goddard know. The inevitable result was that "Hearts of Three" may not be very vertebrate, although it is certainly consecutive.[72]

While not using this mode of literary production as an excuse for the novel's unusual structure or pacing, London tries to convey a material sense of this unusual relationship between the written word and the moving image. London rethinks the notion of authorship based upon the mechanics of this new relationship to his own production: Not knowing where the story was taking him, he accommodated narrative whims over which he apparently had no control. This was a new economy for London, whose authorial autonomy had been largely based upon a rigorous concept of isolated daily labor and production, however much he may have "borrowed" materials that were circulating in the culture at large or purchased ideas from which his fiction grew.[73] London's efforts recognize that the culture of authorship was undergoing a significant change.

London concludes the "Introduction" by addressing authorial rights in a situation in which concepts of "ownership" have been impossibly blurred:

> If this adventure of "Hearts of Three" be collaboration, I am transported by it. But alack!—I fear me Mr. Goddard must then be the one collaborator in a million. We have never had a word, an argument, nor a discussion. But then, I must be a jewel of a collaborator myself. Have I not, without whisper or whimper of complaint, let him "register" through fifteen episodes or scenario, through thirteen hundred scenes and thirty-one thousand feet of film, through one hundred and eleven thousand words of novelization? Just the same, having completed the task, I wish I'd never written it—for the reason that I'd like to read it myself to see if it reads along. I am curious to know.[74]

London's curiosity about the outcome of his project leads us to the text itself. A comparison between Goddard's screenplay and London's novelization reveals that London did provide substantial elaboration and invention for his "half" of the deal. Rather than simply adding a few details to Goddard's screenplay, London made great descriptive departures, sometimes recounting for an entire page what Goddard attended to in a sentence; word and image, as London already realized, had relative economies. Goddard's scenario attends to its characters as if describing the movement of pawns in a game of chess, transporting them about the Panamanian landscape with little elaboration. London's novel takes Goddard's skeletal descriptions and runs with them, filling in the picture for his readers based upon the suggestions offered up by Goddard in an attempt to restore a descriptive, novelistic quality to the minimal details of the photoplay.

Perhaps not surprisingly, *Hearts of Three* takes many of its formal and contextual clues from the already-established conventions of the motion picture. When Francis ends up in a gun and knife fight with a stranger, he makes a statement that blatantly invokes the industry: "Too bad there isn't a moving picture camera to film this."[75] This comment's appearance in the novel, in addition to a later reference to a character's "ideal 'film' face," demonstrates on the most superficial level that the motion picture industry had become part of London's literary consciousness.[76] More to the point, however, is the formal structure of the novel, which, consciously or not, reflects the language of the cinema. In London's draft of the novel, this is so much the case that there are installment numbers instead of chapters, no doubt to help the author chart his progress through the structure provided in Goddard's scenarios.[77] But this slippage in form goes both ways:

in the headings for Goddard's scenarios, he alternately refers to the sections as episodes, chapters, and installments.[78]

The cinematic influence is particularly evident in London's use of the flashback, a cinematic convention that he adapts to the novelistic form in *Hearts of Three*. Charles Musser claims that the Selig Company used the flashback device in *When We Were Boys* (1907), and Eileen Bowser locates the term's first application in a manual for moving picture scenario writers by Harold Weston, *The Art of Photo-Play Writing* (1916); she also notes that the device was referred to more commonly as "memory flashes."[79] The *Oxford English Dictionary* also finds the term's cinematic origins in 1916, but in an October issue of *Variety*; the term's first usage in relation to literature occurred much later, in 1928. Regardless of the terminology, the concept of the flashback was articulated in relation to the cinematic medium in the early twentieth century. The *OED* defines it in its 1916 usage as "a scene which is a return to a previous action in the film, a cut-back; hence, a revival of the memory of past events, as in a pictorial or written presentation."

This is precisely how London deploys the concept—a kind of psychological editing, as Gunning has described it—in his novel. Used as an interiorizing device, the flashback allows viewers a glimpse into the minds of its characters. In London's iterations, the flashback retains its principal function by similar formal markers that appear on the page instead of on the screen. An extended passage, which occurs after Francis's newly found half brother, Henry, puts on their father's old pirate clothes, illustrates London's use of the device:

As the young man, picking the strings of a guitar, began to sing the old buccaneer rouse, it seemed to him that the picture of his forebear faded into another picture and that he saw:

The old forebear himself, back to a mainmast, cutlass out and flashing, facing a semicircle of fantastically clad sailor cutthroats, while behind him, on the opposite side of the mast, another similarly garbed and accoutered man, with cutlass flashing, faced the other semi-circle of cutthroats that completed the ring about the mast.

The vivid vision of his fancy was broken by the breaking of a guitar-string which he had thrummed too passionately. And in the sharp pause of silence, it seemed that a fresh vision of old Sir Henry came to him, down out of the frame and beside him, real in all seeming, plucking at his sleeve to lead him out of the hut and whispering the ghostly repetition of:

"Back to back against the mainmast,
Held at bay the entire crew."

The young man obeyed his shadowy guide, or some prompting of his own of profound intuition, and went out the door and down to the beach, where, gazing across the narrow channel, on the beach of the Bull, he saw his late antagonist, [Francis] backed up against the great bowlder of coral rock, standing off an attack of sack-clouted, machete-wielding Indians with wide sweeping strokes of a driftwood timber.[80]

A combination of vision and flashback, this narration relies upon a familial memory invoked by the donned attire rather than solely by Henry's personal memory of his father. I would argue that the way that London chooses to narrate this scene is entirely cinematic. London's methods here, where skipped lines are equated with fades and cuts, reflect the ways that moving-picture makers had pioneered such formal notions of representing memory, with the first space in the text functioning as a kind of literary dissolve, taking the reader from the present into a scene from the past without having to explain the transition *with words*. In fact, the representational mechanisms established by cinema and its modes of representation save the author the necessity of using language to convey this effect.

This flashback contrasts with London's earlier representations of memory, which function on similar principles but which, mostly written prior to London's involvement with the motion picture industry, share little with the cinematic formalism of *Hearts of Three*.[81] In *The Call of The Wild* (1903), for example, the novel's canine protagonist, Buck, experiences two memories that are narrated rather than envisioned in this cinematic fashion. Like the scene in *Hearts of Three*, the first also involves a curious merging of vision and memory, when Buck "remembered back to the youth of the breed, to the time the wild dogs ranged in packs through the primeval forest and killed their meat as they ran it down."[82] This vision lacks any formal indication of its status as image, whereas in *Hearts of Three* Henry's flashback is almost entirely visual, reading very much like a scene description. Buck's second memory is decidedly more visual, but no less literary in its remembrance of the happy days, people, and places of his past along with earlier ancestral memories, akin to the kind Henry has in *Hearts of Three*.[83] In sum, London does use the device of memory in *The Call of the Wild*, but these uses bear little resemblance to the cinematically derived concept of the flashback as it is deployed in the representation of Henry's memory in *Hearts of Three*.

So is the case with *The Sea-Wolf* (1904), in which Wolf Larsen tells Humphrey Van Weyden about his impoverished personal history despite his notable utterance: "I do not care to remember."[84] As in *The Call of the Wild*, this extended scene is not rendered as a flashback; rather, it is told through descriptive dialogue that provides background materials to advance the plot. This goal is not dissimilar from the use of the flashback in *Hearts of Three*, but it is formally incomparable. Where Wolf's speech presents this material, Henry's narration is notably silent. There are reasons for this that further suggest London's appropriation of a cinematic formalism: Silent films naturally avoid complicated verbal explications in favor of comprehensible visual signs, precisely the kind that London describes in his narration of *Hearts of Three*.

Martin Eden (1909) comes the closest to achieving a cinematically oriented textual reflexivity. Written well into the period of London's cinematic awareness, the novel is replete with visions and mental pictures, with Martin's mind at one point even turning into "a vast camera obscura, and he saw arrayed around his consciousness endless pictures from his life."[85] Mental pictures make up a critical part of Martin's inner consciousness, suggesting the influence of projection upon the author's ability to imagine his character; however, there are no textual markers reminiscent of cinema's formal properties. The movie flashback typically relies upon the use of the dissolve, and the literal space used by London to initiate his flashback in *Hearts of Three* is the equivalent of this cinematic device. Although the use of spatial separations to connote a shift in scenario was not of cinema born, it is a device that London uses rampantly in *Hearts of Three*, as he does nowhere else. There were, of course, practical reasons for this given the rapid pace of action throughout the novel, no doubt out of necessity for advancing such a manic plot. His earlier novel *The Sea-Wolf* does have this kind of division between narrative action, but only on rare occasions to separate one scene from the next within a chapter.[86] The technique was an established part of the cinematic vocabulary by the time London employed it so heavily in *Hearts of Three*. As a condition of having to approximate the visual narratives fed to him by Goddard, London appears to have been compelled to use the literary approximation of the dissolve in order to get from one moment of the story to the next.

One of the consequences of London's use of the literary dissolve (itself a result of Goddard's serialized photoplays) is the unusual prevalence of parallel action in *Hearts of Three*. There are at least as many examples of this device as there are chapters: Francis and Leoncia struggle in a cave with the treasure while elsewhere Henry is jailed and waiting for release; Francis takes care of his business in New York while Henry carries on in Panama; and Torres tries to get at the hidden treasure while several different events occupy the Solano family. As with the cinematic serial, the pace of London's story gets progressively faster, with shorter segments between the spaces that signify these dissolves.

London's literary deployment of these visual and cinematic properties was not only a reflection of what Goddard was handing him. One scene rendered by both Goddard and London illustrates the degree to which London was responding in his writing to more than just his need to follow Goddard's photoplay. After Francis marries the Queen and brings her to New York, Goddard's photoplay suggests her entrance into this unfamiliar, civilized world: "Francis kissed her as in the dream and she asks what the stock ticker is. Francis starts to explain, picks up the tape sees something that scares him and jumps to telephone."[87] London elaborates upon Goddard's scenario by having the Queen ask Francis about the mysterious stock market ticker:

He opened his mouth to reply to her last question, halted, and said nothing, realizing the impossibility of conveying comprehension to her, the while, under his eyelids, or at the foreground of his brain, burned pictures of great railroad and steamship lines, of teeming terminals and noisy docks; of miners toiling in Alaska, in Montana, in Death Valley; of bridled rivers, and harnessed waterfalls, and of power-lines stilting across lowlands and swamps and marshes on two-hundred-foot towers; and of all the mechanics and economics and finances of the twentieth century machine-civilization.[88]

With or without Goddard's cues, London's literary techniques here are highly visual and explicitly cinematic: *pictures burning in the foreground of a character's brain* describe the cinema's techniques for explicating character consciousness, and they are also key to London's desire to "to get the images living in my brains into the brains of others." This is narration recast as cinema, or perhaps it is cinema reinscribed as narration. Such language recalls London's earlier experimentation with visually oriented narration in *Martin Eden*. As in the 1909 novel, this character doesn't merely contemplate these images but enforces a literary approximation of spectatorship upon the reader. But the style, while interestingly cinematic, is also fundamentally descriptive. Motion pictures embodied the "twentieth century machine-civilization" that London invokes; they also facilitated a reinvention of literary convention and a rethinking of the relationship between the written word and the moving image.

Although *Hearts of Three* appears to have failed, as both a novel and a motion picture, London's letters just months before his death remain optimistic regarding a future with the motion picture industry despite his merely minor successes and substantial frustrations. London was hoping to get William Randolph Hearst to produce a film version simultaneously alongside the publication of what would be the final novel released during his lifetime, *The Little Lady of the Big House* (1916). In a telegram to London on September 4, 1914, Sisson concurred with London's idea about the novel's cinematic possibilities: "Believe your progressing novel lends itself to simultaneous magazine and movie production many of Forrest's early adventures are pictorial so is tank riding scene who is person with whom to start planning to work out mutually profitable arrangement."[89] By 1916, London thought it almost obligatory that his writings would have their day on screen at some point. He even reflected upon his works' inadequacies with regard to motion picture production, writing to Sisson that:

> I have written to Mr. Garbutt sending him the text of THE LITTLE LADY OF THE BIG HOUSE so far as I have it written. I am doubtful myself that the ending is happy enough to make it a successful moving picture affair; however I have written to Mr. Garbutt and you may also understand the same thing from me—namely, that I give to the scenario writer free fist to change my plot ending and anything and everything necessary to turn the story into a successful moving picture.[90]

London seems to admit here, without any hint of regret, his own resignation, of sorts. In so doing, London permits himself to think of authorship differently, less heroically, less romantically. He had become a highly visible laborer, one of many, producing novels to be fleshed out or stripped down by more cinematically inclined personnel for his product's secondary (or tertiary) lives. London's acknowledgment that his novel's ending was perhaps not ideally cinematic also implies that he did not think of himself as writing a movie scenario; rather, he was creating a product-in-progress whose ultimate destination was the silver screen. Although this may have increased his cultural cachet, it simultaneously eroded certain notions of autonomous and heroic authorship, increasingly creaky concepts that had begun to diminish over the course of the Gilded Age in favor of a model more akin to the production line, an appropriate conceptualization at which to arrive on the cusp of the 1920s.

London's cinematic dealings, then, would suggest that his relationship to the motion picture industry signaled his rejection of the sacred status of the singular author. This is not to say that the loss was not compensated for in alternate ways, since London's image and his reputation were poised to become all the more visible and valuable despite his virtual alienation from "his" cinematic products. When Christopher Wilson declared that "nearly a century after writers began their quest for the recognition of their intellectual property, they have become, in the jargon of the agent, 'properties' themselves," he could have been describing the deliberate outcome of Jack London's own reputation making, his willingness to sell himself.[91]

Although London's writing came to reflect the language and form of motion pictures, he seemed content with, and perhaps even intent upon, following a literary path with only limited involvement in the actual business of motion picture production. This path, however, led to a seemingly inevitable cinematic afterlife for his works. The author's aims for his literary production had therefore undergone a significant conceptual shift with the addition of motion picture distribution to his chain of literary economics. London may not have had "a successful moving picture affair," but he was willing to relinquish and, in so doing, debunk the sanctity of authorship in the name of his future successes in the more loosely defined field of popular culture, foreshadowing the fates of dozens of established American authors who later sought to make their reputations, and their money, by transporting their works to Hollywood.

4

MAKING *IT* IN HOLLYWOOD

CLARA BOW AND THE CYCLE OF THE FAN MAGAZINE

When fame and public scrutiny became too much for actress Clara Bow, she exiled herself to a desert ranch in Nevada with cowboy actor Rex Bell, enacting an interesting counterpoint to the direction Wyatt Earp took in the latter part of his life. While Earp tried to memorialize his legend in Hollywood and resuscitate his Wild West mythos by guiding the movie cameras in his direction, Bow sought to salvage her reputation, health, and sanity by removing herself, at least geographically, from the perpetual limelight of Hollywood. Living in a barely furnished "board shack," she showered outdoors, dodged lizards, and shot rabbits for supper, at least according to the fan magazines, which were reluctant to let Bow disappear entirely from their pages, perhaps only as much as Bow was unwilling to give up the spotlight entirely. In her exile, Bow appeared to be trying to avoid the often-pernicious scrutiny of the press and public. However, a 1931 *Photoplay* piece entitled "Roughing It with Clara" provides a glimpse at Bow's post-Hollywood existence, its author quoting Bow: "It's the first time in years that I've been able to be just myself. No people, so I don't have to act."[1] It is, of course, ironic that Bow offers this information to a *Photoplay* writer, thereby presenting this new, reclusive version of herself to still-curious fans, for whom Bow's movies were virtually a thing of the past.

In many ways, Bow's reputation is both the most and the least deliberately "self-made" of those examined in this book, since Bow became a star and was dethroned via official mechanisms of the celebrity industry. She also had the least at stake in her initial Hollywood foray: Raised haphazardly in Brooklyn by a mentally ill mother and an abrasive, alcoholic father, Bow was a devoted movie fan with a seventh-grade education who used the movies and their stars to construct a dream life outside of her own less-than-ideal reality.[2] But Bow did more than dream of another life;

she obtained one by winning a "Fame and Fortune" contest sponsored by Brewster Publications (publisher of *Motion Picture*, *Motion Picture Classic*, and *Shadowland*), which led initially to a cross-country train trip to Hollywood and some minor film roles. Although she undertook the least risk in attempting to do so, Bow is in other ways the most audacious Hollywood aspirant to appear within these pages, for she struck out to Hollywood with nothing but her own ambitions behind her. She would eventually ascend to the apex of movie stardom at Paramount, become the subject of seemingly endless gossip in media outlets that ran the gamut from scandal sheets to the same fan magazines that had promoted her, and then disappear from Tinseltown altogether.

To examine the process through which Bow was made and then unmade in Hollywood, this chapter will pay particular attention to her career in relation to star and fan culture. By the time of Bow's arrival in the mid-1920s, Hollywood's star-making capabilities, which first emerged a decade earlier, were fully in place. The studios—vertically integrated, powerful corporate entities—sought out and groomed a hierarchy of talent, reserving the greatest resources for those at the star or near-star level, who in turn helped the studios ensure that audiences would return to their theaters for the next "star X" picture. Publicity departments determined the histories, personalities, and even the names of a large roster of studio talent, fabricating whenever it was potentially lucrative to do so. The motivation to follow the directions of the studio bigwigs was not just Pavlovian (do this and you'll get a better role in the next picture): The performers were all under long-term contracts obliging them to adhere to any manner of behavior that might benefit the studio's plans for them; what they wore, who they dated, how much they weighed, might all be part of the deal. Publicity departments arranged photo opportunities, public appearances, and product endorsements—what Daniel Boorstin thought of as pseudo-events because they took place only because they would be reported—that helped to craft the image of the star or starlet and to keep them circulating in the media: the newspapers, of course, but especially the fan magazines.

The fan magazines were not hard-hitting journalistic enterprises, employing ambitious investigative reporter types hoping to get at the truth about the stars and the industry. Instead, they relied upon the studios for information that they in turn processed and fed to the star-hungry public. Much of that material was generated by the studio's own publicity departments, who wrote copy—often purportedly by the stars themselves—that helped the magazines fill their pages with "authorized" and "exclusive" material. The fan magazines were *the* major purveyors of information about the stars to the public, and they contain a wealth of information pertaining to 1920s Hollywood consumption: images, products, stars, and films. Mining their pages will help to illuminate the ways that reputational entrepreneurs, to use Gary Fine's term—the fans, the studios, the media, the star herself—interacted to shape Clara Bow's public image. In addition to the fan magazines, *It* (the 1927 Paramount production directed by Clarence Badger) will serve as the cinematic text that supports reading Bow in the context of Hollywood's particular influence on female identity and commercial culture as it illustrates the ways that consumption was tied into ideas of reputation on both star and fan levels. *It* is a significant film in part because it directly addresses issues of commerce, class, and desire, important elements of fan magazine culture; and in part because Bow's reputation hinged on the identity of this particular role, which helped to solidify her standing as a New Woman among her rapidly growing audience.

Bow's career is especially instructive with regard to the media's role in the mediation of reputations given its ongoing fascination with Hollywood celebrity. Robert Sklar argues that, by the end of the 1920s, "movie players could speak to the public about their divorces and love affairs with at least some of the frankness they used among themselves."[3] Although this might be oversimplifying the case, especially considering the studios' attempts to regulate such information, the playful circulation of 1920s publicity concerning public figures' lives differed radically from the late-nineteenth-century belief that curiosity about others—even public figures—was crude and improper. Public figures began to respond to these perceptual shifts at the end of the nineteenth century, in part to "cope with such an assertive press and the unflattering claims that its representatives were willing to publish," by allowing the press more access to the selves they wished to present, thereby avoiding potentially more pernicious speculation.[4]

The April 1895 issue of *Celebrities Monthly*, discussed in chapter one, represents the earlier mentality in its biographical note for actress and society woman Mrs. George Gould by reflecting upon her admirable behavior during "the trying time of the marriage of Miss Anna Gould and Count de Castellane, when vulgar curiosity was most rampant," noting that "she managed the affair with admirable discretion." If curiosity was still widely considered vulgar at the turn of the century, by the 1920s it had been institutionalized and in effect normalized, especially in relation to the movie industry, whose studio publicity departments and marginally independent fan magazines fed the public information (however fabricated) about stars' lives. As "noted psycho-analyst" Louis E. Bisch promoted the concept in the pages *Photoplay*, "curiosity is a highly valuable and healthy trait," an unsurprising endorsement to appear in a magazine whose existence rested upon satiating this attribute.[5]

Making Reputations in Print

Women are less markedly affected by acting than are men. Women are always acting more or less, anyways, whether they be professionals or not. —Dr. Louis E. Bisch[6]

Clara Bow's rise and fall in Tinseltown were meteoric. She inauspiciously arrived in Hollywood in 1923. By the late 1920s, she received more fan mail than any other star. By 1931, *Movie Classic* magazine published an article about her entitled "Can She Ever Come Back?"[7] Bow made fourteen films in 1925, eight in 1926, six in 1927, four in 1928, three in 1929, four in 1930, and only four between 1931 and 1933, when she made her final appearance in Frank Lloyd's *Hoopla*, retiring permanently at the age of twenty-eight. She received 45,000 fan letters a week at the peak of her career in 1929, a period during which henna sales tripled as a result of adoring fans who wanted their hair to be the wild red color of Clara Bow's.[8] Such "colorful" knowledge likely would have been gained through fan magazine articles and pictures, since Bow's films were, of course, in black and white.[9]

The first would-be fan magazine, *Motion Picture Story Magazine*, appeared in February 1911, with new magazines following on an almost yearly basis through the early 1940s.[10] Perusing fan magazines of the late nineteen-teens and early twenties, one frequently encounters readers' questions about the color of stars' hair and eyes. The fan magazines gladly offered this information in their pages, creating a discourse that shaped fans' perceptions of stars and made their personal lives appear accessible and real, however otherworldly and fantastic.[11] Details about hair color, eye color, favorite perfume, and so on also made Bow an imitable commodity, as is suggested by the increase in henna sales in the late 1920s. In conjunction with the films themselves, which, as Charles Eckert has demonstrated, "functioned as living display windows for all that they contained," the fan magazines cultivated commercial desires in their readers that also would be tended to over the course of the 1930s in more direct ways by the studios, who licensed star clothing lines to retail shops around the country.[12] Not only were the details of the star's life made public, they "belonged" to the public and were readily available—and purchasable—through the fan magazine.

The National Guide to Motion Pictures

PHOTOPLAY

FEBRUARY
25 CENTS

Clara Bow

The Dramatic Story of Clara Bow's Life
Told For The First Time

FIGURE 11: It may be "told for the first time," but not for the last: Clara Bow's life is the cover story of *Photoplay*'s February 1928 issue. Originally published in color. *Collection of the author.*

The fan magazines were not a direct line of communication between the stars and their fans, since the studios functioned as the filter, fabricator, and mediator between them. Although the studios tried to control their stars' lives, publicity departments did not always succeed in repairing perceived "moral lapses," particularly in the post–Fatty Arbuckle era.[13] The evidence provided in the fan magazines suggests that Bow was ultimately not treated like other valuable star commodities, who were better protected by the powerful studios that contractually owned them. Bow's status at Paramount in the late 1920s was rather unique: In an era of immense control over stars, she was the only actress at the studio who did not have to sign a morals clause as part of her contract, which she negotiated after three smash hits had put her in a position to ask for almost anything she wanted.[14] In some ways, her press treatment can be understood as a test case for the degree to which personal star information could be mishandled, reminding us of the consequences that stars' reputations faced at the hands of an increasingly personality-focused media. In fact, as Charles Ponce de Leon points out, stars in the early twentieth century had to be cautious about their "ability to sell things—including themselves" to an "assertive press" by adjusting their media images to suit—or at least not to offend—public tastes.[15]

Bow's turbulent tenure in Hollywood demonstrates the reciprocal and dependent nature of stardom and media culture during the 1920s, suggesting the degree to which star reputation existed at a tenuous intersection between competing reputational forces. Her particular story begins with the Brewster Publications contest call that appeared in the January 1921 issue of *Motion Picture* magazine. "The Fame and Fortune Contest of 1921" used a catchy slogan—"HISTORY REPEATS ITSELF!"—to solicit photographs from aspiring stars (see figure 12).[16] The history referred to in the announcement is the highly successful (according to the magazine) contest of the previous year. The slogan taps into the fantasies of its readers, who as participants seek to become a part of this future history, attesting to the symbolic, if not realistic, opportunities offered to the fan magazine reader.

Fans have historically been defined, as Joli Jenson points out, "as a *response* to the star system" and thereby as passive, "brought into (enthralled) existence by the modern celebrity system, via the mass media."[17] The contest, however, endows a sense of active involvement upon its participants, even as it does so in a misleading fashion: "The Golden Key of Opportunity Is in Your Hands—Turn the Key in the Doorway of Success and thru the portal of the Fame and Fortune Contest you may enter the kingdom of the screen." The language of the contest promises fans a chance, with seemingly minimal effort or risk, to transform themselves into the images they gazed at in the pages of the magazine and on the silver screen; the language is of the cinema-age fairy tale, and the reader is the imagined princess.

The contest unites, then, issues of spectatorship, consumerism, and celebrity. The very desire to move beyond the passive position of *seeing* to the active position of *being* reveals much about the psychological import of celebrity in American culture, particularly to an understanding of female

Making *It* in Hollywood 105

> ## HISTORY REPEATS ITSELF!
>
> ## The Fame and Fortune Contest of 1921
>
> The phenomenal success of the Fame and Fortune Contest which has been conducted for the past year by THE MOTION PICTURE MAGAZINE, THE CLASSIC and SHADOWLAND has firmly decided the heads of the Brewster Publications that another contest, even more far-reaching in its power, should be started immediately for the year 1921.
>
> ### The Golden Key of Opportunity Is in Your Hands—Turn the Key in the Doorway of Success
>
> and thru the portal of the Fame and Fortune Contest you may enter the kingdom of the screen.
>
> ### Photographs May Be Entered at Once
>
> and the first honor roll winners will appear in the January issues of each of our publications.
>
> ### Send in Your Photograph Early
>
> We know that you get tired of reading this notice, but if you could have seen the avalanche of pictures which flooded the offices at the last moment, and could realize that there must ensue tremendous confusion, unnecessary work and an inevitable delay in the announcement of the final winners, you would appreciate the value of this warning. Those who have failed in previous contests are eligible to enter the next contest.
>
> ### Fill Out the Coupon Below at Once
>
> FAME AND FORTUNE CONTEST
>
> ----------------- MAGAZINE ENTRANCE COUPON -----------------
>
> Name ....
> Address .... Street ....
> City .... State ....
> Previous stage or screen experience in detail, if any ....
>
> When born .... Blonde or brunette ....
> Weight .... Height ....
>
> (This coupon, or a similar one of your own making, must be secured to the back of each photo submitted.)

FIGURE 12: The Brewster Publications 1921 "Fame and Fortune Contest" encouraged movie fans to fantasize about and to act on their Hollywood ambitions. *Motion Picture* (January 1921): 122.

participation in that culture. The contest reproduces spectators not only as consumers but as *actors*, giving them the opportunity to recreate themselves by literally sending their images into the public sphere. In other words, this contest—and others like it—allowed fans to experiment with ideas of personal revision, of moving beyond the more passive role of consumer/spectator by "turning the key in the doorway of success." Although participation endowed a degree of activity upon the fan, especially if we understand fandom in the context of hobby culture, the fan still gave up her image, passed it on, and awaited judgment that would almost certainly be rejection. Bow thus stood as a symbol for the many who remained on the other side of the portal, a symbol of both the promise and the pretense of the necessarily exclusive star system. A fan from Queensland, Australia, testifies to the significance of this symbolic power: "I remember when you won a beauty contest some years ago & I still have the picture framed."[18] Bow was a tangible reminder of the cinema's ability to *transform* the spectator, here quite literally.

Viewed in this fashion, Bow's participation in the contest was an active (if prepackaged) mode of response to cinematic images, one that had radical consequences for her position as both spectator and consumer. Just as the movie industry had made a consumer out of Bow (of films, fan magazines, fantasies), the fan magazines were ultimately responsible for transforming her into an object of consumption. The relationship between spectatorship and consumption, then, was clearly not limited to movie audiences but had logical consequences for the fan magazine reader. Kathryn Fuller writes that *Photoplay* editor James Quirk "argued that the movies had created a breed of 'perfect consumers' who had an almost complete dependence on motion pictures to generate their needs and desires."[19] Following Quirk's logic, spectatorship and consumerism converged in the figure of the fan, who desired and pursued information to supplement her movie-going knowledge and sought out products to aid in her emulation. Fuller aptly claims that such assumptions reflect both Quirk's and the other fan magazine editors' "growing awareness of women's purchasing power."[20] With increasing numbers of "New Women" entering the job market and becoming wage earners, women were being taken seriously as economic forces, particularly by the movie industry.

Although fan magazines were imbued with Hollywood's corporate ideology, they still offered a way for women to become actively involved with movie culture and, in the process, to negotiate their own identities beyond their everyday, lived experiences. In the pages of the magazines, women were encouraged to evaluate star reputations, and to consider their own existence in relation to the stars. The fan magazines linked women in particular to the public space of the movie theaters, to patterns of consumption, and to a broad network of fans and spectators. The fan magazines were advertisements and their pitch was attainability: If you buy this, you can be *like* star X. Bow was an ideal kind of advertisement for the star system, in part because she perpetuated the illusion of possibility for fans. One fan explained this sense of proximity to Bow, responding to the news of Bow's

FIGURE 13: According to Adela Rogers St. Johns in her February 1928 *Photoplay* cover story, this is the first professional photograph taken of the contest-era, pre-star Bow. *Collection of the author.*

trip to a sanitarium: "It seemed as if I knew you real well. It sort of seemed as if a real friend of mine, and not a movie star far beyond my reach, was lying sick and probably tired of the whole mess of being a star."[21]

Such feelings of intimacy emerged partly as a result of the familiarizing discourse promoted in the fan magazines, which often situated stars as storytellers, confidants, advisers, and friends to their fans. By the 1920s, there was a general understanding that spectators could be influenced—emotionally, psychologically, behaviorally—both by on-screen images and by the discourse contained within the pages of the fan magazine.[22] The perceived danger of this scenario, as Janet Staiger points out, was that the confluence of advertising, publicity, and exploitation could influence "people not only to buy the movie show but also the lifestyles and ideologies represented in the film."[23] The fan magazines did address lifestyle issues alongside the fantastic stuff of stardom; their advertising content might be understood as linking these two realms.

The post-suffrage Jazz Age was rife with debates over women's social position, especially concerning the 1920s New Woman, who was notably different from her late-nineteenth-century counterpart in two important ways: her class and sexuality.[24] Jeanine Basinger observes that the movie flapper "acted out the change that was taking place for women in fashion, sex, social awareness, and politics."[25] The 1920s New Woman, at least as she was configured by the popular press and cinema, was largely working class, like the shop girl that Bow plays in her definitive *It* role; furthermore, the New Woman's sexual behavior was much more visible, less unspeakable, and therefore more subject to debate. Women's lives were becoming more public, made so not only by employment and wages but also through such "acceptable" leisure activities as going to the movies.[26]

One way to understand the fan magazines and the contests is as a tool to mediate and, in effect, to control the aspirations of female audiences, in particular. The pages of the fan magazines are littered with Hollywood horror stories, particularly for the young girl who hopes to make it on her own in Tinseltown.[27] The fan magazines had their cake and ate it too by offering such simultaneously seductive and cautionary tales that encouraged their readers' aspirations for stardom to transpire more locally, more domestically. One means of achieving this was to create desire for a kind of personal transformation that could be attained by adulation and imitation, something along the lines of buying a star-endorsed product, copying a star's hairstyle, or participating in one of the "Fame and Fortune" contests. Readers might attain a kind of mirror-image of star status by following the commercial cues provided within the pages of the magazines. A woman's Hollywood ambitions, in other words, need not remove her from her home, except to take a trip to the movie theater, the photo-booth, the salon, or the department or drug store, in order to transform herself into someone star-like. Changing hairstyles or perfumes was one thing; acting like a movie star, or getting on a westward bus to become one, was another.

The fan magazines participated in the debate over women's changing roles in the family and society, in part, one suspects, to address the conflicting images of ordinary and star behavior. In other words, the fan magazines concerned themselves not just with star reputations, with which they were deeply involved, but with the daily reputational dilemmas facing their readers. *Photoplay*, for example, had a monthly column on "Girls' Problems." In the March 1927 column, Carolyn Van Wyck posits this modern gender dilemma with a Shakespearean flourish: "To work or not to work is the problem of many married women today."[28] As Van Wyck explains, "they don't want kitchen duty and no wages but a real outside job and real wages."[29] The equation of "real" jobs with "real" wages resonates particularly in this post-war era. In an August 1927 *Motion Picture* article, "What Do Men Want?" Bow comments about the status of modern sex relations, acknowledging that shifting gender roles during the war acclimated men and women to a new mode of living: "I wouldn't give up my work for marriage . . . I think the modern girl is capable of keeping both a job and a husband."[30] Perhaps this statement was a response, of sorts, to a fan letter Bow saved from 1926, in which a female fan expresses one of her fears: "Goodness, I hope you don't get married and retire. If you marry please don't desert us, you will disappoint all your fans."[31] The reciprocity here—of fan letters, advice columns, and celebrity statements—suggests a dynamic interrelationship between the public, the press, and the star; the subject matter also duly reflects the social and political relevance of the discourse contained in the magazines.

Such advice as that which issued from Bow helped to feed her reputation as a turbulent New Woman willing to speak out on behalf of women's changing roles in society. That a fan magazine deemed such discourse worthy of publication within its pages—otherwise filled with images and stories that had little to do with real-world issues and everything to do with perpetuating the fantastic nature of Hollywood lives—suggests the importance of women's economic and social roles to Hollywood and its satellite industries. Modernity, consumerism, and female identity were increasingly intertwined, and the movie industry seemed especially adept at articulating these connections. As Nicholas Daly argues, a "newly integrative national consumer culture" was linking "commodity-based happiness with the 'modern' sexuality of the American Girl."[32] But there is also a significant discordance worth noting here, for while statistically women were becoming more independent (financially and socially), Hollywood stars existed in an utterly different world and had unusual relationships to the "realities" of gender.[33] So while fan magazines may have presented an economically and even socially optimistic imagining of women's social roles, one need only note the number of advertisements for jewelry and clothing, for example, much of which was made affordable through payment plans or other gimmicks, to suggest the aspirational glamour being peddled to fans along with the star-images. These modified, watered-down, commercialized Hollywood ambitions relied upon the atypical economic power of the female star.

Although it may be true that more women opted to work in the 1920s, few could find career paths as profitable as movie stardom. Movie stars became the diversions of working girls' leisure time and the stuff of their fantasy lives. The fan magazines of the 1920s, costing between five and twenty-five cents, with circulations of almost half a million each, created an alternative discourse to middle-class, family-oriented periodicals such as *Ladies Home Journal*.[34] The subject matter of Bow's films usually reflects the social status of these fans—working girls with sufficient wages but even bigger dreams. American women's aspirations were certainly perceived as being directly influenced by Hollywood, and not always in positive ways. In 1921, the same Elinor Glyn who would a few years later create the "It" label that defined the era and its wild child, Clara Bow, wrote an article for *Cosmopolitan* entitled "What's the Matter with *You* American Women?" This interrogational, early-twenties piece expresses anxiety over women's liberated and promiscuous behavior, which Glyn claimed was threatening the character of American women: "Has the American girl no innate modesty—no subconscious self-respect, no reserve, no dignity? I know what I think of them."[35] According to Glyn, American women needed to attend to their "chastity, mental and physical," to reject the "age of the body" in order to nurture their neglected spirits.[36] But by the late 1920s, Glyn would be singing another tune in the pages of the same magazine, celebrating women (and men) who had "It" (though Glyn repeatedly and unconvincingly denied that "it" was equivalent to sex appeal) and could use "It" to get what and who they wanted.

The disparity between these two pieces, published less than a decade apart, reflects the tremendous changes of the 1920s, both in women's roles and in the culture's evaluation of their attitudes, appearances, and actions. Bow became a symbol of the behavioral possibilities opened up by women's post-suffrage liberation in this era of prosperity and gaiety, at least according to Hollywood's depiction of the contemporary world. Movies helped create the nation's mood, luring post-war audiences into theaters with films that embodied and begat excitement, fun, and the spirit of rampant consumerism. Bow thus embodied New Women's behavior and fans responded to her image, particularly as a model for identification and mimicry. Fan letters to Bow often inadvertently reveal the function of the star image in their daily lives, such as a 1926 letter from Connie Romero, which explains the significance of the star photo: "Fans should have an autographed photograph of their favorite star so that they can look at it all day and get inspiration and ambition."[37] The entire Hollywood system operated on the fundamental precept of constructing fans as consumers of stars and, as deCordova argues, the point of star discourse was to extend "the boundaries of the cinema as institution so that it could more fully occupy people's lives."[38] Fan magazines are the most obvious form of this deliberate encroachment of cinematic discourse into people's daily lives. Through their countless stories of stars' lives, fashions, makeup, hair, loves, and homes, the magazines created numerous identificatory modes for the magazine reader, who was encouraged to emulate elements of the star lifestyle.[39]

According to Dr. Bisch's problematic assertion in the epigraph to this section, women are always acting, always performing. Such notions of female behavior are suspect, of course, yet fan culture did everything to foster such mimicry. The 1933 Blumer study, *Movies and Conduct*, offers several examples of the type of imitative fan behavior inspired by Bow, a star with whom fans appear to have been especially eager to identify. The study cites an eighteen-year-old, white, female high school senior: "Clara Bow has been my ideal girl, and I have tried to imitate some of her mannerisms. The way she wears her hair . . . how she rolls her eyes, her quick smile, and all her little actions."[40] Bow is figured here as an imagistic role model, the source of the girl's desires and self-imaging. Her mimicry confirms the reciprocal nature of fan culture and the way that on-screen images resonated outside of the theater. The girl's observations also appear to derive from the films themselves (as opposed to the fan magazines), as is suggested by her articulation of a mimicry of movement: eyes rolling, a "quick smile," and the "little actions." Because Bow was so readily the object of identification and mimicry, she was also a symbol of the medium's possible impact on off-screen behavior, revealing the potentially negative side effects of fan culture.

What is It?: *Making Reputations on Film*

Entertainment was conceived up in the Garden of Eden. Eve gave the first show the day she slipped into a fig leaf. Adam, the audience, enjoyed himself so much, that he decided to go into the show business. From then on, shows were made by men for men. —Beth Brown[41]

Clara Bow's 1927 film *It* can be understood as a parable about fan culture, particularly the ways that fan magazines constructed female readers and Hollywood films positioned female spectators.[42] *It* is replete with the interplay between plenitude and lack, with the elemental bases of spectatorial identification, and with the processes of personal reevaluation that were central to the workings of female fandom in the 1920s. The film plays with notions of spectatorial agency through a romantic plot revolving around female persistence. Like fan culture, which encouraged women to imagine and, on occasion, to act out certain fantasies about their identities in relation to star culture, *It* enacts a fantastic narrative of female sexual aggression and class transcendence. The film also illustrates the building of Bow's reputation as a turbulent but also moral New Woman, offering a counternarrative to her media undoing, which will be addressed in the final section of this chapter.

It was a cinematic response to the resignification of this previously innocuous pronoun by writer Elinor Glyn, whose story about "It" appeared earlier the same year in *Cosmopolitan*. After some studio negotiating, Glyn publicly proclaimed that Clara Bow was the real "It" girl, relying on popcultural amnesia to erase the fact that in a February 1926 *Photoplay* piece Glyn had named Gloria Swanson and Vilma Banky as "the only two actresses on the screen who have IT."[43] At this point she had sold the "It" story to Paramount for $50,000 and, as Basinger observes, deserved "credit for her canny exploitation of the press and the complete understanding she had of the nonsense of her day."[44] Glyn was given a cameo role in *It* and became part of the publicity machine for the film, whose catchy title and general concept alone derived from Glyn's story. The film exemplifies both formally and contextually the status and the ambitions of the New Woman, primarily through the device of the gaze.

Contrary to Beth Brown's ironic Edenic metaphor for Hollywood, *It* is a film that invites the gaze of its female spectator, largely to identify with the film's heroine and with her decidedly sexualized and empowered modes of seeing and being. The film celebrates its female star's rebellion against conventional modes of female behavior and complicates her relationship to the process of objectification. In other words, *It* seems every bit as much made for the male gaze as for its female counterpart. As a consequence, the film can be understood as offering its female spectators—who were major constituents in the construction of Bow's reputation—a subversive and ultimately successful variation of "ordinary" women's behavior.

It depicts the career of Betty Lou (Clara Bow) and her romantic pursuit of the department store owner's heir, Cyrus Waltham (Antonio Moreno), the "new boss" at the department store where Betty Lou works as a salesgirl. While the plot is hardly remarkable, the mechanics of the film's nar-

Making *It* in Hollywood   113

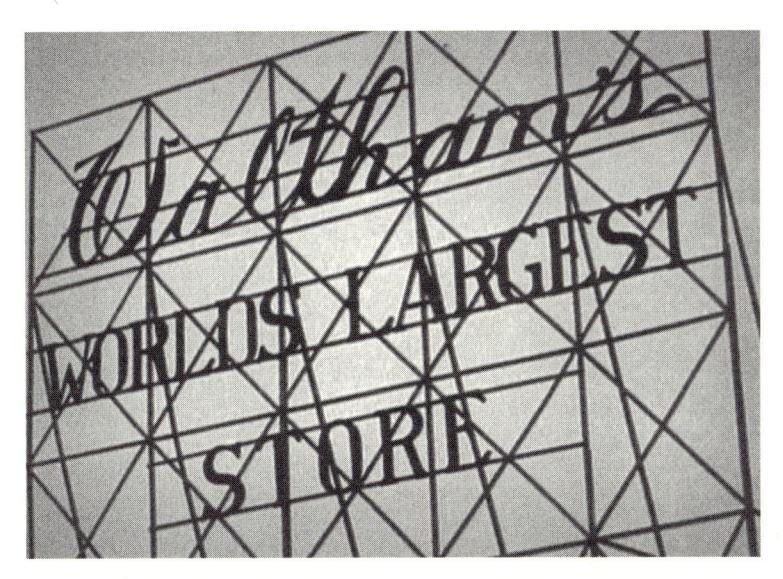

FIGURE 14: The opening shot of *It* invokes the film's consumer-driven narrative by referencing both the store where Betty Lou (Clara Bow) works as a salesgirl and the man, Cyrus Waltham (Antonio Moreno), whom she will eventually acquire. *Paramount Pictures, 1927.*

rative and its star performance set it apart from the typical class-crossed romance.[45] The establishing shot zooms out to reveal a sign on top of a massive brick building that reads "Waltham's, World's Largest Store," signaling from the outset that this film will be concerned primarily with the workings of consumer culture (see figure 14). The camera pans down to a view of the bustling street and zooms in toward the store's entrance to show many people coming in and out; here, the film already suggests, is modern American life manifest in the hustle and bustle of consumerism.[46] In the second sequence, we enter the store and see the active life within; shot from a high angle, the masses of customers and workers moving about have the appearance of so many busy ants at a picnic.

As established in the opening sequence, consumption serves as the paradigm for the entire film and the basis for Betty Lou's desire. However, this desire is hardly limited to Betty Lou, for so much of spectatorship has to do with the logic of consumption. Miriam Hansen has discussed the degree to which film spectatorship echoed conventions already well established by commercial advertising, especially the ability to create needs and desires: "Besides turning visual fascination itself into a commodity, the cinema generated a metadiscourse of consumption . . . a phantasmagoric environment in which boundaries between 'looking' and 'having' were

FIGURE 15: *It* is preoccupied with the processes of looking and acquiring. Our first glimpse of Betty Lou playfully encourages voyeuristic pleasure. *Paramount Pictures, 1927.*

blurred."[47] Waltham's department store, in which much of this narrative is located, formalizes the spectatorial concerns of the film, for it is a place (just like the movie theater) where one is expected to look, to desire, and to experience pleasure through fantasies of acquisition. Those fantasies of acquisition, however, are more easily actualized in the department store than in the movie theater, as the fan magazines unintentionally acknowledged throughout their pages.

This "phantasmagoric environment" is dramatized when we get our first glimpse of Betty Lou, who holds a piece of lingerie in front of her clothed body to show an older, respectable-looking couple what they might expect from their purchase (see figure 15). Couched in the decency of the on-looking couple, whose "decorousness" justifies exposing the lingerie (or at least adds a comic element to the image's overt sexuality), the film allows its spectator momentarily to enjoy looking at the wide-eyed Betty Lou with no more than a hint of the lingerie's sexual implications.[48] As the man and woman smile and nod, the division that Hansen notes between "looking" and "having" is blurred. Since both the department store consumer and the cinema spectator are expected to desire that which they see, the scene appropriately figures consumption as both an economic exchange and a mode of ideologically sanctioned visual pleasure. As Daly observes, "tying Glyn's story to the department-store daydream in particular, also had the effect of tying sex appeal to consumer desire."[49] Here, in fact, sex appeal is represented as the literal tool of the marketplace.

This flirtatious looking is fleeting, however, for another salesgirl interrupts to point out Cyrus Waltham as the "new boss." From this moment, the film reverses the gaze prevalent in dominant Hollywood cinema away from a male appraisal (singular or collective) of the attractive on-screen woman. Here, the male character, Waltham, is situated on the passive, receiving end of the sexualized gaze. The preceding lingerie scene serves as a brief reminder of Betty Lou's to-be-looked-at-ness, to borrow a well-known phrase from Laura Mulvey; however, Betty Lou is hardly the object here.[50] This shift is crucial for two primary reasons: First, it acknowledges that behavioral upheavals of this nature were part of the continual dramatization of the New Woman; second, it recognizes that working-class women in particular had access to this gaze, primarily through their roles as *independent consumers*.

I would like to suggest that the scenes that follow enact an inversion that indicates the changing nature of the New Woman and of female fandom, which allowed Bow to transcend class, location, and upbringing to become a Hollywood star. The film continues to mirror the foundations of fan culture, replicating the desires solicited by fan magazines, which encouraged women to look, desire, and become. *It*, however, achieves something a bit more dangerous by depicting a gaze that moves out of the living room and the darkened movie theatre onto the street and into the marketplace. This gaze hinges not on some notion of identification, masquerade, or envy but on explicit, active, heterosexual desire, something akin to sexual purchasing power. *It*, however, celebrates this desire in the safe realm of fiction, however potentially imitable.

The scene proceeds as a series of shot/reverse-shots, atypical in that the camera's eye recognizes only half of the gaze relays: the woman's (or women's) half. Betty Lou gets wide-eyed and stares directly at Waltham, the object of her visibly increasing desire. In the mise-en-scène of the department store, a business with the sole purpose of creating and then satisfying desires, Betty Lou is the ideal customer: She sees, she wants, and in the end she gets. But not without first undergoing some struggle, for in the reverse shot of Waltham, he remains oblivious to Betty Lou's gaze. Furthermore, Betty Lou's desires diverge from the material objects of consumption—the things that purport to complete the lacking subject/consumer—to Waltham himself, a man who represents the sum total of consumerism, the star, if you will, of the commodity system. Betty Lou is

FIGURE 16: Betty Lou and the other salesgirls in *It* take a moment to stare unabashedly at their new boss, Cyrus Waltham, thereby reversing the traditional economy of gazes. *Paramount Pictures, 1927.*

not intimidated by Waltham's class-based star power, something the other shop girls deem an impossible divide. Betty Lou runs full steam ahead into her task, just as Bow did with that other seemingly impossible divide with the star search contest.

The next reverse shot shows Betty Lou still agog, with nine more female clerks behind her in similar stages of ogling (see figure 16). Betty Lou is up front with her chin on her hand, enjoying the act of looking to an unusual degree and for an unusually sustained duration for a female character. Hers is an unabashed voyeurism, a proud display of her visual pleasure. In yet another reverse-shot of Waltham, he remains oblivious to the fact that he has become a spectacle. A medium shot of Betty Lou follows with the intertitle "Sweet Santa Claus, give me *him*!" This scene articulates concerns over 1920s women's behavior through a concise series of shots that empower Betty Lou with an active, *consuming* look while making Waltham the unknowing, sexualized spectacle.

Betty Lou's visual empowerment can be understood as an inversion of the politics of looking in the cinema, which has relied upon the spectacle of women and the privileging of the male gaze. Ironically, the press kit for *It* misrepresents the film on this level through an image of Betty Lou surrounded by a group of staring men (see figure 17).[51] This advertisement is a lie, of sorts, since this configuration appears in the film in the opposite fashion when Betty Lou and the other shop girls rapaciously stare at

Making *It* in Hollywood   117

SAY "IT" WITH POSTERS!

FIGURE 17: In the press kit for *It*, a group of men leering at Clara Bow are a reminder of the star's spectacular nature, since the film's narrative offers the opposite scenario. *Courtesy Library of Congress Moving Image Section.*

Waltham. The press kit perpetuates the idea of women as the object of the gaze. Removed from its cinematic context, the image of a group of men staring at Clara Bow also seems perfectly logical given her studio marketing. In fact, the press kit image says more about Clara Bow as a star than about Betty Lou as a character, for Bow's publicity was reliant on her spectacular sexual appeal. While Betty Lou as a character spends the first part of the film fighting her way into Waltham's visual register, Clara Bow the actress seemed hard-pressed to exist outside of the intense visual scrutiny of the public and the media. The distance that Bow at least partly achieved by removing herself to the Nevada desert at the end of her career resulted in the kind of seclusion that would have been disastrous for Betty Lou's romantic conquest.

But *It* presents more than just a reversal of the status quo, a transposition of the traditional male role with the traditional female role. On the one hand, this scene of Betty Lou and the other shop girls staring at Waltham is hardly radical, for the premise of the film still revolves around a classed inequity linked to Betty Lou's "type" (the independent working *girl*) as well as Waltham's (the rich capitalist *man*), the end result being, predictably, the promise of marriage and a reconciliation of this divide. There is also a tacit understanding that while Betty Lou appears to be a relatively carefree working girl, she would rather be an otherwise-occupied wife of a rich businessman. In other words, she is a working girl only because she has to be.[52] She sells lingerie but ultimately sells herself, even if this final transaction is enacted on her terms. On the other hand, the scene says something important about the 1920s woman precisely because Betty Lou is able to look, desire, and pursue without being punished or condemned. In fact, by film's end she is substantially compensated—materially, emotionally, and morally—for her aggressive behavior.

Ultimately, the gift that Betty Lou receives is Waltham, but Santa has little to do with this acquisition. Rather, it is Betty Lou's ability to perform that enables her to capture Waltham's previously absent gaze and consolidate her active, aggressive modes of seeing and being with a retained, albeit revised, sense of femininity. As spectators, we join Betty Lou as she experiences the various impediments to her romantic pursuit. In particular, Betty Lou's dilemma is how to redirect Waltham's heretofore absent gaze. Much as Bow repositioned herself from spectator to spectacle, from consumer to consumed, through the fan magazine contest, Betty Lou turns the tables on Waltham's gaze in order to enact a strikingly similar negation of obscurity. By participating in the fan magazine contest, Bow rejected the idea of being an anonymous fan much as Betty Lou rejects being an anonymous employee.

It therefore replicates the paradigm of plenitude and lack that constitutes not only the foundation of stardom but also the motivating premise of the fan magazine contest. As empowering as Betty Lou's active looking may appear to be, in order to realize her goal she needs to furnish what has been absent by attracting Waltham's gaze; she must get him to actively complete the companion shot to the earlier relay of gazes in which he is an unknowing and unseeing object; she must reposition herself as an object in order to gain *her* object; she must advertise herself. So when Waltham wanders by Betty Lou's lingerie counter with his back to her and then leans on a piece of fabric, Betty Lou gets an ingenious look on her face and pulls the fabric in an attempt to attract his gaze. Her desire is to direct Waltham, but she fails here (as she does in successive attempts) as he nonchalantly proceeds.

It takes Waltham's bumbling and foppish pal Monty (William Austin)—who is on a mission to find an "It Girl" in the store after reading the Glyn piece in *Cosmopolitan*—to notice Betty Lou, in whom he immediately recognizes the mysterious quality that has gone unnoticed by the oblivious Waltham. Monty's own "desires," feeble as they are, are dictated by the *Cosmopolitan* article—he's told about this "it" and goes to find it. Thus, the film also suggests that the press has power over desire, mirroring the rationale behind the fan magazine and its consumer-oriented discourse.

While Monty looks at Betty Lou with an ineffectual, easy-to-dismiss, even effeminate longing, Betty Lou continues to gaze salaciously at Waltham. *It* presents a world in which it is acceptable to behave in this unabashed fashion. In the character of Betty Lou, *It* presents an ideal of spectatorship made literal: Like the department store consumer, she sees, she wants, and she gets.[53] But while this last component of possession remains safely in the realm of fantasy for the film spectator, whose pleasure is based upon the constant deferment of desire, Betty Lou acts out and rewards spectatorial fantasies by becoming aggressive, plotting, and sexually predatory without apology and without coming off as threatening. There is a related satisfaction to be found in the fan magazine contests: They alleviated the chronic postponement of fan adoration by allowing the spectator/reader to *do something*; so too the star-endorsed products that fans were encouraged to purchase in order to live like the stars.

Bow's characters were appealing for the same reason: They allowed audiences to experience a kind of sexual liberation and moral reward that was not available in such a coherent fashion outside of the realm of fiction. Even as Bow's reputation veered into the realm of scandal, it still retained its appeal and value for many of her fans precisely because of its subversive qualities. As Paula Fass points out, the 1920s were "a turning point, a critical juncture between the strict double standard of the age of Victoria and the permissive sexuality of the age of Freud."[54] Betty Lou's "newness" is precisely what makes her so attractive to Monty and, eventually, to Waltham. Betty Lou's embodiment of the unabashed modern woman legitimizes female desire, be it sexual or economic. The fact that her wants are made attractive here, neither dangerous nor scandalous, suggests that the film's spectators might desire similar values; after all, as Richard Ohmann suggests, part of magazine-reading culture (and I would add by implication movie-going culture) involves joining an ideological community, sharing experiences and values. Betty Lou, as a model for the female spectator, constitutes the triumph of feminine independence over the constraints of class and culture; but, of course, this is only a fictional transcendence. Her role validates the fantasies of spectatorship and fandom discussed earlier in this chapter, in part by articulating a cultural permissiveness for new modes of women's behavior. The film—like the fan magazine contest that propelled Clara Bow to fame—provided an opportunity for women to envision rule-shattering behavior.

Betty Lou's uniqueness, particularly her willingness to ignore convention, is unquestionably appealing in the context of the film. The film proceeds as an examination of all those things that make Betty Lou different, and as a result desirable, as the spectator is increasingly aligned with her ambitious pursuit of Waltham. Her foil, Adela Van Norman (Jacqueline Gadsdon), is everything that Betty Lou is not: rich, well dressed, well mannered, reserved, and perfectly predictable. But Betty Lou's presence reveals that Adela is no more than an outmoded type. Betty Lou, who has to improvise her evening wear, who cannot read a menu in French, and who would prefer going to Coney Island than the Ritz, is appealing precisely because she defies Waltham's expectations of bourgeois womanhood.

While it takes some work to capture Waltham's gaze, Betty Lou controls the remaining action of the film in virtually every scene: When Monty offers her a ride home, she pushes him onto her crowded double-decker bus, much to his surprise and consternation; when Monty asks if she'd like to have dinner, she agrees on the condition that he take her to the place where Waltham is dining; when her roommate, an unwed mother, is unable to work because she is sick, Betty Lou cheerfully takes care of her; and when this same woman is faced with losing her baby to nosy reformists, Betty Lou charges in and claims the baby as her own despite the stigma attached to single motherhood and its real consequences for her reputation and her romance. Her character's dynamism makes her the visual and moral center of every scene she inhabits. Her attractiveness—as both an object of desire and of identification—is undeniable.

But what is it in Waltham that Betty Lou desires? Her lust for him is seemingly instantaneous, but it is mediated by her knowledge of what he is: rich, the owner of the largest department store in the world. The film stops well short of making Betty Lou a gold digger, but Waltham seems to have little that is attractive except for his wealth and status. In fact, Betty Lou proves (perhaps to audiences as much as to Waltham) her moral correctness when she refuses the denigration of Waltham's offer to maintain her as a mistress after he suspects that she is just after his money.

The classed nature of Betty Lou's desire is displayed both while she prepares for her evening out with Monty and when they arrive at their destination, the Ritz. As Betty Lou uses scissors to alter one of her dresses into evening wear, her eyes land on a newspaper advertisement for Waltham's (see figure 18). Betty Lou appears dreamy-eyed over the advertisement, but it is not clear precisely what is behind this same love-dazed expression that we witnessed earlier when she first set eyes on Waltham. Not only does Betty Lou see the name Waltham, which signifies both the man and the "largest store in the world," but the advertisement is also headlined by an announcement of "New Dresses at $11" and the "Latest Fashions from Paris." In his study of women and department stores, William Leach imagines an analogous scenario as exampling one of "the more grim

FIGURE 18: While Betty Lou makes a homemade dress for her night out at the Ritz, she spies an advertisement that reminds her of both the material things she lacks and the man who embodies those things. *Paramount Pictures, 1927.*

components of consumer experience": "the misery many poor women must have felt as they passed the windows of city retail stores, which revealed to them an unobtainable world of luxury."[55] In *It*, however, this is only a temporarily grim experience.

The newspaper advertisement is another version of the shop window, which Betty Lou gazes at as she fabricates her own poor imitation of the "latest fashions" with scissors and pins, suggesting a doubling of her desire: it is at once for Waltham and also for what he represents in consumer culture. Betty Lou's desire for Waltham and his gaze is integral to her aspiration to be recognized by and within consumer culture, for as a working girl it seems that only a man like Waltham (interchangeable as his name is with the department store itself) can satisfy her consuming desires. The advertisement is therefore both a reminder of what she currently cannot have (the store-bought dresses, the latest Paris fashions) and of what she might be able to get (Waltham); the one, of course, follows from the acquisition of the other. Daly argues that "*It* was an advertisement for fun, modern sexuality."[56] More precisely, *It* is an advertisement for a specifically female sexuality linked to the idea of the aspiring female consumer. This scene provides yet another reminder of the powerful print culture—here a newspaper advertisement, elsewhere a fan magazine—that mediates fan/consumer desire.

The degree to which class and desire are united in Betty Lou's lack is

FIGURE 19: The prim and proper Adela Van Norman (Jacqueline Gadsden) cannot compete with Betty Lou's playful physicality, as is evident when Betty Lou and Waltham frolic on the appropriately named Social Mixer during their first date in *It*. Paramount Pictures, 1927.

depicted further when she and Monty arrive at the Ritz. The *maître d'* sizes up Betty Lou—as do we, aligned as we are here with the camera's perusal of her—and detects the flaws that indicate her class. As she is led to what has been termed a "quiet table," Betty Lou scours the restaurant, looking for Waltham; her gaze is searching, predatory. When she spots him, she does a double take as we inhabit her point of view, and the shot rapidly dollies in to a close-up on his face. This is an unusually fast dolly, which disrupts the established visual pacing of the film. Her frantic desire is evident in the dolly; ideologically, we are aligned with Betty Lou and her quest—both visual and literal—for Waltham. When Betty Lou drags Monty to a more centrally located table, again controlling the action of the scene in her attempt to direct Waltham's gaze, she finally gets what she's been working for when the two make eye contact. Once Betty Lou has attracted Waltham's gaze, the rest is quick to follow.

Their ensuing romance is predicated partly on Waltham's fetishization of Betty Lou's class, or, perhaps more precisely, on the way that her class allows her to behave outside of certain class-bound conventions. Betty Lou demonstrates a physicality that is absent in the affluent Adela, manifest most obviously in Betty Lou's frenetic onscreen movement. When Betty Lou suggests that she and Waltham go to an amusement park for their first date, they dine on hot dogs and revel in the physical delights offered at the park (see figure 19). At the end of their date, however, when Betty

Lou returns Waltham's kiss with a slap, the intertitle reads, "So you're one of those Minute Men—the minute you know a girl you think you can kiss her!"[57] In contrast to several other Bow films from the same year, such as Victor Fleming's *Hula* or Dorothy Arzner's *Get Your Man*, necking is not a part of the otherwise playful New Woman's vocabulary in *It*. This is somewhat surprising, if only because until this point Betty Lou's interest in Waltham has been decidedly sexual.

Betty Lou's slap is an interesting nod to "the real world" and to the complexity of her otherwise liberated behavior. Within the context of the narrative, her behavior is explicable, for hers is both a defensive and performative reaction, defensive because she has nothing to fall back on and performative because, to a certain degree, she is acting out what she suspects she *should* do in response to Waltham's physical advances. To have embraced Waltham's kiss would have been to compromise her goal, for Betty Lou wants nothing less than marriage, of course, and therefore tries to conform to how she suspects a marriageable girl might behave.[58] When Waltham later ignores her after he mistakenly thinks that she does, in fact, have an out-of-wedlock baby, Betty Lou thinks he is mad that she slapped him and apologizes: "I'm sorry—but a girl *has* to do that. You know how those things are!" Betty Lou here acknowledges that her reactions are not based upon what she wants, but on what she must do to survive. Sexual freedom is revealed to be little more than an outward performance; the rules of propriety and morality appear to have changed little, even if attire and behavior seems to suggest otherwise.

Betty Lou's behavior here, in some ways, is consistent with Bow's own life, testament as it is to the ultimately conservative public allowance for unconventional New Womanish behavior. While the film offers Betty Lou the safely respectable culmination of marriage, Clara Bow's real-life affairs lacked this kind of tidy, recuperative closure. When Monty reads the *Cosmopolitan* in which the Glyn piece appears at the film's beginning, the camera lingers on a section of text in order to define the subject of the film: "The possessor of 'IT' must be absolutely unself-conscious, and must have that magnetic 'sex appeal' which is irresistible." Herein lies the falsity of Glyn's concept in the context of the 1920s and of *It*, for there is nothing about Betty Lou's "it-ness" that is unself-conscious. Rather, it is precisely the sexual nature of the New Woman's "It" that necessitates an increasing realization of the dangers of the "magnetic 'sex appeal'" that Glyn claims is "It"; for examples, we only need turn to Clara Bow's career-long lack of self-consciousness, which resulted in an impressive track record of scandals. Betty Lou's apparent need to always consider how she is being perceived by Waltham—how her reputation is standing up in the face of so

FIGURE 20: Although the film doesn't end with a wedding, Betty Lou triumphs as she and Waltham emerge from the water to embrace on his yacht with "IT" momentarily between them. *Paramount Pictures, 1927.*

many possible compromises to it—has everything to do with the "It" of the film's title and with her character's ability, literally, as it turns out, to climb out of her class.

This same magnetic appeal that Betty Lou slaps away when Waltham tries to kiss her is also what Waltham thinks she has succumbed to when he falsely assumes she is an unwed mother. Although the circumstances surrounding Betty Lou's roommate's pregnancy are not disclosed in the film's story, Molly is certainly a cautionary figure, representing the potential casualties of the New Woman's sexual liberation. Betty Lou escapes this fate, but only by *self-consciously* keeping within the traditional parameters for pre-marital interactions, something we might remember as we turn to Clara Bow's turbulent reputation and her eventual Hollywood exile (see figure 20).

It is worth returning here to the already-noted fragile boundary between public and private that is as much a part of the politics of *It* as it was of the life of the movie star. The fan magazines exploited female audiences' desire for the ingredients of movie stardom by redirecting and extending the spectatorial gaze and personal ambition to commercial products. *It* enacts a similar manipulation of the gaze—by both Betty Lou and the female spectator. Although Alexander Walker contends that "'It' boomed with the financial independence of the young female wage-earner who wanted to acquire not social status, but sexual attractiveness to match her spending power," it is truer to the film to argue that Betty Lou in fact controls the gaze through a knowledge of her sexual attractiveness, which enables her eventually to gain social status.[59] It is not an either/or proposition, since consumption and social status remain inextricably linked in the film's narrative. Both Betty Lou and Clara Bow sought new ways to negotiate the modern world and to construct a reputation. *It* merely dramatizes the commercial matrix in which all reputations exist, and the degree to which female agency might function entrepreneurially in such endeavors.

Fan magazines, department stores, and films such as *It* all demonstrate the goal of creating personal desire in their readers/customers/spectators. Both Betty Lou and Clara Bow occupied such atmospheres of consumption, one of the commodity and the other of the commodified image. The fan magazines extended the fantasy world of the cinema, providing pages full of stars with extraordinary lives for ordinary women to ponder; these magazines were themselves a kind of department store catalogue selling images of the stars. Clara Bow, the star commodity, existed in this atmosphere of celebrity and commerce. In 1926, a fan magazine author could matter-of-factly assert that Bow "represented an investment," concluding with the Hollywood bottom line that, "an investment must be profitable."[60] In fact, Paramount eventually labeled Bow's films by the seasons: "Fall Bow," "Spring Bow," and so on—designations that reinforced her status as a commodity not at all unlike those offered in the commercial realm of the department store or in the many advertisements littering the pages of fan magazines.

Unmaking A Reputation

Ten million breakfasts halted—
  Ten million grapefruit waited—
Ten million voices whispered—
  Ten million breaths were bated.
The mightiest words of tongue or pen
  Were Clara Bow's engaged again!
              —Cal York[61]

Whereas in the fictional department store, Betty Lou controlled the gaze, Bow had no such luck navigating the media landscape of the late 1920s and early 1930s. Just a few years after making *It*, her reputation was unmade, in large part by the very studio-media empire that made her stardom possible in the first place. *It* inspired discussions over contemporary women's behavior, particularly because Betty Lou emerges victorious, morally correct, and self-satisfied at film's end. But where Betty Lou was rewarded for her behavior by getting her man in the end, off-screen Bow was increasingly compromised by the media's sensational reporting, which figured her behavior as lacking the neatness of a happy Hollywood ending and as defying the moral standards being peddled as part of the "post-scandal," censorship-avoiding, reformed Hollywood.[62]

What began as a series of highly public affairs (some real, but most fabricated as studio publicity) and broken engagements evolved into an alienation of affection lawsuit; a trial involving her former secretary and confident, Daisy DeVoe, which detoured into a relentless exposé of Bow's promiscuity; wildly proliferating rumors, such as one that claimed Bow had "entertained" the entire USC football team; to her very real nervous breakdown that led her to a sanitarium and, eventually, back "through the portal of the Fame and Fortune Contest" and away from Tinseltown.[63] David Stenn sums up a false but damaging, three-week-long, 1931 *Coast Reporter* series on Bow that reads like the worse kind of smear campaign: "Promiscuity and exhibitionism, kinkiness and incest, lesbianism and bestiality, drug addiction and alcoholism, venereal disease and family insanity . . . no movie star had ever been vilified in such an obscene and brazen manner."[64]

Scandals reveal much about the beliefs of a culture, as Adrienne McLean notes in her introduction to *Headline Hollywood*, exposing the ways that "private behavior, public conduct, gender roles, family relationships, and film art" are perceived in terms of their acceptability or deviance.[65] Bow's prominent headline presence certainly demonstrates the ways in which she functioned as a kind of litmus test for the behavior of women, both in and out of Hollywood, as well as for Hollywood's need to represent its moral universe in a particular light. During the 1920s, the Hollywood studio system needed to find ways to generate admiration despite the presence of scandal.[66] Bow's star text, to use Richard Dyer's terminology, offers us insight into this matrix of politics and representation. Her unmaking can be understood as a response to the debates over scandal, morality, and sexuality that were circulating in the industry and in the culture at large.

Criticism of the New Woman's often-scandalous behavior came from both inside and outside of the motion picture industry. Although Elinor Glyn may have changed her mind about the New Woman between the early and late 1920s, not everyone had. In the same year that saw the release of *It*, the silent film actor Harrison Ford proclaimed that,

The tendency [of the flapper] is toward mannish sophistication, a devil-may-care attitude that is in direct contrast to the feminine charm that marked the girl of 1890. I am not at all sure that the fault lies entirely with the twentieth-century girl, for she was forced by the war to depend on herself, and such dependence naturally led her to abandon her feminine qualities for the less attractive mannerisms of today.[67]

Ford's evaluation of the flapper blames cultural forces behind her behavior, which he implies had an especially unattractive component. The New Woman's sexual aggressiveness is surely part of what he represents as "mannish," as opposed to that equally ambiguous notion of "feminine charm." Bow herself rejected the illusion of innocence expected of women, no doubt the same illusion that Ford terms "feminine charm": "Why pretend that they still want the old-fashioned girl with the hoop skirts who coyly asks, 'What is beer, papa?'"[68] Bow repeatedly made public rebuffs to outmoded pretenses of virtue and inexperience, sexual or otherwise, to make the case for a new acceptance, even a celebration, of women who could shed such performances in favor of a more honest worldliness. Such progressiveness tested the limits of what her reputation as a star could bear. Her on-screen roles and reported off-screen behavior conspired to excessively sexualized the flapper-era woman in ways both appealing and threatening, especially given the widespread perception that "women's changing desire" was being promoted by the film industry.[69] Bow learned the hard way that there was a downside to being a most obvious representation of these changes.

Interviews with Bow that appeared in the fan magazines reveal an unusual candidness about her own past and present, particularly in comparison to her colleagues who divulged few truths about their personal lives.[70] In a Ruth Biery interview that appeared in the November 1928 *Motion Picture*, Bow describes her impoverished background, her mother's mental illness and death, and the details of her love life: "Why, of course, I'll tell you about my love-life story. There is no secret about it."[71] As her biographer, David Stenn, argues, Bow's transgression was that "in an industry trying to forget its outcast past and adopt affectations to suit its exalted present, Clara had remained herself, and as such was a constant reminder of her and, by implication, everyone else's lowly background."[72] Her unusual frankness about her past, sexual or otherwise, proved to be a mistake as public opinion—*at least* as it was represented by the print media—shifted from admiration to condemnation.

The media's condemnation of Bow should not, however, simply be conflated with fans' responses to the flapper idol. We should always remain suspect of the degree to which the mainstream press and fan magazines reflect the public's feelings or desires. Fan letters received by Bow during this era echo each other in their lamentations for the press coverage she received and support Basinger's claim that "despite her off-screen didoes, audiences loved her, because she always seemed to be giving it everything she had."[73] "I wish there was some way of giving those reporters a taste of their own medicine," asserts Cecilia Radnovich in a June 9, 1931, fan letter. Marjorie Derr, an "ever faithful fan," commiserates with Bow in a letter from 1931: "we all sympathized with you in that DeVoe trial—and would have loved to inject some rat poison [sic] in a few reporter's [sic] systems." Repeating a similar refrain, Marion Clarke wrote to Bow on June 24, 1931, that "I've been reading so much about you since your misfortune. I think its [sic] just terrible for the press to print such lies and scandal. Of course, many people enjoy reading that type of news, but believe me—anyone with at least a few ounces of brains knows that half of the things which are printed are lies—awful ones, too." In the process of expressing their anger over the desecration of their idol, some fans employed these events to demonstrate the degree to which the press coverage failed to reflect *or* to affect their feelings. Edna Dolores McGloin from Brooklyn, Bow's home town, wrote on June 9, 1931, that "I have not missed any of the press reports about you for the sake of my idolatry, and while some of these reports have been extremely painful to me, you have never ceased to be my screen favorite."

These letters cumulatively suggest the ways that fans frequently rebelled against press representations of the stars. By no means regurgitating the prevailing current of the media, these fans express their own opinions about Bow and her scandals to reveal their understanding of the media as suspect, mendacious, even vicious. They certainly do not give the impression that the headlines had any effect upon their feelings about their favorite star, or her potential as an actress. Such seeming solidarity from these "devoted admirers" stands in contrast with what was being published in the fan magazines, which conspired to gradually unmake Bow's reputation. The title of Leonard Hall's 1930 *Photoplay* article indicates the tenor of this widespread coverage: "What About Clara Bow? Will the Immortal Flapper Learn Self-Discipline? Or is She Fated to Dance Her Way to Oblivion?"[74] This implicit disapproval reflects the degree to which Hollywood and its publicity industries relied upon the illusion of the star's "right" to occupy such a culturally privileged position, despite the fact that this may have stood in the face of fans' interpretation of the same reported acts.

Bow's sexuality became the primary subject of the fan magazines who covered her, and these magazines were increasingly comfortable with passing judgment on Bow's not-so-personal life. The copious references made in the fan magazines to Bow's many "engagements" were thinly veiled references to Bow's sexual conquests.[75] As the caption reads under a picture of Bow looking devilishly at Harry Richman, who is motioning to put a ring on Bow's finger: "Clara Bow has been engaged many times. The list of loved and left is staggering. Now she is engaged again, and this time the name is Harry Richman . . . Or is he just another playboy?"[76] In addition to a barrage of questions about Bow's personal life, which afforded the magazines the opportunity to speculate frivolously, information about Bow's scandals was often contained within articles that themselves warned about the disingenuous nature of publicity from within the media. In "Misinformation," Ruth Biery argues that, "Hollywood is the home of Misinformation. No place in the world do rumors charge about with such electrical swiftness and power as in the motion picture city."[77] As evidence for her case, Biery explains that, "if Clara Bow is seen twice with the same man, it is a love affair. Three times means an engagement."[78] Embedded within the very scandal reporting that it seeks to criticize, these articles contain feeble apologies, of sorts, for the stuff that really sold the magazines.

Clara Bow is also the primary subject of Mildred Spain's May 1931 *Photoplay* piece, "Those Awful Reporters!"[79] Spain blames the entire panoply of publicity—reporters, press agents, and producers—for dragging Bow's reputation through the mud, but to make her case Spain includes the details of Bow's scandalous press treatment. When Carl Vonnel wants to express the truthfulness of his "Clara Bow—Housewife of Rancho Clarito" story, he does so by claiming that Bow's domestication "is no press-agent yarn."[80] This internal criticism and questioning of the facts co-exists with the scandal-reporting, resulting in a body of writing that tries simultaneously to exploit and to sympathize in order to play every marketing angle.[81]

A September 1930 *Motion Picture Classic* parody by Cedric Belfrage, "Classic Holds Open Court," humorously points out the silliness and hypocrisy of the scandal-reporting while also exploiting its more sensational appeals. A scantily clad and smiling Bow is pictured standing in cruciform. Her face is framed by the "case": "The charge:—Sex appeal is a crime. The Plaintiffs:—The Prodnose Family. The Defendant:—Clara Bow."[82] The summary of the case against Bow reads as follows: "Defendant was charged with possession of sex appeal without a license, contrary to law, with wholesale enchantment and corruption of young manhood through insidious celluloid exhibitions of herself, and with general conspiracy against public morals in the first, second and third degrees."[83] While the tone of the piece is comic, it predicts the kind of scrutiny that Bow would, in fact, subsequently undergo. Even in jest, the fan magazine hits upon the precise mode of criticism that sent Clara Bow into exile.

The premise of the *Motion Picture Classic* mock case raises an interesting point about the nature of 1920s cinema by invoking the "insidious celluloid exhibitions" that were both immensely profitable for Hollywood studios and the subject of debate for those concerned with the moral state of the country and cinema's effect on that state. Among the religious and governmental groups, the scientific and pseudo-scientific researchers, the media, and the fans themselves, there was a prevailing sense that Hollywood's morality was under the looking glass and that Bow was, indeed, being tried as part of this larger inquiry into the industry; it was not only Bow's reputation at stake, but (more importantly) Hollywood's. In the mock case, Bow is interrogated about the most highly debated component of this moral universe, her sexuality: "The fact is that, by your own admission, you not only possess sex appeal for all practical purposes, but you persist in broadcasting it so as to weaken the moral fiber of millions of young men who see your films."[84] The utterance of this fictional threat reminds us that while young women were considered the primary readers of fan magazines, and while women's behavior was the primary focus of these magazines, critics of the day were equally concerned with the immodest arousal of male spectators. A 1926 letter to Bow, written by a fan after he saw *The Plastic Age*, confirms the romantic impact of Bow's celebrity: "Very few young fellows whom I know can see one of your pictures without 'falling,' I fell!"[85] Although this is a rather innocent statement, many of Bow's films—plot-thin and flesh-baring as they often are—do seem little more than pretenses for erotic display. In the now-legitimate space of the movie palace, one could go inexpensively and respectably to see a Bow picture and be assured that sexually charged images would be a part of the package.

These 1920s films were studio products and Bow, of course, had nothing to do with what they were about or how she appeared in them. The public, however, may not have been aware of this, as indicated by one fan's query in a 1931 letter begging for Bow to make a serious come-back: "Can't you have any rôle you wish? I'd just love to see you once more in a dramatic picture."[86] Bow's films rely upon her characters' electrifying physicality and irrepressible flirtation but are hardly the stuff of serious drama, which she repeatedly was barred from by studio executives who sought to profit from the reputation they already had created for Bow. What Bow did play was cookie-cutter flapper girls who flirted with "girl's problems," to use the language of the *Photoplay* column. In *The Plastic Age* (1925), for example, Bow plays Cynthia Day, who has designs on college-student Hugh Carver (Donald Keith). Instead of waiting to be courted, Cynthia's character actively pursues the less-savvy Hugh, even enticing him with such clichéd pickup lines as, "If there's a moon tonight would you like to take a walk?" When the two do go for a walk, Cynthia takes advantage of their remoteness by pulling Hugh into a dark area to kiss him passionately. It is a decidedly bold and shocking move—to use Ford's term, "mannish"—especially to the surprised Hugh. Cynthia's sexual aggression functions as a kind of reversal, since her kiss triggers the formerly repressed Hugh's sexual urges. After awakening his desire, Cynthia flees. The power that she derived from being aggressive and in control of the situation is shifted away from her when Hugh takes on a frighteningly active role. The narrative itself plays out much like Bow's career: Awakening popular sexual desire and exciting the public, Bow eventually was compelled to flee from the scrutiny her celebrity would carry with it. Hugh runs after Cynthia, eventually catching up with her in the distance. The scene ends with an eerie long shot of the two, as Cynthia is caught and struggles to get out of Hugh's arms.

This unusual transition—from Cynthia's aggressive sexual advances to her fleeing from the aroused Hugh—is suggestive of the spectrum of gendered behavior in Bow's 1920s films. Within seconds, Cynthia appears to be both seductress and innocent; but the scene ends abruptly, even awkwardly (not unlike Bow's career), since we are unsure what will result from Hugh's pursuit and capture. It is an uncomfortable cut, a moment in which ideas of rape seem implausible yet hard to dismiss. The film's overall jovial tone works against such a sinister reading; surely both characters are caught up in nothing more than a juvenile sexual game, neither really knowing how to conduct themselves. The point of this otherwise relatively frivolous film, in fact, seems to be that there are no right or wrong ways to behave. This is the plastic age, as the film's title tells us, and the rules are bending for everyone and everything. The film ends with Cynthia brazenly declaring her right to choose between Hugh and Carl Peters (played by Gilbert Roland, one of Bow's reported fiancés). Here Cynthia declares, "Listen to me! I'll go with whomever I wish!" Such freedom—of behavior, of choice—is the ongoing premise for women in the flapper-era films. But Bow's controversial media reputation is testament to the ways that women's sexual freedom, in particular, could be indicted despite the cinematic celebration of the same.

Hula (1929), directed by another of Bow's alleged fiancés, Victor Fleming, in fact opens with a highly sexualized image of Bow swimming naked on her back in a lagoon. The erotic shot is preceded by an opening title that sets the scene for the rest of the film: "A Hawaiian isle—a land of singing seas and swinging hips—where volcanoes are often active—and maidens always are." There is no question about what the allure of such films was: They relied upon the sex appeal of their star. *Hula* is about a wild child who falls for Anthony Haldane (Clive Brook), a man who has come to Hawaii to build a dam, a rather appropriate sexual metaphor for the film to dance around, particularly given the fact that Hula (Bow) triumphantly blows up the dam at film's end. The film does, in fact, posit a curious dichotomy that has to do with "civilized" and "savage" behavior, one that is suggestive of modern morality and, not surprisingly, one that revolves around issues largely sexual in nature. When Hula chases after her dog and first meets Anthony in his guest room, she is wearing only her robe. Much like Betty Lou in *It*, Hula is visibly enthralled with this handsome stranger. When Hula leaves Anthony's room, she is scolded: "Hula, you can't go into a man's room half-dressed, it's shocking!" When she questions her faux pas, she is again chided: "Really—you've lived among natives so much—you've become as primitive as they are."

In this first invocation of the "raw" native as a symbol of sexual impropriety, civilized behavior, not surprisingly, is linked to conservative behavior. Although Hula is scolded for this uncivilized action, the audience is clearly supposed to enjoy and desire to see more of such adventurousness. But this desire to see Hula (and Bow more generally) act out such "primitive" behavior is also an acknowledgment of the tangible barriers to liberated sexual behavior outside the theater doors. The appeal of such a plot (repeated as it was in only slightly altered variations across the body of Bow's work) is that audiences could see still-taboo behavior on-screen. With increasing disapproval directed at Bow as her public scandals escalated, she became a sign of how the prevailing morality of the culture could be pushed and, conversely, how it couldn't. She would not be the only one, of course, with vastly more serious accusations being leveled at stars beginning in the early 1920s, such as those that led to the immensely public Hollywood purging of Fatty Arbuckle.[87] But it is not an overstatement to claim that Bow acted out the repressed and repressive materials of a culture at war with its own sexual revolution.

Fixed in the discursive realm of the "native" by the popular press amidst a decidedly "civilized" cultural framework, Bow (like Hula) was characterized as pushing the boundaries of sexual identity. In the relative simplicity of the cinematic world, the answer was easy: Go native, follow the id, blow up the dam, get your man. And Hula does just this, initiating her sexual victory during a later luau scene in which Anthony is watching the other hula dancers instead of Hula. Realizing her need to relocate Anthony's gaze—the same necessity as Betty Lou's in *It*—Hula grabs a hula girl and borrows her clothes. When Hula emerges to do her own hula, she controls Anthony's gaze by calling attention to her scantily clad body. Hula's exhibitionism pleases Anthony and presumably pleases the film spectator; both get a glimpse at the spectacle of a woman set on sexual conquest in the face of civilized restraints placed upon even the most sacred of cultural institutions: marriage. She is sexual without guilt and without consequences, a perfect cinematic fantasy. Hula's behavior is rewarded because it defies the sexual rules of the culture; Bow's was excoriated for the same reason.

Even in the "respectable" Academy Award–winning William Wellman war picture, *Wings* (1927), Bow's tomboy character Mary Preston learns the lesson of becoming a sexualized spectacle by film's end. While on leave in Paris, Mary sees her beloved Jack Powell (Charles Rogers) necking with a woman in a nightclub. Upset, Mary runs crying into the bathroom, where she is advised by a French woman about how to properly trap a man. Providing Mary with a very low-cut dress to take the place of her uniform, the French woman teaches her about that quality which Bow possesses in every one of her roles: the means to attract attention. This is the key to Bow's cinematic reputation; it is the lure of stardom based on an audience's sexual response, precisely what Bow is tried for in the mock court case and in those very real litigious encounters she had in the 1930s.

Bow came full circle even in the pages of the fan magazine, from being discovered to being exiled, quite literally, from their pages. But even as these press-related incidents contributed to the unmaking of her reputation, the media continued to acknowledge its effect upon her, often with a sympathetic tone. Paul Jarvis's 1931 *Photoplay* article is explicit: "It's quite true that Clara lacks the armor of pretense and evasion with which a more sophisticated girl might have protected herself . . . She never learned the cycle of newspaper personality."[88] Also in *Photoplay*, Harry Lang mused, "You may say to yourself, when you read those sob-sister stories about how Clara has suffered, that it's ninety per cent hooey. But look at those eyes, and you begin to understand."[89] Like the cautionary Hollywood stories that appeared in the same pages that made glamour and celebrity seem an attainable ideal—think, for example, of the fan magazine contest with which this chapter began—such information reminds us of how contradictory public discourse in the Golden Age could be, particularly when profit was the bottom line, and a lot of people stood to profit from Clara Bow.

A letter from David O. Selznick to B. P. Schulberg aptly represents the cold economics of the star and studio system, reflecting the star's reputation as a fluctuating and fragile commodity. Discussing a potential pairing of Bow with George Bancroft in a 1931 letter, Selznick writes "But now, with Bow on her way out . . . we would be extracting the last ounce of value out of Bow before letting her go."[90] The callous language of this letter cuts to the unflattering core of the business of Hollywood studios. The image it conjures is bleak: male studio executives pondering how to squeeze every last cent out of their rundown female property. Bow was in every way a product on its way out; she was last year's fashion, to invoke the seasonal rhetoric used by the studios themselves. From a business perspective, there was no room for sentiment or sympathy.

In the early 1930s, Bow tried unsuccessfully to get out of her Paramount contract in an attempt to avoid having to shoot another film in the nervous state she was in. She wrote an explanatory letter to B. P. Schulberg in which she sums up the perils of publicity and the trauma of being unmade so publicly: "I am sick in heart as well as body and I am only going away to try and regain my health . . . I have always tried to be decent and nice to everyone and I think the people who know me well understand the real Clara Bow."[91] By this point in her career, Bow espoused the realistic understanding that "any industry must keep going regardless of anything, or anybody, still a human mind and body can only stand so much punishment."[92] Bow dramatically points to the division here between the industry—imagined as a machine driving on despite its constituent parts—and the individual body, mind, and soul of the actress.

Although made by the fan magazines, Bow was ultimately sustained by her fans, whose letters did not cease when her career did. "Down here at the Motor Vehicle," Marjorie Derr averred in her response to hearing that Paramount had released Bow's contract, "you are a favorite with all—young and old. We read all the reviews of your pictures—and never miss a movie magazine that contains a write-up about you. I have yet to hear someone say they did not care for your acting in a single picture you've played in."[93] Derr makes a case for the role that the movies and the fan magazines played in the leisure-time occupations of women as spectators, readers, and participants in a cultural debate about celebrity and worth. She also articulates a rejection of the dominant media and studio logic of the time, which was that Clara Bow's career was finished and her audience diminished.

It seems, then, that the reception of Bow's reputation was quite differ-

Making *It* in Hollywood   135

FIGURE 21: In this misleading illustration from Herb Howe's September 1931 article, "The Hollywood Boulevardier," a defiant Bow is imagined as bravely striking out from Paramount for a new, independent career. *The New Movie Magazine. Courtesy Laura Boyes.*

Clara Bow packs her lipsticks and leaves the old manse, otherwise the Paramount Studios. Clara says she is going to try her luck as an independent star.

ent from its representation. Bow had only minimal control over "her life story," or its reception, during or after the media-frenzied peak of her fame, demonstrating the degree to which reputation is an ultimately uncontrollable thing, made and unmade by forces, both great and small, that often transcend its possessor. More often than not, it is shaped only partly by the person in question, and equally by the workings of the culture industry, to borrow Adorno and Horkheimer's term. What had been a case of extreme proximity—between on- and off-screen character, as has been illustrated through my readings of her films—became, for Bow, a case of extreme distance. Bow's absurdly simple answer to her unmaking was to remove herself physically from Hollywood, to make herself relatively unpublic by redirecting her ambitions away from the motion picture capital. In fact, Bow planned her final attempt at reputation-making to transpire not during her life, but after: Her burial arrangements, dated August 13, 1960, request Forest Lawn Undertakers to make up her corpse to appear "as nearly life-like as possible" by looking at still pictures "from my last two talking pictures namely, Call Her Savage or Hoopla."[94]

5

"If We Are Ever to Be in Hollywood"

GERTRUDE STEIN'S MOVING IMAGES

Even taxi drivers knew her. One of them led me into a corner, asked if that was the famous Stein, and said he missed *Four Saints* in Hartford and guessed he'd "wait till it gets in the movies, because the movies makes them easier."
—W. G. Rogers, *When This You See Remember Me*[1]

This chapter is about something that never happened. Modernist author, art collector, and cultural provocateur Gertrude Stein did not get to "be" in Hollywood in the manner she imagined; her works were never made into films; nor did she succeed in making herself the affluent celebrity she imagined she might become. But the failure of her Hollywood plan is less relevant than the existence of the scheme itself. Scholars have largely overlooked Stein's desire "to be in Hollywood," but this aspect of her career is crucial to an understanding of cinema's momentous impact on American culture and of Stein's sense of her standing in that culture. Stein's pursuit of a Hollywood career forced her to articulate important ideas about success and the nature of authorial personality that suggest the degree to which the popularization of cinema was a catalyst for her rethinking. As Stein began, often cagily, to explore the culture that insisted on recognizing her according to the personality-based terms of celebrity—*Time* magazine, for example, called her "one of the least-read and most-publicized writers of the day" in their 1933 cover story[2]—she also began to consider what a cinematic representation of herself or her works might provide. As has been argued throughout this book, Hollywood and its product made people reorganize their perceptions of the world and of themselves. This literary expatriate and modernist innovator was no exception.

The current literature about modernist authors and cinema revolves almost exclusively around avant-garde filmmaking and film criticism. The epicenter of these discussions is the journal *Close-Up*, published between 1927 and 1933 by a collective that included the poet H.D. *Close-Up* focused on noncommercial cinema and solicited writings from modernists including Stein, who contributed two prose pieces to the journal in 1927. Referring to Stein's "Mrs. Emerson," published in *Close-Up* in August 1927, Anne Friedberg argues that to interpret it "literally as about cinema would be forcing meanings on Stein's intentionally slippery polysemic play."[3] Stein's publication in this journal, then, both resists literal interpretation and refuses to be "about" the journal's purported subject. Despite this anti-literal tendency, which was not exclusively characteristic of Stein but rather of any number of modernist authors, it is widely agreed upon that Stein "identified cinema as a foundational term for the syntax of modernism" and that the cinema greatly affected many modernist writers.[4] Neglected in these formulations are the ways in which Hollywood and mainstream commercial cinema exerted their influence not just on modernist thinking and writing, but on modernist ambition as well.[5]

As we will see throughout this chapter, the critical tendency to associate Stein with the non-narrative films of the avant-garde neglects a very significant connection that she had to Hollywood, or at least that she tried to have. This view, which tends to dismiss mainstream cinema's impact on the avant-garde and on Stein in particular, will be challenged in the following pages by looking to Stein's consideration of the Hollywood motion picture industry in relationship to the trajectory of her own career. Although Stein's desire for celebrity predated her Hollywood ambitions, Hollywood altered the nature, location, and magnitude of the celebrity she imagined for herself. Stein's understanding of her potential relationship with Hollywood, with what we might call the center of *popular* culture, signals a move toward postmodernity's eventual blurring of the barriers separating high and low.

In contrast to her experimental writing, the steady stream of letters that Stein penned throughout the 1930s reveal a surprising shift in her aspirations, away from the shadow of the avant-garde and into the glare of the mainstream. Stein began looking to the motion picture capital in the mid-1930s, expressing envy for writers who already had made it there, especially those who seemed able to get something for nothing. She wrote to fellow author and regular correspondent Thornton Wilder in 1936, "I just read in this morning's paper that [P. G.] Wodehouse says that they give him $104,000 for doing nothing at Hollywood they keep him there but they do not use what they ask him to do, now that would just suit us fine."[6] Stein gushed at the possibilities implied by Wodehouse's deal, proclaiming that

> we want a payed [sic] [vacation] which is à la mode here now, and of course we are not valuable like he is, but for considerable less would we write dialogue and titles that they do not want to use, not at all do we insist that they use our works printed or unprinted not at all, we just want to run around and do nothing and be payed [sic] largely for it ... we are just pining for pleasant xtravagance [sic], so keep your eyes and ears open, if they want us we will come, we would love to be payed [sic] largely and we are kind of tired of just staying here.[7]

Authorial status was being translated into fantastic rewards in Hollywood as literary reputation was used as leverage to broker deals. As London and numerous other authors had done before her, Stein was beginning to envision herself as a potential player in this market.

But Stein was hardly a populist of the London variety, so can she be taken seriously here (and elsewhere) even as she seems to make such suggestions fancifully? The sheer repetition of such requests to Wilder and many others, as this chapter will illustrate, affirms that Stein did not take her Hollywood idea lightly, even if she coated it in enough whimsy to make its failure less biting. Stein had "discovered" Hollywood during her lecture tour of the United States over the course of 1934 and 1935, which followed on the heels of the most dramatic event of Stein's literary life: After years of self-publication, paltry book sales, and nonexistent profits, Stein struck literary gold in 1933 with the publication and best-selling success of *The Autobiography of Alice B. Toklas*. In the wake of the attending onslaught of good publicity, Stein and Toklas, who was referred to in the contemporary press as the author's devoted secretary and companion, boarded the S.S. *Champlain* and arrived in New York on October 24, 1934.[8]

Up until this point, Stein was best known for not being read despite having written hundreds of novels, essays, poems, operas, and plays, many of which intentionally flaunt their disregard for these formal designations. She was also renowned for the salon she kept with Toklas, filled floor to ceiling with shockingly modern art, at 27 Rue de Fleurus in Paris. Here, Stein presided over gatherings of such early-twentieth-century luminaries as Ernest Hemingway, Sherwood Anderson, Pablo Picasso, and Henri Matisse, while also producing, but not necessarily publishing, an impressive battery of manuscripts, all typed out from Stein's virtually illegible handwriting by Toklas.

The Autobiography of Alice B. Toklas changed the nature of Stein's fame. The book was unlike anything that Stein had published before. As Friedberg and many others have observed, Stein's writing had been characterized largely by its intentional playfulness, determined opacity, and rigorous opposition to conventional prose narration.[9] Anecdotal, witty, and hardly repetitive, *The Autobiography* was readable and it was read. As a charming account of Paris, among other things, the novel—more a playful biography of Stein than an autobiography of Toklas—bounds from discussions of futurism to French cooking, from the making of sentences to the latest fashion in hats (accoutrements much loved by Alice). Stein herself would explain with her usual flare for turning the public's perceptions around that "the style of *The Autobiography of Alice B. Toklas* is not peculiar at all. The only peculiar thing is that I wrote it myself."[10]

Stein's biographer James Mellow observes that *The Autobiography of Alice B. Toklas* provided Stein with her first substantial income from her writing. The initial printing of 5,400 copies sold out nine days before the official publication date and Stein's royalties from Harcourt alone added up to almost $4,500. The novel was serialized in *Atlantic Monthly*, sold for $3,000 to the Literary Guild for a subscriber special edition, and translated into several languages, all unprecedented successes for Stein.[11] Compared to her experience with the publication of *Three Lives* in 1909, which she shopped around for several years before paying Grafton Press $660 to produce 1,000 printed and 500 bound copies, Stein had pulled off a literary coup.[12] Although she and her brother, Leo, had lived well in Paris on their "modest but comfortable income from San Francisco properties," this was income of a different sort and, perhaps most importantly, all her own.[13]

The immense popularity of *The Autobiography of Alice B. Toklas*—the book most responsible for propelling Stein into the public eye, the most read of her works, and the text that most informed the public's perception of her—forced Stein to acknowledge that she might be remembered more for her famous associations and charming anecdotes than for what she considered her masterpieces, especially her magnum opus, the thousand-page *The Making of Americans* (1925). As Bob Perelman bluntly puts it, "*The Autobiography of Alice B. Toklas* would be damned as mere entertainment," perhaps as much by Stein as by anyone else.[14] Following its success, Stein experienced an unprecedented battle with writer's block and some not-so-unprecedented concerns with her own immortality and place in the history of American letters. After much deliberation, she also decided that her newfound popular fame might be exploited to enlarge her reading public, and after over thirty years of expatriation Stein decided to return to the United States for a lecture tour over the course of 1934 and 1935.

While Stein had long been fascinated with the workings of fame and had experienced a certain degree of renown as an expatriate writer and friend to the avant-garde, her tour plunged her into the life of a popular celebrity, American style. Richard Bridgman points out that the American trip forced her "to confront all the sophisticated means of exploiting a 'personality.'"[15] Seeing her name in lights in Times Square, being recognized on the streets, seeing her books in shop windows and her name in the press, receiving an invitation to the White House, and meeting virtually any public figure she desired, over the course of these seven months in America, Stein was experiencing a life almost fully revolving around public and publicized encounters. Though enchanted by this newfound fame, Stein was equally wary of, even uncomfortable with the trappings of such a spectacular lifestyle. As Stein grapples in her own writing with the need to be remembered as an important writer, not merely as an eccentric personality, she provides insight into the tensions between celebrity and reputation while also revealing her conflicted relationship to the very Hollywood-based notion of star power as it was developing alongside her own career.

Already well established as the center of the motion picture industry by the time that Stein arrived there in 1935, Hollywood was defying the economic decline of the nation as a whole. Stein's brief visit to Hollywood—an island of opulence amidst of a sea of fiscal despair—informed her views on the inner workings of fame and the outer workings of prosperity. Hollywood became the place in which she envisioned her own dramatic transformation—brokered on the basis of her current literary reputation—from unprofitable expatriate intellectual to affluent American celebrity. But Stein was not one to concede so crassly to wanting merely fame and fortune; literary reputation had always been her raison d'être. Rather, she began imagining the innovations of her own work as coincidental with those of the cinema.[16]

By embracing the technology of the moving image, Stein tried to ensure her alignment with this popular medium for highly self-conscious and, as always, cleverly self-promotional reasons. Following the post-cinematic reconceptualization of celebrity during the early twentieth century, it became clear that Hollywood was the place where the most spectacular personalities were being made, a place where public visibility was churned out as a seemingly effortless commodity. One could not afford, for reasons of posterity as well as economy, to ignore that Hollywood was making and maintaining reputations in proportions previously unheard of, however different these kinds of reputations might be. In fact, the concept of reputation was being revised, at least in certain circles—and certainly in the mind of Stein—to include the signifiers of success endowed by Hollywood: money, leisure, mass recognition, not to mention an illusory notion of freedom. Stein realized, perhaps only after her visit in 1935, that Hollywood was making history, myth, and an unprecedented impact on the way that the world, including herself, perceived success (literary or otherwise). It was therefore only natural, as Stein might have said, that she was drawn to Hollywood and that Hollywood became the focus of her post-tour drive to make an American "comeback."

"Perhaps Hollywood Too is That Thing": Celebrity In America

Stein and Toklas arrived in Los Angeles with considerable fanfare, at least by literary standards, in the spring of 1935.[17] A representative for Warner Bros. met the ladies at the airport with an invitation to "come to their cinema place to see them," as Stein put it.[18] Here were some of the gatekeepers of Tinseltown throwing open their doors and, according to her own account, Stein demurred. As she explained without really explaining anything, "when the Warners asked us to come and lunch we did not go."[19] Her inexplicable hesitancy to meet the powerful brothers Warner suggests, at minimum, that Stein had not yet come to terms with her commercial aspirations, or with the role such a powerful studio might have played in their realization. She represents herself in press interviews of the period and in her own writing as similarly nonchalant about films and the industry from which they derive. Brushing off the Warners' invitation seems consistent with Stein's pre-tour attitude, which was altered in the wake of suggestions that she might profit dramatically from such a relationship.

In a letter postmarked April 2, 1935, from the Hotel Vista del Arroyo in Pasadena, Stein seemed to be warming up to the Hollywood experience. She wrote to art and culture impresario Carl Van Vechten about a party that one of his friends, Beverly Hills denizen Lillian Ehrman, threw for them: "we have had a most amusing time and thanks to you met everybody we wanted to meet, Mrs. [Lillian May] Ehrman gave a party last night for us Charlie Chaplin, Dashiel [sic] Hammett, the highest payed [sic] directors, Anita Loos, and John Emerson and all and everything and it was most amusing."[20] Stein's ability to attract this roster of famous Hollywood players to a dinner party testifies to the amount of curiosity her presence inspired during the tour. It also suggests that Stein may have been nurturing more than a little interest in celebrities of the Hollywood variety.

The gathering made the society editor's column in the *Hollywood Citizen-News*: "Mrs. Lillian May Ehrman of Beverly Hills held the spotlight of the week as the hostess of Gertrude Stein, modern writer whose three day visit in the Southland caused a flurry of excitement."[21] Stein seemed quite taken with all of this attention. "It is very nice being a celebrity," she wrote, "a real celebrity who can decide who they want to meet and say so and they come or do not come as you want them. I never imagined that would happen to me to be a celebrity like that but it did and when it did I liked it."[22] Stein's admission of surprise—her acknowledgment that celebrity of this scale was a shock, though a pleasing one—alerts us to a transformational moment in the author's self-perception. She had already tested her understanding of celebrity power by asking Ehrman if she could meet Dashiell Hammett, whose detective writing she greatly admired. Lo and behold, Stein informs us, "We went to dinner that evening and there was Dashiell Hammett."[23] Within these tales lurks a lesson from which Stein's post-tour writings would emerge: Even in celebrity-mad Hollywood, Stein could stand her own. Her reputation—both as a writer and as a personality—could be used as a tool to reorient herself in this other constellation.

Triggered in part by these brushes with the Tinseltown elite, Stein tried to process her feelings of increasingly grandiose personal importance. She was acutely aware of the fact that her encounter with celebrity during the American tour changed the way she thought about herself and her writing, not all for the better. Although Stein certainly had been around celebrity before—in some ways, she had always surrounded herself with it—it had never been of the Hollywood variety. William G. Rogers—"The Kiddie," as she and Alice affectionately called him—an American G.I. whom Stein and Toklas befriended during the First World War, received a letter during the tour in which she wrote: "Have we had a hectic time it is unbelievable ... everybody knows us on the Street ... you go into a store anywhere to buy anything and they say how do you do Miss Stein and Alice goes anywhere they say how do you do Miss Toklas and they so pleasantly speak to us on the street, its [sic] unbelievable."[24]

Stein pondered the implications such fame had for her future, as she also did in reaction to her success with *The Autobiography of Alice B. Toklas*. In *Everybody's Autobiography* (1937) she wrote that, "I had never made any money before [the *Autobiography of Alice B. Toklas*] in my life and I was most excited."[25] Treating herself to an unusually extravagant shopping spree, she purchased a "new eight cylinder Ford car and the most expensive coat made to order by Hermès . . . for Basket the white poodle," and ended up with a lingering case of literary performance anxiety in the form of writer's block.[26] Armed with the knowledge that her writing could be more than merely controversial—it could be translated into cash, so much that even the dog could live in style—Stein attributed the profitable aspect of the *Autobiography* to the fact that "I feel differently now about everything."[27] How differently would emerge only after she left the *gloire* of America and returned to the relative isolation of her Paris life.

Stein already had made a career of writing with the explicit goal of showcasing her distinct literary personality. In this way she was like Jack London, an earlier pioneer of authorial personality and autobiographical reinvention. But while London was widely considered readable, Stein was widely considered inaccessible. In its 1933 cover story, *Time* magazine described her as "the man-in-the-street's" synonym for "the cult of unintelligibility."[28] Frequently refusing narrative altogether, Stein favored an understanding of texts not only as literary works but as monuments to and reflections of their authors. Stein became increasingly disdainful of plot and narrative because she felt that they detracted from the most important feature of the modernist work: the presence of the author in the text. Exploring the budding culture of personality, Stein's understanding of authorship mirrored, in some ways, the star-driven premises of the Hollywood system. The Hollywood studio film was fueled by the presence of its star(s) much as Stein's oeuvre relied upon making her own presence tangible; the one, however, did not so easily equal the other.

Authorship historically has been associated with renown to some degree, but the early twentieth century witnessed the making of authors into full-blown celebrities, occasionally nearing the heights of those carefully managed celebrities of the screen. While such a conceptualization of the author as celebrity dates back to the nineteenth-century Romantic tradition, the proliferation of media, particularly visual media, in the twentieth century resulted in a veritable explosion of authorial celebrity. Stein was acutely aware of the difference between the kind of renown she could achieve as an expatriate author of works that were for the most part considered "difficult," versus the fame and fortune that was being bestowed upon both cinematic and mainstream literary figures in Hollywood. Furthermore, as Kevin Starr observes, "film and literature were competing, some would claim irreconcilable, modes of expression; and in the 1930s, film—by which is meant the assembly-line product of the industrialized studio system—outperformed literature as both an art form and a social necessity."[29]

The disparity between what Stein could achieve in France, both financially and in terms of her reputation, and what others were achieving in the motion picture capital has to do with the most basic principals of supply and demand economics. But it also indicates a cultural shift in notions of achievement, in which ideas of celebrity and success were becoming undifferentiated concepts.[30] Stein's sense of authorial prominence, particularly her need to invoke her presence doggedly within her works, makes sense within this matrix of modern celebrity. But Stein was also torn between being a celebrity in the Hollywood sense and being a seriously read author; the two were so readily confused precisely because this was an era in which both reputation and celebrity were evolving in response to the impact of Hollywood. Although Stein seemed to conceive of her ideal reputation as a genius, she also recognized that this designation could only get her so far.[31] Stein appreciated the ways that her difficulty as a writer was often ascribed to her genius, deducing that this idea of genius might be marketable in Hollywood, that celebrity might not be incompatible with genius after all.[32]

For proof of Hollywood's impact on Stein's understanding of her literary reputation, we need only look to the author's correspondence, much of which tried to assure her of her place in the American popular imagination. Thornton Wilder, Carl Van Vechten, and a host of other correspondents provided Stein with reassurances of her stature and legacy, which Stein encouraged. Even before her American lecture tour, much of this reassurance came in the form of Hollywood-related analogies. In these, Stein is often compared to a movie star, as in a September 19, 1933, letter from Max Ewing replete with flattery that is typical of these correspondences: "I wonder if you know that you are more discussed in Hollywood these days than Greta Garbo? The autobiography is delightful."[33] In a letter dated just two days later on September 21, 1933, Van Vechten echoes the sentiment: "You are on every tongue like Greta Garbo!"[34] Garbo was, of course, one of the most luminous—not to mention sexually mysterious—female stars of Hollywood during this era, and her 1933 star vehicle, Rouben Mamoulian's *Queen Christina*, about a young queen's quest for true love, was a box office hit. The point was being made implicitly: Movie stardom of the Hollywood variety was the measure by which other public personalities were judged.

This hierarchy of celebrity is confirmed by a blurb Van Vechten wrote about Stein for a Gotham Book Mart Deluxe Catalogue. Enclosed in a September 13, 1939, letter to Stein, the publicity notes that, "In the matter of fans you can only compare her with a moving picture star in Hollywood."[35] As metaphors, these comparisons playfully exaggerate Stein's success by making claims that are at once flattering and misleading, ultimately reinforcing the primacy of Hollywood celebrity. An author wants readers, not fans; Stein bemoaned this regularly. This is the very crisis of celebrity culture as Stein would understand it: how to attract readers without changing the nature of her writing, which she did to a certain degree with *The Autobiography of Alice B. Toklas*, and which she eventually seemed willing to do if she could get a deal in Hollywood. These early suggestions of celebrity imply, however loosely, that Stein could in fact sustain a literary version of Garbo-magnitude fame. Such complimentary epistolary mythologizations presage Stein's fantasies of Hollywood celebrity. Since she could make herself the star of her literary works, perhaps the system in place in Hollywood would be the profitable next step.

Stein was not satisfied with the nature or magnitude of her fame, even when she was to witness in person the degree of her recognition in America and despite countless reassurances, such as the one contained in Henry McBride's March 20, 1934, missive: "Did Carl [Van Vechten] send you one of his photographs of your name in electric lights on Broadway? It seems to me that ought to content you with fame."[36] Such testimonies that Stein had "made it" due to the success of the *Autobiography* were not adequate, for Stein knew very well the difference between seeing her name fleetingly in lights and keeping her name in the minds of Americans present and future. Electric lights were no indication of permanent literary canonization, and they apparently did little to enhance the sale of Stein's other books. Sherwood Anderson reassured Stein of this very thing, writing on September 29, 1937, that, "the impression of you, in America, goes on—a powerful rich thing."[37] In her absence, both before and after the tour, Stein lacked the ability to keep herself in the foreground of the American scene, a cultural landscape informed more and more by media (both print and moving), more interested in the written about than the written.

According to the logic of celebrity in the age of Hollywood, this lingering impression of Stein could only recede with time since her presence was needed to facilitate a substantial furthering of her reputation. As she noted in her March 30, 1935, *New York Herald Tribune* article: "Do you see what I mean when I say anybody *in America* can be a public one . . . anybody who can have his picture where it is to be seen by anybody."[38] Stein is geographically specific here about the nature of publicity, noting the uniquely American proclivity to make people so readily and perhaps even unworthily known to the public. Losing out on the usual possibilities for

Gertrude Stein Home After Thirty-One Years

Famous Literary Figure, Here for a Lecture Tour, Maintains She Is a Realist Despite Her Eccentric Use of Words

In Gertrude Stein's opera, "Four Saints in Three Acts," there appears, among others, this verse:

"To know to know to love her so.
Four Saints prepare for Saints.
It makes it well fish.
Four Saints prepare for Saints it makes it well."

From the wards of the Glasgow Mental Hospital an unknown author wrote:

"One two three sugars
Aunt Jilly filled her pockets
Dickey birds its the highest
You can roll around as much as you like."

When Gertrude Stein arrived in New York last week for her first visit to her native country in thirty-one years, reporters hastened to ask her opinion on this odd similarity which psychologist Lawrence Gould called "self-induced pseudo-mania." Miss Stein easily explained: "After all, James the psychologist. She soon became absorbed in psychology, poetry, and the interpretation and development of art, and acquired a strong feeling for words as materials. Her habit of repetition of words and phrases in her writings has had much to do with her fame as a literary eccentric; but she maintains she is a realist.

Her early volumes, "The Making of "Americans" and "Tender Buttons," her now famous experimental works in prose, brought praise from rational critics and wonder and puzzlement from the average reader. But she has influenced a generation of writers such as her pupil, Ernest Hemingway, and Sherwood Anderson. An intellectual in her writings rather than in personal appearance, she has a small opinion of intellectuals in practical affairs: "The best governors are always the men who respond to instinct."

Arriving in this

Keystone photographs
Gertrude Stein (left), and Alice B. Toklas

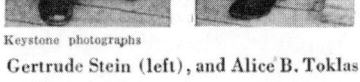

FIGURE 22: Gertrude Stein's homecoming tour of America inspired significant media attention, which tended to focus equally on her fame and her "eccentricity." Note that Stein and Toklas are both pictured, but that their images are separated despite the fact that it looks like the photograph was taken at the same time and place. *Literary Digest*, 1934.

publicity by virtue of her absence, Stein worked toward this end abroad by continuing to produce literary works to generate interest from afar.

Despite these efforts, the *Literary Digest*'s "Gertrude Stein Home after Thirty-One Years" describes her as a writer who "*has been* a famous literary figure *in France*" (see figure 22).[39] It is glaring that this success is deemed so specific to a locale that Stein cared little for in relation to her literary reputation. *Time* magazine characterized her as having "made herself a background place in the literary panorama" *until* the American tour, which allowed her to move "from the legendary borders of literature into the very market-place."[40] The value of her physical presence in America was reaffirmed by such statements, particularly through *Time*'s reference to the economic reward gained through this repositioning. As Stein herself succinctly put it in *Everybody's Autobiography*, "It is very nice being a celebrity"; but "being" a celebrity in this fashion can only happen when one is, in fact, "being" a celebrity, when one is present to generate the publicity that celebrity in the modern age required.[41]

In her absence, however, Stein was not entirely forgotten. She made occasional headlines in press parodies as well as serious literary magazines, appeared in some comics, and garnered a few references in the movies. In *Top Hat* (1935), starring Fred Astaire and Ginger Rogers, Rogers jokingly mistakes Stein as the author of a confusing telegram replete with incomplete sentences and "stops."[42] We can only assume that the majority of the film's audience got the joke; the existence of such a reference in this immensely popular film reveals the degree to which Stein was widely and well known, for the studios cared little for obscure references. But while the audience probably knew who Stein was and what she was known for, this only supports the supposition that Stein was known to the vast majority of Americans as a caricature and as little more than a curiosity.

Stein's persona thus lingered on the fringe of the celebrity culture produced by Hollywood even while she resided abroad. Even Stein, who professed little interest in going to the movies, would identify Wyatt Earp's Hollywood friend and correspondent William S. Hart as an acting favorite and would be sure to list other important movie celebrities that she met during her tour.[43] Stein duly noted the peculiar and occasionally upsetting sensation of autographing, being recognized on the streets, and seeing her name in lights while on her own version of the Hollywood publicity tour: "it does give me a little shock of recognition and nonrecognition."[44] But Stein also depicts her conflicted feeling on this issue, reporting in her radio interview with Lundell that "I who am easily frightened by anything unexpected find this spontaneous considerate contact with all and any New Yorker touching and pleasing and I am deeply moved and awfully happy in it."[45]

Stein was wont to discuss these experiences of celebrity; they fascinated her because they changed the way she thought about herself and her writing while they also made tangible the alluring potential of American publicity. And while it may have been an awakening for Stein to learn that fame of this magnitude had its price, in Hollywood these sacrifices were precisely what made celebrity so enduring in the public's imagination. Perceptions of film celebrities were largely tied to the star's economic independence: "The ability to own a mansion, the opportunity to partake of prohibitively expensive forms of leisure, like yachting or polo, and the time to travel widely are some of the kinds of privileges associated with stardom."[46] As is evident in reading Stein's letters, the economic lure of Hollywood was irresistible. Stein appears to have been charmed by images of affluent celebrity, which were depicted regularly in the press and which she experienced during her stay in America. Although Stein repeatedly expressed a lack of interest in cinema—she claimed rarely to see films—Hollywood's promotion of its mythic opulence appears to have convinced the literary lion of the potential reward a Hollywood alliance might provide.

By the end of her lecture tour, Stein seems to have bought into the myth of Hollywood success. This despite the fact that Toklas wrote to Rogers during their return voyage that, "some day we'll come back . . . but not [to] California because G. hated it."[47] In a letter postmarked May 1, 1940, to Samuel Steward, a professor and novelist with whom Stein corresponded regularly, Stein signals a significant departure from her supposed aversion to California by expressing a fantasy that itself seems straight out of the movies: "and it does seem if we ever are to be in Hollywood it will be the work of Sammy Dear Sammy, wouldn't it be nice if they wanted us and gave us so much money we could buy a car and drive a car we and Sammy at the wheel."[48] This is just one of the many instances in which Stein whimsically represents her enchantment with the Hollywood myth of overnight success. She often reduces the mechanisms of Hollywood achievement to a simplistic endowment of money based merely, it seems, on being "wanted." Through fan magazines, newsreels, and the mainstream press, Hollywood had marketed and sold itself as nothing less than the stuff that dreams were made of. Stein represents herself as complacent with the fantasy, if she can only figure out a way to participate in it.

In a letter to Steward just three months earlier, postmarked February 13, 1940, Stein makes inquiries while further expressing her investment in the fantasy of Hollywood stardom:

say I hear he had to do with movies, could he not arrange that The World is Round, or the Autobiography of Alice B. Toklas be done by Hollywood, if he could he could be our agent and we could go and sit out there for large sums and everybody would be happy, do have him do that, I like him and would like him so much better if he could do that, the Autobiography would make a swell film, so would The World is Round, either or both . . .[49]

Stein is resolute but indiscriminate here, enthusiastic and flippant, professing to care neither which of her works would be made into a film nor how such arrangements would be made. She appears to accept the fact that she has this desire to make it in Hollywood while her almost childlike tone mocks this same desire. Like Denise in the first line of Stein's 1940s play "Yes Is For a Very Young Man," we can picture Stein saying, "Oh dear I am so tired of working I wish I could be rich again, oh dear."[50] Did Stein understand what going to Hollywood would actually mean? Did she want merely to make money, or did other motives lurk behind making a name for herself through the translation of her works into films? In marked contrast to Jack London's labor-intensive vision of his own Hollywood contributions, Stein depicts her end-goal as the act of leisurely accumulation, of sitting around and collecting money. In other letters, Stein refers to film projects involving works about a variety of figures such as Benjamin Franklin, Daniel Webster, Pablo Picasso, and Alice B. Toklas, making her appear much more interested in the perks of Hollywood fame than the substance of her product.[51] Playful or not, Stein's frequent musings on the subject of Hollywood fame reveal a certain tentativeness about the future of her reputation as uncompromising literary modern or Hollywood writer. The question was, could one be both at the same time?

Stein's comments also require consideration in the context of her writings on success, failure, and her first taste of American fame. Stein reacted to her success with *The Autobiography of Alice B. Toklas* in ways that point to her intentions with Hollywood. Looking back upon her career, as in her 1946 "Transatlantic Interview," Stein struggled with the consequences of the stylistic departure of *The Autobiography*, musing that "I became interested in how you could tell this thing in a way that anybody could understand and at the same time keep true to your values, and the thing bothered me a great deal at the time."[52] Stein circuitously alludes to the problem of writing a popular work without sacrificing the values underlying her literary experimentation. This idea perplexed her, and was a central part of her consideration of Hollywood, with its unabashed commercial goals and rewards. Particularly for those high modernists whose writings were intentionally exclusive, success in a mass cultural sense suggested intellectual compromise and debasement.[53]

Success also brought Stein's career into the currents of popular culture and criticism, sometimes in unflattering ways. T. S. Matthews's 1934 piece in *The New Republic* presents us with just one of the reactions to Stein's visit that must have troubled her with regard to her reputation as an important author in America. The tone of the piece is mocking, but serious:

> She knows we have come here because we are interested—not so much in her as in her writing. We know better. We are here because we are curious—not so much about her writing, which we have never read, and probably never shall, as about herself—an apparently sensible, perhaps really sane woman who has spent most of her life writing absolute balderdash, and then, by gum, a year ago published a book that was perfectly plain sailing, and got her on the bestseller lists. We want to see what this creature looks like, we want to hear what she has to say for herself.[54]

There is the implication of carnivalesque curiosity here, with Stein depicted as a naïve who fails to realize that her popularity has nothing to do with literary merit. Matthews deems Stein an eccentric novelty, dismissing her literary status with the kind of blunt commentary that Stein was well aware she was up against. "Practically nobody does read her . . . we have read what the newspapers have to say about her," Matthews continues, articulating precisely Stein's "problem of publicity."[55] While her writings made Stein's personality such a central issue, they are also purposefully difficult, drawing attention to the personality who would dare make such a thing and call it not just art, but genius. *The Autobiography* compounded this by making Stein the very comprehensible novel's subject, again bringing her carefully constructed and performed personality to the foreground and sparking a new kind of curiosity from the public.

Stein made a case for the ruthless infusion of the personal into the modernist literary text in her "Transatlantic Interview," in which she explains "why biographies have been more successful than novels . . . in part [due to] this enormous publicity business."[56] *The Autobiography* supports Stein's thesis, though it does not solve her problem of publicity. However, it is certainly Stein's pivotal work in terms of the formation of her ideas about success and fame; it is also the book that forced her to realize something about her material worth as an author. Stein grappled with this authorial dilemma, reiterating concerns particularly over her post-*Autobiography* success: "Henry McBride always said that success spoils one and he always used to say to me that he hoped that I would not have any and now I was having some."[57] Bernard Fay quotes a similarly concerned Stein in the *Saturday Review of Literature*: "Don't you know that all writers, good or bad, at a time try to sell themselves and to sell their souls. They do, but all of them do not succeed. It is not given to everybody to be cheap."[58] These public iterations of anxiety over success of this nature, concerns that reflect a perceived incompatibility of literary genius and commercial rewards, suggest a filtering down of Hollywood values for Stein, who appeared willing—even eager—to "sell out" in her later musings on the entertainment capital. Although Stein appears disdainful of such cheap success, she did not remain so reluctant even as she publicly articulated the conflicts between modernism and commercialism. Edmund Wilson, in his review of *The Autobiography*, also notes Stein's perplexing attitude: "Success in itself seems to imply for her some imposture or deterioration."[59] This is all the more the case, as Wilson notes, because of Stein's penchant for irony; but there is also a sense that Stein rationalized her glory in failure largely because before *The Autobiography* she had yet to encounter unqualified success. The tone of her Hollywood-related epistles reflects a similar move in the name of protecting the author's carefully constructed literary ego.

In *Everybody's Autobiography*, the sequel to *The Autobiography of Alice B. Toklas* and a veritable study of celebrity and publicity, Stein documents her American tour and her experiences of celebrity—her own and others'—on American soil. It is here that Stein's dabbling with cinematic metaphors convenes with her personal experiences, all of which lead to her post-tour desires to join the ranks of the "everybodys" making their fortunes on Hollywood soil. *Everybody's Autobiography* also functions as an extension of Stein's self-promotional tour of America. As a literary representation intended to bolster Stein's celebrity in absentia, the text is nothing less than an advertisement for herself.

Publicity is at the center of *Everybody's Autobiography* and is addressed most evidently in the sections of the book involving Stein's encounters with movie celebrities. At a tea party in New York, Stein met Mary Pickford, who went from enthusiastically suggesting that they be photographed together to rushing off before this photograph could be taken. Stein narrates this anecdote to expose the workings of publicity by asking the other guests about Pickford's unusual behavior as part of her interest "to know just what they know about what is good publicity and what is not."[60] The guests surmise that Pickford was both unsure about how a picture of herself with Stein might be interpreted by her (Pickford's) audience and whether Stein's endorsement of the photograph meant that Stein would benefit more from the photograph than herself. When one imagines the image it becomes clear that the two are impossibly incongruous figures, one so tailor-made for mainstream audiences and the other so anomalous within the context of movie-star iconography. Pickford has been discussed as one of the first highly manipulated celebrity personas to come out of Hollywood, making such deductions about public image seem tenable. But perhaps the greater moral of the story here is that without Pickford, Stein was not photographed. Pickford's Hollywood star power allows her to say that "it would be easy to get the Journal photographer to come over," while Stein is left asking why the picture never happened.[61]

The formal structure of *Everybody's Autobiography* reinforces Stein's aforementioned concerns about publicity and the effect her tour had upon her status as an author and a celebrity. The five chapters—"What Happened After the Autobiography of Alice B. Toklas," "What Was the Effect Upon Me of the Autobiography," "Preparations for Going to America," "America," and "Back Again"—imply a legible, linear narrative. They also designate the anxieties of both text and person, and situate the geographical anchor of America in relation to Stein's celebrity (here largely a result of the publication of the *Autobiography*). The vague "Back Again" that concludes the volume indicates the undetermined nature of Stein's future; while referring to France in a literal sense, Stein's interest in coming back again to America is the actual subject of her epistolary energies of the era coterminous with the writing of *Everybody's Autobiography* through the war period. The dilemmas of absence and presence (of author and of readers in America) were becoming inescapable for Stein, who increasingly linked her presence in America to the perpetuation of her own publicity and celebrity.

Compensating for Stein's absence from the American scene, *Everybody's Autobiography* functions both as a document of Stein's American experience and as a continuation of her American tour de force—a promotional substitute for her literal absence. In it, Stein repeatedly asserts her place in American letters. Pairing herself with Einstein, whom she terms "the creative philosophic mind of the century" (and who, coincidentally, had visited Hollywood just prior to Stein in 1931), Stein states that, "I have been the creative literary mind of the century."[62] Later, she matter-of-factly asserts that, "I know that I am the most important writer writing today."[63] Beyond the amazing self-assurance of these statements lurks the biographical Stein, who elsewhere appears less than certain that others would agree with such valuations. Considered another way, perhaps this is evidence of Stein's real confidence in her literary stature, enabling her to shed her serious literary chrysalis for a new version of herself who could guiltlessly enjoy the indulgent gratifications of wealth and celebrity. As "the most important writer writing today," Stein's conceptualization of cinema and celebrity drives home one of the premises of this book: that the movies changed the very nature of how individuals perceived both the value of their reputations and how they could be used.

By understanding *Everybody's Autobiography* as a study of celebrity and publicity, we can better understand the lessons learned by Stein in America that led her to formulate her Hollywood ambitions. Discovering firsthand the way that American audiences responded to her presence and the way that publicity—and potentially the movie industry—could transform her and the public's reaction to her, Stein meditates over how to reconcile her absence with the desire to further her presence. She argued in her "Transatlantic Interview" that the novel was dead in the twentieth century because, unlike the nineteenth century, there is now "this enormous publicity": "the novel supplied imagination where now you have it in publicity, and this changed the whole cast of the novel."[64] Following from this observation, *Everybody's Autobiography* is as much a celebration and promotion of Stein's genius as it is a record of her transformation, a résumé detailing her past successes, and an effort to inspire her popular ascension. In addition to touting herself as the creative literary genius of her generation, she also provides a series of commercial blurbs for her many unread and unpublished works, much as she does in *Lectures in America*. Although the book fails to answer Stein's questions about the fate of her literary reputation, it makes it plain that she was acting as her own publicity agent, of sorts. But Stein would have to look not just to America, but more specifically to Hollywood in order to articulate her future plans, and even then these would be wrought with a confusing mixture of desperation, fantasy, silliness, earnestness, and hope.

Cinematic Writing and the Quest for an Audience

In her 1920 play "A Movie"—titled such for no reason that is made apparent within the play itself—Stein raises concerns about audience in a few pages of wonderfully abstract, allegorical "theatricality." The scenario involves an American painter working in France who bemoans at play's beginning, "Where are American tourists to buy my pictures."[65] It is not a stretch to imagine that this American painter is a literary embodiment of Stein herself, pondering her poor book sales and lack of American recognition as a writer living abroad, particularly during these pre-*Autobiography* years.

In the play, this painter becomes a taxi driver in order to make money and eventually uses his driving skills to aid in the war effort, a scenario only marginally different from Stein's own wartime occupation. But the point of this is not just that "A Movie" presents a theatrical biography that uncannily mirrors Stein's career; in fact, in many ways this painter's story bears little resemblance to Stein's own. Rather, what is most remarkable is the recurrence of audience-related concerns for the expatriate artist, gathered under a title that signifies an industry that would attract Stein's curiosity in her later career.

The seemingly arbitrary relationship between these concepts of audience and genre—a painting versus a movie—points the way to what Stein would ultimately posit: that the cinema offered a potential solution to her dilemmas of reputation and audience. In the same year as "A Movie," another play, "Photograph," ponders similar issues, noting that, "For a photograph we need a wall. Star gazing. Photographs are small. They reproduce well. I enlarge better."[66] This associative chain links notions of celebrity, representation, reproduction, and distribution in ways that extend Stein's fanciful imaginings of cinema as an option for herself and her writing. Her conclusion here, that "I enlarge better," also recognizes the power of her presence while it acknowledges that series reproduction has worked wonders for others. But this is a thought contained within a larger question that exists throughout Stein's prose: Could "a movie" solve the artist's problem of audience?

Well after "A Movie," *The Autobiography of Alice B. Toklas* rekindled Stein's ruminations on this subject. In his article on Gertrude Stein and the manifesto, Alan Knight writes that Stein's post-*Autobiography* writer's "block, along with her lack of satisfaction in the fame she had achieved, started her thinking about the relationship between the writer and her audience."[67] Knight deems this shift in thought as the motivating factor behind her *Lectures in America* (1935); however, it is more importantly the case that Stein's thinking through her writer's block led her quite literally to the gates of Hollywood and to her musings on cinema's relationship to her writing. Stein's audience-related concerns were focused largely on the nature of the lecture circuit and her potential to cultivate a larger reading audience through her American talks. The American movie industry, as Stein recognized, had developed methods of distribution that commanded audiences of proportions unheard of with other artistic mediums.

It is therefore no surprise that in *Lectures in America* Stein repeatedly associates herself with movies, despite the fact that elsewhere she claimed little interest in them other than in her post-tour efforts to "be" in Hollywood. It also seems appropriate that Stein's emphasis on the cinematic logic of her literary practice would be presented to audiences in the country that dominated motion picture production.[68] Stein suggested that she and the cinema operated on similar formal principles, primarily upon the device of repetition. In the case of *The Autobiography of Alice B. Toklas*, Stein also relied upon the presentation of a star-studded cast: Picasso, Hemingway, Matisse, and the like. Although Stein drew on the success of *The Autobiography of Alice B. Toklas* to attract audiences to her lectures, she turned the tables on her audience's expectations during the American lectures. As James Mellow asserts, "if her listeners had expected intimate accounts of her friendships with modern painters, she disappointed them."[69] Stein instead used the lectures to introduce audiences already curious about her persona and her lifestyle (which they knew of via the *Autobiography*) to her "more important" unread works and to the literary theories that made her write the way she did. These lectures functioned like cinematic trailers, although instead of anticipating new releases they redirected the audience to already existing texts.

Elucidating her own methodology within these lectures, Stein links her techniques to the technological innovations that reinvented mobility in the early twentieth century: the automobile, the train, and most importantly the cinema. By writing herself into the apparatus of modernity through such deliberate linkages, Stein tries to assure her own position as literary innovator and ultra-modern. Seeing America as a symbol of progress, Stein situates herself at least symbolically within its borders and in relation to its advancements. In so doing, however, she also reveals the extent to which she relied upon technology, including that of the cinematic image, to express an understanding of her own literary style. Stein's descriptive strategies expose the process of her own mythmaking, for in these analogies we witness her attempts to express, assert, and even understand her own literary importance. By aligning herself with the cinema, she presages what later will become a desire to see cinema do something for her beyond the metaphorical connections she makes in the *Lectures*. In fact, without the aforementioned technological innovations, Stein would have been deprived of the vocabulary with which to express her intentions; she also would have lost an important connection to the most popular medium of the early twentieth century.

The cinematic metaphor employed by Stein demonstrates that, even before her pilgrimage to the United States, she acknowledged the potency of the medium. Likening her technique of "repetition with a difference" to individual frames of film, Stein insists on a similar effect of movement and progression in her own writing. In *Lectures in America* she explains,

> in the Making of Americans, I was doing what the cinema was doing, I was making a continuous succession of the statement of what that person was until I had not many things but one thing . . . I of course did not think of it in terms of the cinema, in fact I doubt whether at that time I had ever seen a cinema but, and I cannot repeat this too often any one is of one's period and this our period was undoubtedly the period of the cinema and series production.[70]

As she was becoming more aware of her potential audience and its cinematic predilections, Stein seemed eager to compare her work to the medium that was wooing the masses. Stein aligns herself here with the movie camera, suggesting a kind of verbal cinema that employs the formal methods of this visual medium. Her considerable forays into verbal portraiture attest to Stein's fascination with the relationships among sight, sound, and memory as functions of writing. Here, however, Stein does not position herself as analog to the human painter, but rather to the movie camera, suggesting that this effect had been dictated by the *cinematic moment* in history. The camera is capable of precisely capturing both space and time, an appealing idea for someone who claimed to be investigating the possibilities of containing such concepts in her own writing. Stein is forthcoming here about making such claims of similarity between her prose and the cinema in retrospect; however, her notion of simultaneity is still based upon the premise that this coincidence attests to her aptitude for enacting a literary expression of the modern age, one that is in sync with current tastes and trends.

Written for her lecture tour of the United States, Stein's musings on the cinema also suggest an awareness of her audience's familiarity with what was by then the most popular form of American entertainment. By the 1930s, movies and movie stars had become so much a part of America's popular cultural imagination that they had, in their brief existence since the turn of the century, become subject to scrutiny, criticism, and regulation. From the twelve-part Payne Fund Studies of the 1930s, which attempted to assess the ramifications of film-going on the American public, to the 1930 Motion Picture Production Code and the establishment of the Hays Office in 1934, the impact of film on its spectators was being recognized, theorized, and regulated. Definitions of art and entertainment were forever altered by the popularization of this medium, which by the economically catastrophic 1930s still managed to attract an impressive percentage of the population to its theaters on a regular basis.[71]

"If We Are Ever to Be in Hollywood" 157

This must not have escaped Stein's observant eye. In fact, Stein comments on the power of stars in her discussion of the twentieth-century novel during her "Transatlantic Interview." Here she explains that in the nineteenth century, "People really worried about and felt for these [novelistic] characters. Now, you see, even the cinema doesn't do it for them. A few actors or actresses do, but not the characters they portray."[72] Stein's assertion reflects both her own showcasing of personality and the stars' similar capacity for overshadowing their characters. Stein implies, and rightly so according to the logic of the Hollywood studios, that audiences came to films to see movie stars, not film characters. According to Stein's position, biography and publicity had overshadowed fiction. However, the movies were a potentially more effective conduit for presenting personalities to the public than other art forms. Stein's own *self*-promotion testifies to her belief in the preeminence of autobiography as *the* dominant fiction of the twentieth century. One need only look to Hollywood to affirm this; as stars became household names, the effectiveness of Hollywood's technologically and economically savvy deployment of its human product was undeniable.

Stein needed America, not just because it was her symbolic homeland and a "great nation," but also because its population embraced the importance of personality. Hollywood symbolized the nation's capacity for making reputations, albeit ones substantially different from the one Stein had created for herself. The movies made celebrities—not always, but consistently enough—precisely because films could be reproduced and distributed to a virtually limitless audience; this is a notion that resonated for Stein, who sought the means by which to substantially increase her own audience. Coming to America and traversing it in person was Stein's most aggressive act of self-distribution, a move that Charles Caramello describes as her understanding that "she might have to publish her person in order to publish her work, since her celebrity status, for better or for worse, can be used to provoke interest in her as an artist."[73] Like the film prints that made their way through the movie theater circuit, Stein distributed herself through her lectures. But Stein also realized that the exhausting work of a lecture tour was more tedious and less profitable than the production of a single reproducible cinematic event that could do the laborious footwork for her. As Stein wrote to Van Vechten in a letter postmarked February 15, 1940, regarding a second tour of the United States, "I am not at all sure I would like lecturing, that is in any large quantity, I would like to go over but to lecture three or four times a week for a number of weeks does not really seem to me as if I would like it."[74] The only way out of the financial necessity of lecturing would be through a profitable deal with Hollywood.

But the idea of being cinematically captured and distributed was not entirely pleasing to Stein, despite the numerous letters indicating that she *must* play herself in a Hollywood movie. As she reports in *Everybody's Autobiography* after seeing newsreel footage of herself reading "Pigeons on the Grass": "and when I saw myself almost as large and moving around and talking I did not like it particularly the talking."[75] The newsreel footage is not, of course, an instance of Stein *playing* herself; this is Stein *being* herself. However, one of Stein's most modern attributes was her capacity to play herself, both on the page and in person, again pointing to her conflicting ideas about self-promotion and exploitation. Stein's uncanny reaction is also notable because she reports the flipside of this discomfort, noting that the newsreel was "given in the cinema theaters everywhere and everybody said everybody liked it."[76] Acknowledging both the power of film to reach mass audiences and its ability to produce confusing reflections in the filmed subject, Stein temporarily expresses distaste for the medium. But Stein's conclusion has less to do with her reaction to the medium than with others' reactions, for the newsreel's circulation—its ability to reach "everybody" (though this is less literal than Steinean)—is what most impressed the author.

The relationship between Stein's writing and the cinema is even more complex given her efforts to link herself to a medium to which she professed an indifference. Kenneth O'Hara, a reporter for the *Los Angeles Times*, was among the media representatives awaiting Stein's arrival in Los Angeles during her lecture tour. He asked the author if she was eager to see Hollywood during her tour. "Yes—and—no!" she replied, hardly an assured response. As he wrote under the headline "Doesn't Care for Films": "the films have never interested her."[77] "When they became so solemn," Stein clarified with her particular knack for turning a response into a riddle, "I lost interest."[78] Though the films themselves may have left no great impression upon Stein, the apparatus of the film industry appealed to her sensibilities. Further explaining to the *Times* author the way that "the movement of her time forced" her writing upon her, Stein articulates a concept of being "of one's period" that suggests simultaneity and spontaneity, a move Stein was apt to make given her ardent desire to be so "of one's period" as to define it. The cultural phenomenon of the motion picture industry is notable not only for its introduction of a new form of entertainment, but as a reorganization of perception and a realignment of sensory experiences.

Stein insisted on connections between the movies and her writing, using the formal properties of film to justify and explain her use of repetition, especially in her literary portraits (of Picasso and Matisse, for example): "Funnily enough the cinema has offered a solution of this thing. By a continuously moving picture of any one there is no memory of any other thing and there is that thing existing, it is in a way if you like one portrait of anything not a number of them."[79] While Stein's logic might be sloppy, it is also a manifestation of her curious determination to promote formal experimentation as a modern form of entertainment, regardless of comprehensibility. For Stein, both the cinema and her writing bear the mark of modernity, and this matters more than a consideration of their real differences. Stein figures repetition (of images, of landscape, of herself) as progression, for "in a cinema picture not two pictures are exactly alike each one is just that much different from the one before, and so in those early portraits there was as I am sure you will realize as I read them to you also as there was in The Making of Americans no repetition."[80] According to Stein, the end-effect of such reconfiguration is not stasis, as some may perceive upon reading her works, but rather the sought-after condition of mobility. Stein observes, "It is not repetition if it is that which you are actually doing because naturally each time the emphasis is different just as the cinema has each time a slightly different thing to make it all be moving."[81]

When considered alongside her thoughts of Hollywood success, Stein's insistence that her work is comparable to the cinema also indicates her own desire for a level of comprehension and popularity that was simply impossible given the very real differences between the difficult nature of her prose and the accessible nature of Hollywood film. So while formal and even theoretical similarities are indisputable, there is no real comparison here between her writing and the movies, and Stein appears to be perfectly happy professing no realization of this. When Stein arrived in Los Angeles on March 28, 1935, for her four-night stay at the Hotel Vista Del Arroyo in Pasadena during the lecture tour, she continued to perpetuate stylistic comparisons between her writing and the movies even outside of her lecture environs. "I don't repeat myself any more than the cinema does," she reported in the front-page *Los Angeles Times* interview.[82] Both accurate and misleading, as any veteran Stein reader knows, Stein was nearing the end of her tour and felt little need to justify this idea further. In fact, Stein rarely felt obliged to explain herself comprehensibly. Now in close proximity to the actual locus of cinematic production, Stein seemed even more intent upon celebrating the naturalness of her connections to cinema: "But, nevertheless, the cinema movement is analogous to succession. It is the spirit of the age."[83] Throughout her career, Stein claimed that only she could truly capture and write the spirit of the age (it was Picasso who could capture the Zeitgeist on canvas), and here she again links herself to the language and cultural significance of movies. Such analogizing is not at all surprising, however, given Hollywood's mastery over that which Stein most ardently desired: a massive captive audience.

Stein grapples with this idea of audience over the duration of her career. When asked at the end of her "Transatlantic Interview" why she published things that were written for herself and not for an audience (something Stein was apt to claim in her writing and in interviews), she replied with unusual clarity: "There is the eternal vanity of the mind. One wants to see one's children in the world and have them admired like any fond parent, and it is a bitter blow to have them refused or mocked . . . Anything you create you want to exist, and its means of existence is in being printed."[84] Stein seems to be speaking equally here of her writing and of her reputation as that thing she created and wanted to exist and live on in the American popular imagination, however much she refuses to articulate a vision that goes beyond the literary. The dissatisfaction expressed here suggests Stein's own perceived failure in the manufacturing of her fame and, as we shall see, of her aborted transportation to Hollywood.

"Nothing May Come of It All": Putting Stein on the Map in Hollywood

The first recorded mention of a movie deal originated not, as one might expect, with Stein or Toklas, but with Lillian Ehrman, who had hosted Stein's Hollywood party. On July 27, 1935, Carl Van Vechten forwarded a letter from Ehrman in which she suggests that *The Gentle Lena* section from *Three Lives*, which was about an unhappy, arranged marriage between a German servant girl and a tailor, be sold to a film studio. Van Vechten responded, "Why didn't somebody think of this before? . . . So you may be going to Hollywood to film The Good [*sic*] Lena!"[85]

Stein's noticeably immediate response, postmarked August 7, 1935, was that "It will make us most happy to have the Gentle Lena in the films most most happy . . . my it will be nice seeing you again and the film will help."[86] In September of 1935, she wrote to Van Vechten that "I have signed the agreement with Mrs. Ehrman's brother," Ivan Kahn, who would act on her behalf marketing *The Gentle Lena* to the studios. "It would be nice if it came off," Stein concluded, casually optimistic that it would.[87] A month later, Stein reported to Van Vechten that she "just had a letter from Kahn at Hol[l]ywood, he is trying the Paramount for the gentle Lena, and is to let me know, we do hope and hope so, it would be lots of fun."[88] While Stein sounds nonchalant about the possibilities of selling her work to get to Hollywood, she would not remain so blasé. Stein's insouciant tone was typical of her mid-1930s letters, which muse lightheartedly about a leisurely life in the motion picture capital, about getting paid for doing nothing. By the end of the 1930s, however, her correspondence took on a more dramatic air, one of guarded despondence if not outright desperation, and with good reason.

Like many Americans who were drawn to movies during both world wars to escape from the realities of war (if only for a few hours), Stein viewed Hollywood as a potential escape from both from the real war that she had so vehemently disavowed and from her more personal battle with success. Settling back into France after her lecture tour, Stein began writing letters regarding the possibility of returning not just to America as someone in the lecturing and literary business, but more specifically to Hollywood as someone in the movie business. Setting her devotees into action, Stein's letter campaign to get to Hollywood seemed nearly successful. But as her enthusiasm was met repeatedly with failure, her playful optimism dwindled. As an unpublished and undated letter written to Mrs. Ehrman on Stein's Bilignin stationary indicates,

I am afraid there is no longer any hope of the Gentle Lena. I often wonder if a film could not be made of the Autobiography of Alice B. Toklas, have you or your brother ever thought of that, I would be very pleased to come out to Hollywood if there was any proposition made to me that was of interest, this is something I have long had in mind.[89]

Stein is not being whimsical or hyperbolic here; rather, this is an unusually sincere missive that indicates a long-term interest in getting to Hollywood. Stein's Hollywood dreams display her hopeful ideas about the value of her reputation, and about the relative economies of literary and cinematic production. These observations are especially important because they illuminate the far-reaching shift toward a cinematically oriented conception of self-representation and publicity.

In a letter to Thornton Wilder (who had himself made several somewhat reluctant forays to Hollywood in an effort to make money) postmarked July 8, 1936, Stein schemes of getting to Hollywood in a way that suggests she had bought into the city's mythology:

I do not know what makes lovely films but that [the *Autobiography of Alice B. Toklas*] might and they could shoot the background here and in Paris and we could be taken in Hollywood including the puppies Basket and Pepe and we would have enough money to make a leisurely trip across the continent and the Mississippi valley taking on a college boy for the more difficult driving and then we could have an installation in Washington Square and go to and fro for ever . . . I'd love you to put us on the Hollywood map, but don't think about it twice only perhaps there is something in it.[90]

Quickly dispensing with the reunion banter, Stein imagines a future for herself that relies upon the financial gains that could be imagined only through a deal with Hollywood. Being put "on the Hollywood map" makes literal Stein's cartographies of fame; it is not just lecturing in America but being "taken in Hollywood" that is appealing. However, Hollywood exists as an embodiment of a metaphor here since making a "lovely" film is figured as Stein's ticket to mobility across the American landscape. Stein infers that Hollywood would enable her to live her own lifestyle unbounded by the restraints of economy and the relative isolation of expatriatism. One might argue that Hollywood exists *only* as a metaphor for Stein, for her understanding of it is so removed from even the fantastic nature of the city itself. As a conceit, Hollywood's presence in Stein's writing establishes both her interest in her own success and the degree to which success of this nature required a connection to Hollywood.

Hollywood recurs throughout Stein's 1930s and early 1940s correspondences. In a March 19, 1940, letter from Van Vechten, he notes that he,

talked to Bennet [Cerf] about the motion picture possibilities of The Autobiography which are ENORMOUS, but motion picture people are peculiar. You can't approach *them*. They must approach *you*. I think the time to take this up is when you are lecturing in Hollywood. Of course you both would have to appear in the picture. Even Greta Garbo and Lillian Gish couldn't be you and Alice. I can't wait for this! It will be wonderful![91]

Although Stein did not want to take up the lecture circuit again, Van Vechten suggests something that Stein was already familiar with: that only with her presence could she be considered, remembered, celebrated. In other words, Van Vechten's suggestion that Stein come to Hollywood to play herself forces the issue of Stein's more general need to return to America. This statement also suggests that Van Vechten, too, understood the unparalleled value of cinematic success.

This insistence on self-representation brings us full circle back to the idea with which this chapter began—that Stein possessed a certain cultural currency that might be leveraged in Hollywood. Stein's image was well known through newsreel footage, pictures, and cartoon parodies of her that appeared in the newspaper, and the various artistic representations of her such as Picasso's famous portrait, made legendary in part through Stein's repeated invocations of it in print and in lectures. The 1933 issue of *Time* magazine, with a cover image of Stein in profile, further contributed to this image dispersion, the article opining that, "If posterity understands present-day art, it is likely that the future will have a pretty good idea what Gertrude Stein looked like. Picasso has painted her, Picabia has drawn her, Jo Davidson has done a joss-like statue of her."[92] In other words, Stein's image already had been distributed through various media; but, as Van Vechten implies, a feature film starring Stein as herself would greatly elevate her position in America's cultural economy.

At issue here is also the concept of authenticity: Van Vechten implies that even Hollywood cannot adequately represent Stein. In Van Vechten's proposition, Stein would not be an actress; she would be herself. His words assure the author that she has a kind of exclusive right to her own image; that to have an actress (Garbo, no less!) pretend to be her would simply never work for precisely the reason of authenticity. Gertrude Stein is Gertrude Stein; Greta Garbo is not. Van Vechten's words, perhaps unwittingly, seem to reinforce Stein's fears regarding the cultural value assigned to her work versus that assigned to her image. In this way, Van Vechten intervenes in Stein's Hollywood fantasies to provide evidence once again to the author that she, and not her writing, is the sought after spectacle.

Stein's persona overwhelmed the kind of fiction favored by the motion picture industry in a fashion incompatible with the nature of its star system. Although we are, of course, speaking of this in the abstract, since Stein never had the opportunity to play herself outside of the newsreel footage of her, there is good sense in what Van Vechten detects as a necessity for self-representation. Virtually since its inception, Hollywood has displayed a knack for transformation, for turning "ordinary" people into characters and stars, and thereby making them over anew, at least temporarily; Clara Bow's career is testament to this. Stein's situation, however, necessitates a different understanding of the purpose of Hollywood, one with more ties to Wyatt Earp's generation of aspirants than to her own. Stein had earned a right to her own image and the public knew her more than it knew her writing. Unlike William Faulkner, F. Scott Fitzgerald, or Thornton Wilder—whose literary renown and names were bought by the industry, and who were not on-screen commodities *per se*—Stein could not generate the same stamp of textual reliability and interest, though she might be marketable in other, *more visible* ways.

Stein had made for herself a kind of celebrity that was different from virtually any other literary figure contemporary to her: She was an author famous for writing that which went largely unread. Stein pursued Hollywood, but she possessed little literary currency with which to generate a response in the form of a contract for writing scenarios or purchasing existing works; her value resided almost entirely in her image. Just two months after Van Vechten's "don't call them, they'll call you" letter, Stein echoes Van Vechten's personification of Hollywood in a pleading letter to Thornton Wilder in May 1940:

> I told you several people are trying to make somebody make a movie of the Auto of Alice B, it might be fun to go over to help them do that if you see anybody who might want to ask to do it you might get them to want to ask, I understand Hollywood is never suggested to, they must have the idea themselves, I think I would rather do that than lectures, after a winter of radio, lecture seems rather a dismal business.[93]

First and foremost, this letter illustrates an unusual acknowledgment on Stein's part that the role of spectacle might be a desirable one. The business of words (here radio), she suggests, is a strain in a way that the business of images might not be. This letter demonstrates not only Stein's wholehearted belief in Van Vechten's authority on the nature of Hollywood, since she reiterates his personification almost verbatim, but also that she was becoming more aggressive about her desire for others to act on her behalf in this venture. With England declaring war just a few months prior to this letter, it is understandable that Stein would feel an urgency about mobilizing her own plans for redirecting her and Alice's future; this despite the fact that she and Alice were given several opportunities to flee France and the couple opted to stay. Still playing the role of the director, Stein encourages her friends to prod Hollywood into action. Hollywood appears here as the entity upon which Stein's future prosperity and happiness, as well as her safety, depends.

Stein's acknowledgment that she was uninterested in lecturing also suggests that the stakes of her Hollywood ambitions had changed. For as *Everybody's Autobiography* and *The Lectures in America* repeatedly evidence, lecturing allowed Stein at least the chance to pique an audience's interest in her writing where previously they might have only cared about her personality. Abandoning the lecture circuit meant also neglecting the explanation of her works in the one forum in which she could stand before her readers and wittily defend that work in the process of persuading audience members to become readers. But Stein also appeared to be growing more comfortable with the idea of herself as spectacle, embracing that which had seemed problematic earlier in her career but which seemed practical now, perhaps even necessary.

Stein's financial situation during this period not only rekindled her desire for Hollywood and the apparent ease of life there; it was, perhaps more importantly, a way to legitimate her consideration of Hollywood, since success seemed so often to represent compromise and betrayal in Stein's ideology. In a letter received by Thornton Wilder on September 10, 1936, Stein ponders that if she cannot "make money there [Hollywood] I may be driven to do a cigarette advertisement they have just asked me, we will like to travel around and not lecture, can't Hollywood do something about it, someone once dreamed of doing the Gentle Lena there but I never did quite see that."[94] There is regret in this letter about Hollywood's inaction as well as the suggestion that Stein had pressing economic motivations. Becoming commercial, either through book sales, lecture tours, product endorsements, or Hollywood contracts, was taking on a patina of urgency. So long a noncommercially successful writer, then getting a break with *The Autobiography of Alice B. Toklas*, it is no wonder that Stein seems willing to compromise a bit by "going commercial" in order to live a life less bounded by financial and geographical restraints. Returning to America is at once a fantasy and a surprisingly sensible venture, something that Stein, in her relentless impracticality, realized.

To Van Vechten, in a letter postmarked February 15, 1940, Stein casually reinforces the economic necessities of her sojourn while still investing Hollywood with a kind of fantasy weight that recurs in her representation of this mythical city:

of course we cannot go over without making money and there it is, I dream that Hollywood might do the Autobiography of Alice Toklas, they could make a very good film out of that and then they would pay us large moneys to go out and sit and consult and that would be all new and I would like that and once over there I could lecture or not as I liked . . . it is just a dream, I would love so to be in America when they are electing a president.[95]

Stein's insistence on the dream-like nature of this venture is consistent with the fact that her vision of Hollywood is often one virtually devoid of labor. Stein frequently imagines her Hollywood experience as financially liberating, while this accumulation is totally reliant on doing as little as possible in exchange. The persistence of the themes of sitting and getting paid run throughout these letters and Stein is so seemingly invested in this idea of easy Hollywood luxury as to appear, at least on the surface, to abandon her previous devotion to her literary works. The appeal of the "new" here reaffirms Stein's willingness to abandon her dogged literary ways of the past in favor of a newly liberated version of herself, one that cares more for the freedom to frolic in the wasteland of American culture than to make a serious literary contribution.

Stein further constructs the potential filming of the *Autobiography* in terms that go beyond economic success by imagining the transportation of her Paris salon guests and *coterie* to Hollywood. In a letter from Stein to Van Vechten postmarked April 1940, she explains that, "they seem to think that Alice B. might be done in Hollywood, perhaps we all could go out and act in it all that are spoken of in the book I think it would be fun to have Papa Woojums and all."[96] Van Vechten's response, dated April 23, 1940, is equally infused with delightfully naive optimism: "The Autobiography in the Cinema would be MARVELOUS, with everybody playing his own part! Hollywood would be AGOG."[97] The egotism of these letters is notable, especially since Stein seems to advocate the transportation of her own star system, which, of course, revolved around her. The mass expatriate mobilization Stein imagines is a reinvention of Hollywood predicated entirely on Stein's terms. The notion of literally transporting Stein's salon and its guests to make a Hollywood movie may sound a bit like a modernist sitcom, but it reflects the dissonance between Stein's isolated sense of celebrity (wherein she is both unchallenged director and star) and Hollywood's version of the same. Although this cast of characters never collectively made it to Hollywood to see the *Autobiography* made into a film, Stein's suggestion resonates with the implied value of authentic literary and artistic personalities. As Stein says, "it is just a dream."

Stein's enthusiasm over this aspect of the venture—of transporting her salon to Hollywood in order to then capture her universe on-screen—also reveals the degree to which she desired the insular support of this extended family. As she reports in an earlier letter to Van Vechten postmarked October 16, 1937, a Hollywood venture might enable Stein to reconstruct not only her expatriate family but, more importantly it seems, her "Woojums family" (as she referred to herself, Toklas, and Van Vechten):

I am awfully happy that you liked Daniel Webster, I have a dream of its being done in Hollywood . . . it would be lots of fun, and give us an xcuse to go to America, to put it on, and it might be a great success, because and this is what because Papa Woojums could tell them just what to do to make it do really something, you see that's what I dream of if you did it, and I think all of us together out there could have a wonderful time and do something, is there any producer, I could write to out there and tell him he ought to have us, you know Carl I do think we could do something there together, I get quite thrilled about it, . . . and I think it would be wonderful if all the Woojums together did Daniel Webster.[98]

The trope of the excuse emerges once again in this letter, suggesting that Hollywood could facilitate both Stein's geographical movement and the reunion of her "family." There is also a wonderful slippage in this letter that robs it of the otherwise stagy reliance upon hyperbole and juvenilia that predominates these exchanges: Stein refers to Van Vechten here not just as Papa Woojums, her playful nickname for him, but as Carl. This dropping of the jovial linguistic game-playing gives Stein's plotting here a particular air of gravity. For all of the irony or humor that might be present in her letters on this subject, there is a thread of earnestness that suggests the sincerity of Stein's ambitions beneath the playful surface. Perhaps Stein adopted this facetious tone because it seemed consistent with the desire for praise that she was loathe to admit; she was certainly aware of the self-centeredness of her Hollywood ideas, articulated, as they often were, like a child's plans to play house with her friends in order to allay her own insecurities with regard to this venture and her investment in its realization.

Stein is fishing with this ever-changing series of potential movies based upon her works—*Three Lives*, *The Autobiography*, *The World Is Round*—waiting for someone in Hollywood to take the bait. Her indiscriminateness indicates the author's reconceptualization of her literary, economic, and geographical ambitions. Stein seemed willing to rethink the very nature of her reputation despite what might be at stake if she changed the trajectory of her career, all in reaction to the model created by and in Hollywood. Like Jack London, who sought to extend the lives of his literary works through the cinema, Stein approached the marketplace during these years with a seemingly cold, economic attitude toward the products of her labor. Her hesitancies and inconsistencies further suggest that while she knew she was being overly eager by (repeatedly) stooping as "low" as Hollywood, by affecting the pose of sitting around and waiting for someone else to negotiate a deal, she might distance herself somewhat from the debasement. After 1940, Stein seems largely to abandon her enthusiasm and effort for this venture, but in the years prior she repeats her queries in a fashion that reveals a surprising willingness to investigate and invest in the Hollywood system.

Throughout her writing and her letters, Stein equates repetition with movement. Stein's repetition of her dream of being taken in by Hollywood, however, resulted in little more than spilled ink. Relying largely on the actions of others—in part, it appears, because Stein's physical removal from America impeded her own intervention, but also because such distancing was safer, one suspects, for both ego and reputation—Stein's repetition of the Hollywood fantasy produced neither the movement she sought in her own writings nor the movement she evinced in her theories of series production and film. Living in France both before and during the Second World War, Stein's vague desire to "do something" was thwarted by her own inability to produce something desired by Hollywood; or, conversely, to produce desire in Hollywood for what she already had produced; or finally, to produce herself in Hollywood.

In the final analysis, Stein's disappointment is not surprising, for besides *The Autobiography of Alice B. Toklas* and *Three Lives*, her work had limited cinematic potential, despite the presumably incorrect report made by *Time* in 1938 that "in Paris, Gertrude Stein sold her first movie scenario ('Really good—an old-fashioned melodrama')."[99] Although the cab driver encountered by Rogers, alluded to in the epigraph to this chapter, thought that he would wait for a comprehensible cinematic version of Stein's writings, such a product is virtually impossible to imagine. Stein's prose, like her film scripts, would have generated laughter from any studio executive considering making a commercially viable film, hence the comic references in popular culture that replicated only the basest sense of Stein's literary experimentation. And while Stein herself may have captivated an American audience, she was undoubtedly no Greta Garbo. She did try her hand at scripting a film; however, the Steinean nature of something like "Film Deux Soeurs Qui Ne Sont Pas Soeurs"—written in 1929 in French and consisting of one page of action featuring the surprising cast of two ladies, their car, and their poodle—makes it difficult to take seriously in the context of any kind of Hollywood production.[100] The screenplay is ridiculous when considered as a screenplay; but it is exceptional for the fact that as early as 1929 Stein considered herself the best subject for cinematic production.

Hollywood thus loomed as a missed opportunity over Stein's later career. Her reluctant optimism about "making it" indicates both her desire for a future other than that which lay before her, and also the prevailing status of Hollywood as a site for such fantasies of success. Although the populist Jack London may have forged an authorial path to Hollywood, the avant-garde Gertrude Stein's interest in following this path suggests an even greater potency of the film industry and its relationship to modern notions of success. In a letter to Thornton Wilder postmarked October 10, 1936, Stein states, "of all sad words of tongue or pen, the saddest are these it might have been, it is sad, [rê the fact that Hollywood did not call this year] it would have been so nice to see the money nice and almost necessary."[101] The necessity Stein expresses in this letter is ambiguous, though it rests on the financial promises that consistently undergird her articulation of the dream. We know that Stein wanted the monetary success of her Hollywood counterparts. On the other hand, it is her unspoken willingness to become image, a tendency with roots in her literature; to become the spectacle that her "audience" already assumed that she was; and, ultimately, to profit from her celebrity status in a media-driven age, that helped to foster Stein's unrealized ambition to return to America and forge connections with Hollywood.

6

Redirecting Reputation

IDA LUPINO'S HOLLYWOOD FICTIONS

More than with "the star" him or herself, this book has concerned itself with the way that Hollywood became a site for re-imagining identities in the twentieth century; with the way concepts of ambition, reputation, and success were reconceived and reshaped in reaction to the motion picture industry; and with the ways that individuals tried to work with the motion picture industry, often on their own terms. Jack London's and Wyatt Earp's desires, with which the book opened, evince an awareness of the moving image's central role in the lives and ambitions of public figures. Earp hoped to take hold of his publicity and cinematically solidify his role in the shaping of the West, while London worked to ensure his currency in a cinematic age. Bow and Stein, though coming at it from radically different directions, both hoped for something more closely approximating our current understanding of stardom: Bow emerging from fandom into a media swirl of publicity and scandal, and Stein emerging from popular neglect with the hopes of reinventing herself as an authorial celebrity flush with the spoils of stardom.

Our current chapter shifts gears once again to consider the complexity of celebrity and its uses, here by Ida Lupino, who tried to remove herself from her spectacularized star position only to find that the new role she sought to play, as a female director, required at least as much acting, if not more. Where the subjects of the previous chapters wanted to create, cement, or exploit their reputations, and to reap the subsequent rewards, Lupino sought to redefine hers in an unconventional and even riskier fashion. Finding herself caught up in the tangle of Hollywood's—and, to a certain extent, the nation's—gendered politics, the feminized and often apparently self-punitive role that Lupino played in this remaking of her career suggests a representational strategy unique to this study: In order to become a pioneering (however much she refused to acknowledge it as such) directorial figure, she used the media and her own films to publicly dramatize her treading into what was widely understood as male territory.

Lupino began her American acting career after being brought to Hollywood from England by Paramount, but she never wanted the kind of long-term security—with its contingent lack of liberty—desired by most actresses.[1] As an actress Lupino typically played, and often fought for, strong roles; Annette Kuhn describes her screen presence as "the brittle, alone-in-the-world moll, outwardly tough and cynical."[2] She signed a contract at Warner Bros. during Bette Davis's reign and frequently was left with the notoriously tempestuous actress's leftover roles. As her biographer William Donati observes, Lupino was positioned to take the roles that Davis rejected so that their number one strong-willed actress's refusals didn't impact the studio's production schedule so devastatingly; little did Jack Warner know that in Lupino he had another resolute personality on his hands. Soon after coming under contract with Warner Bros., Lupino began refusing roles and getting suspended by the studio; she continued to reject projects she felt were inappropriate, leading to periods of studio suspension for refusing roles that she deemed "beneath her dignity as an actress."[3] As Lupino explained to Gladwin Hill in a 1951 *Colliers'* article, "I got tired . . . of always being a coy thing lounging in a boat, listening to someone sing romantic songs—even at $1,750 a week."[4] Dissatisfied with her choices as a contract actress, Lupino decided to mutually dissolve her Warner Bros. commitment; a 1941 *Picturegoer* magazine reported that "she gave up a contract at $1,700 a week rather than play in unsuitable stories."[5] From the beginning, hers was a directorial impulse, even in relation to her attempts to control her own reputation as an actress.

Lupino starred in more than fifty studio films; however, it is her comparatively brief cinematic directorial career that is of interest here, not only because of its rarity but because as a director Lupino took the greatest risks to realize her unconventional ambitions.[6] After cinema's early years of female participation in all areas of film production, women gradually disappeared from the roles of director and producer as the industry took on its corporate shape in the late nineteen-teens and twenties.[7] A November 1925 column in *Motion Picture Magazine* entitled, "Why Are There No Women Directors?" observes that "the invasion of motion pictures by women has been complete except for one last remaining citadel. There are no women directors who are helping make motion picture history."[8] Noting the prior successes of Ida May Park, Mary Jane Wilson, and Lois Weber, the piece concludes that women "fail to qualify" as directors because directing requires "physical strength": "The strain of picture production usually wears out the strongest man in a few years . . . It would have to be a superwoman to stand up under the strain."[9] Such discourse had not disappeared by the time that Lupino entered the fray in the late 1940s; with the exception of Dorothy Arzner, the American studio system had successfully codified directing as a male profession.[10]

Lupino, who hailed from a long line of professional entertainers, appears to have embraced her own highly theatrical fabrication of self to the public in a fashion that was compatible with the industry's penchant for dramatic characterization. Aiding her navigation of the thorny Hollywood hierarchy, Lupino publicly cast herself in a role of canny feminine submission, feeding the fan magazines with stories that played up her anomalous position as a "woman director" instead of trying to conceal the challenges she faced. In interviews, she claimed that it was an "act" to behave "like a man" or, implicitly, "like a woman," indicating the highly performative yet contradictory nature of her role as woman director. As she put it,

well, I don't act like a man. My way of asking a man to do something on a set is not to boss him around. That isn't in me to do that . . . Listen, if a woman came to you and said, "Honey, gee, I don't know what to do. We've finished this and I'm not quite sure whether we should send it down or what grain I should use. I'd like to do this, but, well, what do you think?" You'd want to help me, wouldn't you? Well, all right.[11]

Read cagily, Lupino's language plays with male notions of superiority in a mocking, almost confrontational fashion. But such statements—and there are many others that offer this same self-deprecating posture—are also frustratingly ambiguous. Lupino appears at once pandering and manipulative, passive yet subversive. It is worth remembering that Lupino's comments, like Dorothy Arzner's before her, do not simply reflect the director's thoughts and feelings; they are a product of publicity departments and protocols, and indicate the kind of story-telling favored by movie industry publications and the popular press in general.[12] These discourses repeatedly link success with the ability to be authoritative and commanding, suggesting that "proper" female behavior guarantees failure for women in "male areas" of the public sector. It is this troubling, essentializing paradox that Lupino engages with, perhaps equally motivated by her own conflicted feelings as by the need for publicity to promote her new career. Lupino's writing on the subject proclaimed that, "I hate women who order men around—professionally or personally. I think it is horrible in business or in the home . . . I wouldn't dare do that with my old man."[13] Coming from the mouth of a director, the statement baffles. But there is a playfulness here that undercuts the initial conservatism of the statement. Lupino's invocations of her domestic and private behavior repeatedly emphasize femininity, wifehood, and motherhood *despite* her profession.

J. Robert Moskin's 1958 essay, "Why Do Women Dominate Him?" reminds us of the most reactionary concerns circulating in the post–World War II era. Like the post-war era prior to it, women were encouraged—at least by some—to believe in an ideal of domestic womanhood. A kind of next generation Philip Wylie, Moskin writes that:

> Scientists who study human behavior fear that the American male is now dominated by the American female. These scientists worry that in the years since the end of World War II, he has changed radically and dangerously; that he is no longer the masculine, strong-minded man who pioneered the continent and built America's greatness . . . And the experts pin most of the blame for his new plight squarely on women.[14]

Although Moskin is concerned specifically with the fate of men and masculinity, women and femininity are to blame for the denigration of male strength. Such accusations of cultural feminization were hardly unique to the 1950s; however, the implication of danger here is unusually alarmist. It is also resonant with the fervent anti-communist hysteria with which it co-existed.

Moskin even suggests that the history of the modern world has, in essence, been anti-male, leading progressively, but not irremediably, toward effeminization:

> During World War I, the American woman was called on to do men's work, and the door was opened wide to "emancipation." In the twenties, she "went on a rampage," and in a roaring, flaming decade, jobs for women, "free love," feminine contraception and women's suffrage became fair play. Finally, the great depression gave women an economic excuse to introduce their husbands to dirty dishes and diapers. They became "partners."[15]

Moskin's is just one voice in a sea of concerns—certainly not all this disparaging—about the ways in which women's and men's roles were changing, in part because women were making inroads into previously male domains. "Partnership" here is a dirty word, and we see Lupino reacting directly to this very concept of spousal partnership in *The Bigamist*, a film examined in this chapter. The *Hollywood Citizen-News* explains matters in a less reactionary but similarly concerned tone under a first-page photograph of Lupino in the act of giving directions to her film editor: "Hollywood has succumbed to the modern woman. The ladies, who formerly were content to parade in front of the cameras, have now taken over many of the chores behind the lenses—script writing, producing, and even directing—which formerly were considered strictly male prerogatives."[16]

Although writers like Moskin do not reflect mainstream thinking, they seem to articulate best—perhaps because they are so vehement and uncomplicated in their approach—the type of criticism that inspired the kinds of responses that we encounter in Lupino's publicity. In her reevaluation of Betty Friedan's conclusions in *The Feminine Mystique* (1963), Joanne Meyerowitz points out that post-war antifeminist writers, who "promoted domesticity as a woman's only road to fulfillment," were in the minority—"at the conservative margin rather than at the center"—at least in her journalistic sampling.[17] However, Meyerowitz also affirms the degree to which most women's mass-circulation magazines emphasized "femininity and domesticity" by describing "their successful subjects as pretty, motherly, shapely, happily married, petite, charming, or soft voiced," in an attempt to avert implications of "lesbian, mannish, or man-hating women."[18] Lupino's publicity strategy, then, reminds us precisely of the ways that such public negotiations "helped to legitimate women's public achievements," to borrow Meyerowitz's terming of the ways that "authors attempted to reassure readers that conventional gender distinctions and heterosexuality remained intact even as women competed successfully in work, politics, or sports."[19] Lupino's reputational redirection, then, mirrors the strategies of many authors writing about public women in the mass-circulation periodicals of the era.

Lupino's ambitions in the field of direction were, one the one hand, at best territorially invasive and at worst destabilizing to the allegedly fragile gender divisions in America. However, they were also very much in line with the aspirations of many women who sought out public careers but who also felt compelled to situate—or, perhaps, were compelled to situate—these careers in relation to their domestic lives. Lupino's publicly expressed concerns about making these same inroads are thus in line with the gender drama of the nation; in fact, her articulation of these anxieties is a virtual narration of these tensions between work and home, professionalism and domesticity. Lupino dramatizes a need to both direct and to be directed—the former as a condition of her profession, the latter as a condition of her gender. By publicly reconciling her professional aspirations with her social responsibility as a woman, Lupino appeared to be trying not to be the kind of woman "squarely" pinned with the blame for "male domination," even though all outward signs based upon her professional role would indicate that she was.

FIGURE 23: Articles about Lupino illustrate the tension between being a hardworking professional woman doing what was considered a man's job while still embodying, as this article phrases it, "the essence of femininity" expected of a 1950s woman, wife, and mother. *Colliers*, 1951. *Collection of the author.*

Lupino is an interesting test case for understanding an individual's attempt to use the film industry to manage and recreate reputation. Working both in front of the camera and behind it, Lupino's cinematic tenure can be understood as a varied and complex attempt to control both image and image reception. Unlike Clara Bow before her, Lupino appears to have possessed a real awareness of the way the female image, in particular, was consumed in the cinematic aftermarket, seeming at times to fight against Hollywood's attempts to package her incorrectly, and at others to make of herself something palatable to the public. Lupino stepped behind the camera to control the production of those her lens captured, while also preemptively shaping her new reputation as Hollywood's woman director. By adamantly reiterating the importance of her femininity in the publicity surrounding this career move, Lupino created a very specific discourse to justify her occupation. She also allegorized these aforementioned gender-territory concerns, consciously to one degree or another, in her films, which are almost always about people struggling over their own issues of image-making and particularly about women whose ambitions threaten their own and their families' happiness.

Projecting a Public Persona

Although suffering significant legal and economic setbacks in the late 1940s and early 1950s, which ultimately would lead to the deterioration of the studio system, Hollywood remained a powerful presence in the popular imagination: stars appeared to have enviable wealth and power, although they often seemed personally paralyzed by their fans as well as their studios. Lupino experienced this lifestyle and its complications firsthand as a contract studio actress. Her distaste for the spotlight and for the spectacle of stardom—the private person as public property—was hardly unique. Robert Aldrich, director of several thrillers about the pathological symptoms bred by Hollywood, often cast the industry in a gothic light that seems in some ways to mirror Lupino's aversion, suggesting that Hollywood was inhabited by tragic star-victims in films like *The Big Knife* (1955) and *Whatever Happened to Baby Jane?* (1962). In the former, movie star Charlie Castle (Jack Palance) battles with his demonic studio boss (Rod Steiger) to get out of his contract in order to rebuild his personal life with wife Marion, played by none other than Ida Lupino. Charlie's eventual suicide provides a bleak and surprisingly candid expression of the despair of the studio-bound actor, at once star of and slave to the system. For Aldrich, it seems, everything about this system was conducive to such pessimistic and destructive conclusions.

While Charlie cannot bring himself to break from his studio because of his own secret—a hit-and-run murder covered up by the studio, a form of deceit not unheard of during Hollywood's heyday—Marion insists upon a life outside of the madness of Hollywood. As a symbol of "normal" domesticity, Marion's desire to escape the unreal demands of the life imposed upon Charlie by the studio seems especially poignant given the subject of this chapter. Without being overly dramatic, it is fair to say that Lupino's dilemmas share a kinship with the metaphor of the inescapable gothic castle that Aldrich implied was the domain of the Hollywood star. Like the fictional Marion, Lupino represented herself as seeking out a personal, domestic space safe from the demands and deformations of a Hollywood career.

When Lupino eventually turned down a seven-year contract from Warner Bros., she framed her decision in the context of domesticity: "I had decided that nothing lay ahead of me but the life of the neurotic star with no family and no home."[20] She reiterates the sentiment in an unpublished draft of an interview with Hedda Hopper: "I might be a star—but without any husband or family and having to worry about my face getting lined, etc. etc. I decided there was something else for me in life other than being a big star."[21] Like Aldrich's Marion, Lupino projects an unwillingness to abandon domesticity for the industry. But these refusals (of roles, of contracts) also enabled Lupino to spend her time observing the filming and editing processes, which ultimately enabled her to step into the role of director when the opportunity arose.[22]

The story of Lupino's entree into directing reads like Hollywood legend. Tired of having to answer to the rigid corporate mentality of the major studios, Lupino and her then-husband Collier Young (previously Harry Cohn's executive assistant at Columbia) formed an independent production company whose first film would set the pattern for the controversial subject matter and semi-documentary style the company advanced over the course of the next several years.[23] *Not Wanted* (1949), a film about "illegitimate motherhood," was to be directed by Elmer Clifton, who suffered a heart attack at the beginning of the film's shoot.[24] By Lupino's account, she was then compelled to assume the directorial role because their low-budget production company could not afford anyone else to take on the task. Claiming that she repeatedly looked to Clifton, who remained on the set, for his suggestions and approval, Lupino is uncredited for this first directorial venture and claimed throughout her life that, "I did not set out to be a director."[25]

However unintentional, this foray into direction enabled her to reprise the role the following year with Filmakers's next project, *Never Fear* (1950), suggesting that the experience with *Not Wanted* was not altogether unwanted. To Hedda Hopper she explained that "the money men said they wouldn't finance our second picture unless I directed it. Now I'm faced with whether I'll sign with Zanuck as an actress—or direct. I decided to go independent. I decided I didn't want to be a movie star—with all it entails—and live that way."[26] Although not giving up on acting altogether, Lupino's activities over the next four years suggest that direction was, indeed, the direction she wished her career to take. In fact, Lupino seemed earnestly to desire to leave acting behind; it was primarily the need for money, especially to finance her filmmaking ventures, which drove her occasionally to the other side of the camera.

Part of the strategy for Lupino's re-making of herself as a woman director involved repeatedly making statements about her femininity as an unnatural but essential part of this new role, thereby attempting to construct a specific kind of reputation as a nonthreatening woman doing the best she could at a justifiably male job. Although she acknowledged that a woman director was a kind of oxymoron, Lupino also criticized the passivity and submissiveness that was so much a part of her self-perpetuated public image. Lupino appears to have understood the media's power—an understanding gleaned, no doubt, from her work as an actress—making her a director always concerned to an unusual degree with reputation and image. In fact, while working as a director Lupino maintained an active publicity campaign more befitting, in many ways, of a star than a director. Repeatedly making assertions about the essential differences that she perceived between men and women, her running commentary on the subject suggested that these differences could not be transcended in professional or personal situations. As a screenwriter, she "never wrote just straight women's roles. I liked the strong characters. I don't mean women who have masculine qualities about them, but something that has intestinal fortitude, some guts to it. . . . Playing a nice woman who just sits there, that's my greatest limitation."[27] Lupino aligns passivity here with a kind of paralyzing femininity, while also imagining an idea of female strength that does not compromise femininity.

She echoes these ideas when commenting on her conflicting roles as director and mother, noting that she turned down many directorial offers because they would have kept her away from her home and, later, her daughter. She elaborates, "That's where being a man makes a great deal of difference. I don't suppose the men particularly care about leaving their wives and children. During the vacation period the wife can always fly over and be with him. It's difficult for a wife to say to her husband, come sit on the set and watch."[28] These ideas are very much in line with concerns over women's decreasing role in the family and fears about a sharp increase in separation and divorce. Lupino's statement about sitting and watching, however, is curious given her previously quoted ideas about screenwriting. If her most dreaded role is "playing a nice woman who just sits there," then Lupino has all but admitted to her desire to be more like the "husband-director" of this equation than the "wife-spectator." However performative, her assumptions, which one might deem fairly typical for her time, suggest that professional ambition is a decidedly male attribute, while domestic ambition is markedly female.

Lupino makes explicit claims about the nature of direction that reinforce her intent to make a reputation for herself as one who behaved appropriately along gender lines, rather than professional lines. As she explains, "Look. A man is a man and a woman is a woman, and I believe that. All right, so you probably might consider directing a man's job. Well it is. Physically, directing is extremely rough."[29] The reputation being established by Lupino here distracts us from the fact that within this statement is an admission that directing is, in fact, a woman's job, as well. However, concluding that Lupino's public self-characterization was mere media banter intended to entertain and palliate requires a certain perhaps unjustifiable leap of faith. Because her words and deeds seem virtually incompatible, many have dismissed Lupino's career as nothing more than she herself frequently made of it: not only accidental but aberrant. I therefore turn to three of the films Lupino directed—*Hard, Fast, and Beautiful* (1951), *The Bigamist* (1953), and *The Hitch-Hiker* (1953)—which offer a series of interesting metaphors for the reputation she made as a female director when examined through the gender paradigms that Lupino herself provides.

However problematic a simple auteurist reading of these films might be, for certainly they are the result of a complex collaboration and are not the sole expression of their director, Lupino played an undeniably significant role in the selection and creation of these projects. It is also unusually the case that Lupino's films are, as Donati puts it, about "people with limitations."[30] It so happens that these limitations frequently revolve around issues of gender, ambition, power, and social structures such as marriage, which were the same preoccupations around which Lupino's directorial persona was constructed. Three of Lupino's Filmakers projects will therefore be examined in the context of their director's conflicted utterances about gender and power, in large part because the films perpetuate the conflicted and self-punitive role Lupino consistently dramatized. The close readings that follow, then, suggest the way that these films unearth, in the fictional realm, the sometimes quite violent struggles with reputation and ambition that are analogous to what Lupino faced as a Hollywood director.

Narratives of Female Ambition: The Bigamist *and* Hard, Fast and Beautiful

As a director, Lupino retained many of the performative qualities of an actress, making herself over to the public as a palatable career woman in a man's field. By directing both motion pictures and her public image, Lupino engaged in an ideological battle that allowed her to do the work she did in a cultural climate that was largely hostile to or derisive of women performing such work. In the films she directed, outside of the fascinating but anomalous *The Hitch-Hiker*, which will be discussed in the final section of this chapter, we encounter female characters struggling to figure out their place in environments that mirror the social constraints Lupino faced. Two of these films, *The Bigamist* and *Hard, Fast and Beautiful*, examine both the psychology and the pathology of female ambition. These films offer a glimpse at the causes and consequences of women's professional goals, both films concluding, in a sense, that women's public and nondomestic drives are aberrant at best and destructive at worst. These narratives echo Lupino's personal battles with her professional life in part because they represent the culture's prevailing attitudes toward women in the public sphere. Context aside, the films represent the significant tensions between women's public and private lives.

While not suggesting that a director's films can be read as transparent analogies for the director's life or beliefs, it is unusually (perhaps even uncannily) the case that the films Lupino directed are embedded—obviously, at times—with the ideology she engaged with in her professional and personal life. A number of her films are outwardly critical of go-getting female characters, with implications that inflect upon Lupino's own publicly aired personal dilemmas. Historically speaking, it is not coincidental that the war and post-war era saw a rise in the number of female characters possessing dangerous ambitions; the femme fatales of film noir are a perfect example. As American soldiers returned to a country in which women had taken active roles during their absence, reactionaries like Philip Wylie and later J. Robert Moskin fanned the flames of such cultural anxieties while Hollywood films often explored similar territory.[31] Women had entered the workplace en masse during the war; Lupino's entrance into direction, though not war-related, follows the national trend of women moving outside of the home into professions that previously had been the exclusive domain of men. Of course, as an actress Lupino was never "in the home" to begin with; but since directing was so much a male province her career movement mirrors the mass female entrance into male professions.

The Bigamist can be classed with any number of 1950s films interested in the way that female characters affect male identity, typically—as Moskin so confidently asserted—in a negative fashion. As the title suggests, it is the story of a man's unfortunate, yet in the film's terms understandable, decision to take two wives. Harry Graham (Edmond O'Brien) is a traveling salesman whose wife Eve (Joan Fontaine) has symbolically traded an apron for a business suit as a means of compensating for her inability to have a child. Eve's un-wifely, un-feminine, and un-maternal behavior, the film suggests, is what drives Harry to take up with the Los Angeles–based Phyllis (played by Lupino herself), a working-class woman who wants nothing out of Harry but his company. As the summary of *The Bigamist* for the Breen office indicates, "Eve's drive and ambition for their success even at the sacrifice of their married life" compels Harry's double life.[32] The story is told in Harry's "confessional" flashbacks after he has been caught in his double life by Mr. Jordan (Edmund Gwenn), whose job it is to investigate Eve and Harry because they want to adopt a child.

Narratively speaking, we occupy Harry's perspective throughout the film, making his character the most complex and sympathetic in the film. This is a crucial representational issue, given the political climate in which the film was produced and the very personal, collaborative nature of its production: Lupino directed the film and her by-then ex-husband, Collier Young, wrote the script. Young's authorship of the screenplay significantly complicates and personalizes the film's politics, as does Lupino's performance in one of the film's major roles. Their contributions support an allegorical reading of the film, particularly given the film's subject matter of a marriage destroyed by a woman's problematic professionalism. Young's then-wife, Joan Fontaine, also co-starred with Lupino in *The Bigamist*; Fontaine and Lupino play the two wives of the titular bigamist with Lupino playing the "other" woman. These role assignments are especially intriguing given Lupino's real-life similarities to the role of Eve, the role that she does not play in the film: an ambitious and successful woman concerned about forgetting what it means to be a "good" wife and a "proper" woman.

Considered in the context of Lupino's public expressions regarding femininity and women's roles, Eve can be understood as an embodiment of all of those anxieties surrounding the maleness of the professional world that Lupino countered through her public statements. In the opening scene, Mr. Jordan reports on "Eve's case" into his Dictaphone, utilizing the narrative device used in Billy Wilder's *Double Indemnity* (1944) to tell another story of a man deeply affected by the selfish and cruel ambitions of a woman. In monologue, Jordan introduces the audience to the plot by stating that, "Mrs. Graham is unable to have a family. Her problem is of undetermined origin." Although we have not yet seen Eve, she already has become the subject of the investigator's discourse on reproductive and social abnormality. Jordan's use of the term "family" is intended to stand in for the more specific term "child"; however, it is doubly suggestive of Eve's alienation of her husband through her lack of "normal" female reproductive capabilities and her related entrance into their business.

Eve is thus both infertile and unable to sustain a proper relationship with her husband, largely, it is implied, as a consequence of her infertility.

Eve's mysterious "problem" can thus be read as both biological and behavioral: A woman, the film will suggest, must be neither overly ambitious nor excessively demanding to succeed as a wife. There is also an implication that Eve's ambition has made her frigid, though no scenes explicitly demonstrate this, no doubt in part because the Breen office directly told Filmakers to "Please avoid any emphasis on sex frustration on the part of Harry."[33] However implicit, Harry's sexual frustration is clearly part of the reason he succumbs to an affair. Eve's familial failures are rendered "undetermined," but the ambiguity of this term leaves open the possibility that it is more than her biology that has caused her failed womanhood.

Having been dealt the blow of infertility, Eve overcompensates for her biological lack with an aggressive business sense that is professionally successful but personally disastrous. As Harry implies in one of his many voice-overs, the side effect of Eve's success is the deterioration of their marriage: "When we found out we couldn't have children Eve was bitter, restless. It was my idea, her coming into the business; she caught on fast, so fast she doubled our sales in no time. But our marriage . . . well, it became a business partnership."[34] Harry is a sympathetic character who does not condemn or excessively criticize Eve, but the blame for the failure of their marriage falls squarely on Eve's business achievements in a fashion reminiscent of the Moskin essay discussed earlier. Instead of using the business as a distraction (a form of entertainment, as it was intended to be by Harry) from her "bitter" reaction to her biological inadequacy, it becomes an obsession (an unnatural one in the film's terms) that infiltrates and contaminates her marriage. The business, in other words, is an abnormal substitute for a child. Devoting the time and energy that she does to anything other than a child is a threat to the nature of the family structure, particularly since she has at least matched the performance of her husband by rapidly doubling their sales. Herein lies the real issue: When allowed to participate in their business, Eve succeeds in the public sphere. She is the nightmare of the post-war era: the woman who, like Lupino, has a taste of "male" work and refuses to give it up.

Eve's success thus renders the marriage a "business partnership," implying that she is unable to be worker and wife simultaneously. After all, this modern, two-income family was hardly the ideal in an era that widely promoted women's domestic responsibilities. Eve eventually confesses her own anxieties about letting Harry down regarding her inability to have a child, acknowledging that work has been a poor substitute for that more desirable role of mother. She explains, in a fashion that affirms Harry's earlier interpretation, that her infertility impeded her ability to perform as a wife and mother, concluding that learning of her inability to have a child is "when I became an efficient little white collared girl . . . I forgot some things." This line effectively feeds into the suspicions regarding working women as constructed by someone like Moskin, particularly in this era in which career women were subject to such scrutiny.

Here, too, are Lupino's own purported fears acted out on screen: Have a career, be it acting or directing, and risk forgetting about what really matters: marriage and family. Regardless of the degree to which these anxieties were played up for publicity purposes, Lupino seemed apprehensive about this, so much so that in the margins of a draft of Gladys Hall's article, "Mad Idesy," in which Lupino is quoted as saying "I am divorced from my work when I am at home," Lupino instructed in her own pencil: "Please italicize that statement, You can say that it is a monomania on my part, if you wish. It is."[35] Lupino was determined to maintain what she refers to later in the piece as "all the pretty pleasures of being feminine" by not forgetting what it meant at the end of the day to be a woman, wife, and mother even as she was forging her way as a director.[36]

In *The Bigamist*, Eve's terminology in this scene—"an efficient little white collared girl"—makes light of her business successes, perpetuating a sense of disdain for the working woman. Being a "girl" instead of a "woman" or a "wife" is emblematic of her failure, at least as she articulates the meaninglessness of her ambitions when examined beside the more important family priorities that she has temporarily forgotten. Eve comes full circle during the course of the film, beginning the narrative in the mode of efficient businesswoman and ending the film softened by her desire to adopt a child (thereby embracing the presumably "natural" desire to be a mother despite it all) and humbled by her husband's bigamy. In other words, she has learned her lesson the hard way. Eve's "shortcomings" allow the film to depict Harry's bigamy as a forgivable crime, if only because he is driven by the male need for a compassionate woman who in turn needs him. Eve's ruthless independence and self-sufficiency are the real crime here.

In Harry's first-person narration of his bigamy, he explains that it all began on a "lonely" Sunday in Los Angeles during a business trip. Missing his wife, he phones Eve from his hotel with the hopes of talking about their relationship. As he explains, "we didn't talk about us. She was in one of her executive moods . . . career woman." The derogatory use of these terms—"executive," "career woman"—justifies the film's rendering of the near-criminal nature of Eve's ambitions. The tone Harry takes when narrating this dialogue is also similar to the way that Lupino describes the potentially destabilizing effects of women with career goals. As Seiter points out, "The voice-over is . . . riddled with resentment towards Eve for outstripping him in their business partnership, for being so 'perfect' . . . Through the voice-over Harry shifts the guilt from himself to Eve."[37] But Harry is only subtly resentful; he does blame Eve for the failure of their marriage and in the film's context Harry is clearly in the right. The film seems intent on demonstrating that a wife working as a therapeutic means to forget her infertility is one thing, but a woman who exhibits the "male" (read: successful) qualities of the executive has crossed the line and threatens to undermine the very nature of the family. Phyllis ("the other woman," played by Lupino) is a working woman, too; but a single working woman, which is an altogether different thing, and a waitress, an acceptable, service-oriented position.

The film thus represents Eve's business goals as impeding any chance for a happy marriage, a particularly interesting plotline given Young and Lupino's prior relationship and their roles in the film's production. Eve is depicted as single-minded, the business taking precedent over every aspect of her personal life with Harry. In fact, when Harry calls Eve after meeting and spending his first day with Phyllis (their relationship begins flirtatiously but platonically), he teases Eve about possibly having an affair. Laughing, Eve immediately changes the subject to business; her flippancy legitimizes Harry's continuance of the affair-to-be. Even after developing a stable friendship with Phyllis, Harry again attempts to come "home" to Eve and make things right by getting away for a weekend with her. Harry narrates his desire to rekindle and repair their relationship, "But she had other plans . . . big plans." The candlelight dinner awaiting Harry is dinner for four, not for two. The lawyer and buyer at the table not only intrude on the couple's intimacy (a privacy desired, it seems, only by Harry, whose sexual frustration we are again reminded of), but are also reminiscent of Harry's inadequacies in the business. Since Harry has previously failed with the buyer, Eve gives it a try. Eve's smiling charm is contrasted by shots of Harry's restrained resentment. He is an outsider to this transaction, much as he has become an outsider to their marriage. Eve's is a seduction of another kind, an adultery based upon business, not sexual relations.

When the buyer jokes about why Eve hasn't been a part of things before, Eve responds in a fashion that is reminiscent of Lupino's discussions of her career: "I'm just Harry's little secretary trying to get along. I was afraid you would ask how the thing worked." Much as Lupino presented herself as a woman doing the best she could at a man's job, Eve plays the role of the

Redirecting Reputation 185

FIGURE 24: In *The Bigamist*, Eve plays the "little secretary" role until her dinner party banter eventually reveals her expertise: "We just happen to have a model in the kitchen, and if you have your combination Phillips screwdriver handy, Mr. Forbes, I'd be happy to take the freezer apart for you." *The Filmakers, 1953.*

properly situated woman-helper. Using the term "little" as she did previously to deride her working in the first place, Eve's performance of meekness is abandoned when she provides very detailed technical information to the men at the table (see figure 24). The camera cuts to Harry as Eve continues her highly professional monologue; Harry just looks at her, having been effectively cast aside and relegated to the role of bartender. Eve's "little secretary" comment is thus revealed for what it is: a mere performance; a subtle jab at the status quo of women's roles in business and in marriage; and a statement that can be used to further one's success while not alienating the men — at least some of them — on the other side of the table. It is, in other words, a cinematic version of Lupino's own reputational entrepreneurship.

While Eve's success ultimately has little to do with her womanly charm, her coy performance enables her to seal the deal without *overtly* threatening the established balance of power; she puts on the face of the ineffectual woman despite the fact that all present seem to know that she is not. Despite these efforts, however, the balance of power in her marriage is thrown off. Eve tries to render herself as a kind of novelty, but she fails because she exposes herself for what she really is: a knowledgeable and ambitious woman, a paradox given her station in life and the moment of history she occupies. This was a role Lupino was aware of playing in Hollywood, as well.

Following the dinner party turned business meeting is a scene that takes place in the couple's bedroom, a space often used by Lupino to depict domestic tension. Lying in bed on the night of Eve's business success at the dinner party (for truly the victory is Eve's; Harry is hardly present at the dinner except in reverse shots of his relative blankness), she talks about her happiness, an obvious reaction to her business success. While Harry again wants to discuss their relationship, Eve is tired out from the hard day's work and she rolls over and goes to sleep. The shot of Eve sleeping is followed by a reverse shot of Harry, who looks longingly in her direction. This shot is a visual summary of what has transpired: Eve and Harry have changed places. As Eve becomes increasingly business-driven, she exhibits stereotypically male behavior and Harry becomes increasingly sentimental, even "womanish."

Eve's happiness is contingent on her success in the business; Harry's is dependent upon his relationship with Eve. Phyllis thus provides for him what Eve no longer can: "female" companionship (clearly a nod to sexual companionship), not the company of a business partner. As Harry puts it, "Eve was my whole life." These seem more the words of a dependent housewife than of a successful businessman. While Harry passionately proclaims that, "Our marriage is the only thing that really matters," Eve becomes more and more focused on the business, which is increasingly her whole life; her marriage—one might even say her womanhood—is what is "forgotten." Harry wants to get away with Eve (presumably away from the business and its effects on her), but she puts their relationship on hold, once again, in favor of the success of their business. Eve's masculinization—her becoming too much "like a man"—is the root of their problems.

Sentimentality, however, is part of what makes Harry so likable, his crime so understandable. Depicting him in this sympathetic fashion makes Eve's trespasses all the more reprehensible. In contrast to Eve is Phyllis, who is a fantasy woman in the film: She desires to know nothing of Harry's past, nor does she want anything from him. She is "better" than Eve on yet another obvious level: After only one night together—significantly, on Harry's birthday—Phyllis gets pregnant. This immediate conception is clearly meant to unbalance the scales and to justify Harry's duplicity toward the comparably callous and infertile Eve.

Phyllis does not even inform Harry about her pregnancy; when he finds out about it she still insists that Harry is free because she doesn't "trap" her men. Although Phyllis remains hard on the exterior, her doctor tells Harry that this veneer covers up her need for him, now more than ever. The authoritative voice of the medical establishment enters the film to motivate, perhaps even to legitimate Harry's proposal to Phyllis; finally, it seems, Harry has found a woman who (admit it or not) needs him. Like the beginning of the film in which Eve is diagnosed as a defective wife, the doctor's opinion supports Harry's decision to commit the crime of bigamy. As he tries to explain his bigamy with Phyllis to Mr. Jordan, he states that, "for the first time I felt needed. I loved Eve, but I never felt she needed me." This statement brings us back to Lupino's performance of a womanhood devoid of authority and aggression. Lupino's insistence that she always play the role of the needy woman in real life—needing advice, instructions, *direction*—is justified here by Eve's failure to do the same and the dismal consequences resulting from this decision. The film makes sense out of Lupino's publicity because it represents a personally disastrous outcome for the woman who cannot veil or otherwise disguise her ambitions, who forgets that husband and home come before everything else, and who disregards that she is first and foremost a woman and that this fact determines all other matters.

So while Eve pushes the business along in San Francisco, Harry begins to lead a truly double life: two wives, two houses, but only one child. Phyllis bears Harry a son and even asks him for his forgiveness after she kicks Harry out when she suspects that he is having an affair with Eve. This double life is also defined by the visual nature of each of these spaces: In San Francisco, all of the scenes take place in the couple's meticulous upper-class apartment; in Los Angeles, the scenes are primarily set in public and working-class spaces or a white-picket-fenced and decidedly lived-in-looking home, suggesting a form of institutional entrapment on the one hand, and freedom and domestic bliss on the other. The scenes in Phyllis and Harry's house reveal more of a real domestic atmosphere: The space is messy but cozy, small but lived in.[38] Their house is a home, not an office. Even Mr. Jordan, the moral authority of the film who investigates the qualifications of Eve and Harry as adoptive parents, seems to sense the necessity of this space to Harry's happiness as he sits in the living room hearing Harry's confession.

Since Mr. Jordan's final judgment seems particularly relevant to the film's stance on Harry's criminality, it is worth noting that he has an ambivalent reaction to the story he has just listened to. Saying that he both despises and pities Harry, he concludes that "I don't even want to shake your hand, though I almost wish you luck." It is this dual reaction of moral condemnation and sympathy that makes Harry's character so interesting and unique to a film of this era. Even the judge who presides over the criminal case concludes that "perhaps he even needed them both." Herein lies the truth of the film: Harry's needs—emotional, physical, psychological—cannot be met by Eve, whose career-driven ambitions de-feminize her to the point that she can no longer satisfy Harry as a wife. Eve and Harry are both casualties of women's supposed liberation. Since when Lupino speaks of her own career, she emphasizes the need to "retain every feminine trait," we can read Eve and her rather immense personal failure as an iteration of Lupino's reticence to appear aggressive about her own career. Seiter is thus only partly correct in pointing out that the film provides "an exceptionally pessimistic view of marriage and domestic life"; more importantly, the film paints a bleak picture of the nearsighted career woman whose ambition leads her down an inevitable path of misery and isolation.[39] Had Eve only slowed down a bit to remember her other obligation to Harry as his wife, she might have been able to have the best of both worlds.

Such moral condemnation has ties to the post–World War II emphasis on the nuclear family, with the housewife figured as the smiling, apron-adorned anchor of the home. Although she is discussing *Hard, Fast and Beautiful*, Wendy Dozoretz notes the popular cultural imaginings that helped support the maintenance of the domestic ideology that informs *The Bigamist* as well: "Women's magazines reiterated again and again the image of the happy housewife with a slew of kids. No matter that a higher percentage of women were working outside the home; making extra money to consume more goods was fine, but wives were not to have careers."[40] The very notion of a career signifies ambition, and we have witnessed in Eve the incompatibility of this drive in relation to the institution of the family.

The Bigamist might be understood, then, as dramatizing Lupino's experience with the Hollywood system, linking Eve's fictional ambition to Lupino's own. Lupino's 1951 film, *Hard, Fast and Beautiful*, similarly addresses the danger of female ambition through the story of a middle-class tennis-player whose mother aggressively facilitates her rise to champion. While predominantly about Florence Farley's (Sally Forrest) ascension to tennis-celebrity, the film is also about the crumbling structure of the Farley family: Milly (Claire Trevor), as Mandy Merck has pointed out, is a version of the pushy stage mother who lives vicariously through her daughter's talents;[41] Will (Kenneth Patterson) is the ineffectual father replaced by Florence's promoter, Fletcher Locke (Carleton Young); and Florence is nearly ruined by the possibility of a professional tennis career but is saved—luckily, in the film's terms—by marriage to Gordon McKay (Robert Clarke) and the promise of a normal (read: domestic and nonprofessional) life. A one-sentence summary of the film might read: Mom turns daughter into business and is punished.[42]

The film begins at the Farley home with Milly's first-person voice-over narration accompanying images of Florence practicing tennis against the family garage door. Contrary to its use in *The Bigamist*, the voice-over in this film does not garner our sympathy or compassion for the character who speaks it. From the start, Milly reveals herself to be the ambitious and manipulative mastermind behind Florence's career. Milly's narration gives voice to the daughter's silent image, suggesting the control that she will eventually exert over Milly's future: "I knew that somehow I was going to get the very best there was out of life for you . . . I always wanted something better for you and I made up my mind to get it no matter what I had to do." The vicarious impulse driving Milly is reinforced by her complaints about having married too young, a mistake she will desperately try to stop her daughter from making. Wanting something better for both her daughter and herself, Milly swears that, "By gosh my daughter's going to have everything, everything I missed. She's gonna go places, meet the right people." Milly thus tries to control Florence's life, encouraging—to a certain degree forcing—her to pursue what she perceives as the correct path to success and fame. As in *The Bigamist*, we encounter a directing woman who is unsympathetic and, by film's end, is punished for her (here even more overdrawn) aggressiveness.

Much like Eve in *The Bigamist*, Milly's ambition—although directed within the family—has similarly disastrous effects upon her marriage. In the only bedroom scene between Milly and Will, he tries to kiss her neck as she shrinks away from him. Their beds—positioned head to head so that they cannot even look at each other—work as visual monuments to the state of their divided marriage. Merck points out that the Farleys' twin beds—facing away from each other with the headboard as a barrier between them—"could almost parody the Hays Code restrictions on conjugal intimacy"; but the beds also look strikingly like the layout of a tennis court, reminding the viewer of the game that has divided this marriage and of Milly's obsessive insistence on her daughter's success.[43] From one side of this "court," Will asks Milly the question that cuts to the core of this film: "Can't you love both of us?" This kind of question, asked by a neglected man, should be familiar; we can imagine it being asked in *The Bigamist*, with Harry referring to both the business and himself. While the "other" of this triangle is the daughter, it is also more than just the daughter that is signified here, because Florence has become, for Milly, the sum total of all of her own unrealized aspirations. Milly rolls her eyes on her side of the bed as she fantasizes about Florence's future, ignoring Will's efforts to restore normalcy to their marriage.

In *The Bigamist*, Harry's efforts at marital rehabilitation are also overshadowed by his wife's blinding ambitions. The sympathetic husband is even more so in *Hard, Fast and Beautiful*, not only because Milly is calculating and selfish but because Will—while ineffectual to a certain degree, even falling ill by film's end (typically the woman's fate in melodrama)—offers sympathy and parental encouragement to Florence in an unconditional fashion.[44] Unlike Milly, who is managerial from the start, Will is compassionate, reminding Florence that, "it's only a game; whoever wins, it's just a game." From Milly's perspective, this is far from the truth; the game, as she perceives it, offers Florence her only opportunity to rise out of middle-class mediocrity to enter the social circles of the elite. As Florence begins to do just this, the film provides us not with her response to her success, but her mother's: "Florence was living in a wonderful new world and I was happy, so happy." Accompanied by a close-up of Milly's smiling face, the film suggests again that Milly's desire to have Florence succeed is a vicarious one; in fact, Florence's success eventually allows Milly to escape from her own entrapment with Will, who Milly perceives as impeding her own desire for social mobility.

Much as Eve is masculinized and Harry is feminized in *The Bigamist*, in *Hard, Fast and Beautiful*, the Farleys undergo similar shifts in the traditional familial balance of power. Merck contends that "Milly takes over the paternal function"—at one point even buying a car, the malest of purchases, without consulting Will in an act that signals the end of their already-strained marital relationship.[45] Dozoretz takes this a step further by arguing that Mr. Farley "exhibits the characteristics usually associated with mothers . . . So the mother embodies the negative parts of mothering, while the father takes on the positive ones."[46] It is important to add to these formulations that Milly's aggressive pursuit of Florence's career is more the behavior of a manager than of a mother. Milly even seems willing to act as a kind of prostitute, enacting a seduction of the well-known tennis promoter Fletcher Locke to facilitate Florence's success in the profession.[47] Milly also covertly sells her daughter's image and name for profit despite the fact that these acts compromise Florence's amateur status.

Milly is able to achieve such calculated exploitation only by removing Will from the familial equation, endowing herself with the patriarchal role of decision-maker. This change is suggested by two scenes that transpire at the Farley home in which the characters—Milly, Will, Florence, and country club president Mr. Carpenter (in the first scene) or Fletcher (in the second scene)—visually dramatize the film's plot. The first of these scenes begins with Mr. Carpenter proposing to send Florence away to tennis camp, all expenses paid. Mr. Carpenter, Florence, and Will occupy the foreground while Milly smokes in the deep field and listens to the conversation. Milly then stands and disappears from the frame while the three discuss the potential trip. Not one to be satisfied with such exclusion, Milly addresses Mr. Carpenter from outside of the frame and draws him—along with the camera's gaze—to her in order to try to get herself included in the trip and, one might add, the scene. Florence then joins the two, leaving Will in the background smoking his pipe. When Mr. Carpenter asks Milly to join Florence on the trip, Will is left out of the process altogether.

The scene demonstrates Milly's talent at shifting the spotlight to herself while simultaneously maneuvering Will to the literal and symbolic background. In the second version of this triangularization of power, Fletcher is the third point in the triangle with Will looking on from the back. Unlike Milly, Will does not reconfigure the space to enable himself to regain power in the family; rather, he is left in the background as Florence is sent off to the national championships. Milly effectively replaces Will with Fletcher: After their very first meeting, Fletcher sits with her at Florence's match, taking the father's place from the earlier scenes. This replacement is an outgrowth of Milly's pathological ambition; it also suggests that this ambition can be understood as a displacement of sexuality, a scenario reminiscent of *The Bigamist*. In a voice-over that sounds like it is spoken by a femme fatale in a film noir rather than a mother in a tennis melodrama, Milly explains: "My dreams for you were coming true. Yes, it was coming true and Fletcher Locke played right along with it. He could make or break you and I'd made up my mind which it was going to be." Milly's maniacal determination for her daughter to achieve this goal at any cost makes her, and the capitalist, celebrity-valuing culture that drives her, the true villains of the film. She is a hyperbolic rendering of the potential ugliness of the ambitious woman, that entity that Lupino sought to distance herself from through her own preemptively defensive reputation making.

Milly's ambitions for her daughter are further villainized in comparison with the efforts of Florence's working-class suitor, Gordon. Gordon's marriage proposal—accepted by Florence with the assurance that she'll make Gordon proud of her—creates yet another conflict because it divides

Florence's attentions between tennis and romance. For Milly, this is the ultimate danger, for she has experienced the stultifying effects of marriage on her own ambitions, however shallow they appear to be. When Milly convinces Florence to take a European tour and surprise Gordon with it, their resulting split is explained by Milly to Florence as being "just the beginning." This initiates Florence's transformation as she becomes a parodic, monstrous extreme of precisely who her mother wants her to be. Having lost her connections to reality—both her father, who is left ailing at home, and Gordon, who is discarded for Florence's pursuit of fame and fortune—Florence announces that she will "play the game the way you play it—for money." Embracing the commercial advantages of her reputation, Florence begins making demands and thinking only of her financial gains and the escalation of her celebrity. No longer interested in the game, it seems, Florence starts calling the shots by acting out the worst of her mother's greedy drives. Even Milly is shown, in reverse shot, to disapprove of Florence's new *modus operandi*.

Florence's transformation—a transference from mother to daughter of the most avaricious aspects of ambition—also gives her a cynical edge, largely because it is brought about by her realization that her mother has been exploiting her and directing her every move (including her breakup with Gordon) from the start. In a press interview with her mother and a female reporter, Florence's sarcasm is transparent: "I'm lucky to have such a wonderful mother—great sport."[48] Florence's ironic realization that her professional ambitions have supplanted the opportunity to have a normal family life—that which Lupino claimed was more important than a profession—serve as a reminder that there are consequences for success, particularly, it seems, for women. During this same interview, a telegram arrives announcing that Will is very sick, and while Milly tries to hide it, Florence grabs it away from her and announces that she is going home to see him. Milly, unable to see beyond her goals for Florence, perceives this impulse as a threat to her performance in the match the following day. In contrast, Will humanizes Florence and reminds her of the person she used to be before she was corrupted by her mother's narrow ambitions. Family and home (here the realm of the father) are the desirable antithesis to the cutthroat world of the champion (here the realm of the mother).

When she returns from her visit, Florence is exhausted but manages to win the match "for her father." While she is swooning from exhaustion as she is asked questions after the match, Gordon surprises her by whisking her away with the phrase, "let's go home." The implied ending of the film—marriage for Florence and Gordon, and Florence's retirement from the grueling circuit—was not, however, the original one. As Dozoretz discusses, the novel that the film is based on ends "with the daughter self-sufficient and alone, but in 1951 the studio required an ending consistent with the dominant ideology."[49] Producer William Faidman's intra-departmental memo to Gordon Youngman reads: "This screenplay demands and requires a happy ending in which the heroine relinquishes any idea she might have had of turning professional and decides to marry the boy she has always loved."[50] The legislation of proper female behavior reminds us of what Lupino was up against in her career, faced with similarly rigid notions about what she should relinquish to have a "happy ending." In this context, "happy" signifies the post-war imaginings of the home and family as the most rewarding locale for female productivity, a notion in conflict with the idea of a professional woman in general, and with a career such as Lupino's in particular. Marriage *and* work are out of the question; it seems impossible for the two to coexist in the framework of either of the films discussed here. Dixon reads Florence's decision to give up her life as a tennis champion as Lupino's restatement of "her own desire to remain subservient—at least superficially—to the existing patriarchal order."[51] However, I would argue that Florence's decision is not simply an act of subservience to patriarchal order; rather, it is a rejection of the monstrously ambitious matriarchal model that led her to such an extreme abandonment of both family and morality.

As Florence exits the tournament scene in Gordon's arms, she hands her trophy to her mother, explaining, "This is yours, you've earned it." This moment solidifies the film's striking resentment of the mother figure, the real director within the film. She not only is to blame for perverting the role of good wife and mother, but also for keeping Florence away from what should have been her real goal: the securing of a reliable, caring husband. The film's final, near-silent image summarizes the punishment suitable for such an overly ambitious woman: Milly sits alone in the dark at the tennis stadium; a zoom-out highlights her loneliness, as the ghost sound of balls being struck—traces of her now-absent daughter and her career—accompanies her isolated image. This moment marks Milly as the film's villain and its most pathetic victim. Earlier versions of the script read as a catalogue of similarly desolate endings for this overzealous mother: In the closing shot from the April 19, 1950, draft, Milly's face is captured in a distorted reflection from Florence's trophy, which Milly then uses to shatter her own image in a mirror;[52] the June 30, 1950, draft has Milly make a "pathetic" attempt at composure followed by a desperate voice-over, "I never did anything wrong . . . She'll come back—she must come back—to me."[53] These endings all reflect the film's desire to hold Milly accountable for her misdirected ambitions, making it is easy—even satisfying—to condemn her.

The emphasis on negative aspects of the maternal role in *Hard, Fast and Beautiful* is complicated by Lupino's own investment in a very different sort of maternal metaphor. In the process of asserting her nonassertiveness, Lupino appears to have stumbled upon a metaphor with which to explain her career to her co-workers and her public, a metaphor Lupino best explains herself: "I love being called mother. For when I am working I regard my production company, motion picture or television, as a very special kind of family."[54] Motherhood is an especially interesting metaphor for Lupino's self-imagining given her public discussion of the conflicts between career and family. Being called mother on the set domesticates her work in a way that underplays the public, nonfamilial, nontraditional nature of her directorial role. However, this self-naming also permits Lupino to act "motherly"—both stern and caring, compassionate yet authoritative. These behavioral polarities are precisely those qualities embodied by the two competing female roles in *The Bigamist*: one stern, the other caring; one authoritative, the other compassionate.

Regardless of how playful—even of how tongue-in-cheek—Lupino might have been, this maternal metaphor suggests the power of patriarchal ideology. In a 1966 *TV Guide* piece appropriately titled, "Follow Mother, Here We Go Kiddies!" Lupino's ex-husband Collier Young perpetuates the metaphor: "She is the finest wet nurse in the history of young talent."[55] Imagine John Ford or Alfred Hitchcock being compared to a wet nurse; it is disturbing not only because of its absurdity but also because it is a term that could only be applied to a woman, and only as a reminder of her biological difference. Although her own films dealt with a frustrated nonmother (*The Bigamist*), an unwed mother (*Not Wanted*), and an overly ambitious and destructive mother (*Hard, Fast and Beautiful*), it is curious that Lupino should have either chosen or accepted such a loaded name for herself. But this tension reminds us of the degree to which Lupino made her unusual reputation in order to facilitate her atypical career.

Francine Parker perceives that the "split aspect of the female person is the recurring theme running through all of Lupino's films . . . [symbolizing] . . . the essential schizophrenia of woman's world."[56] However, I think it necessary to apply such a statement beyond Lupino's films to the publicity that facilitated her career as well, which made it clear that there was a price to pay for making one's way in a man's world. While I am tempted to consider the female roles in *The Bigamist* and *Hard, Fast and Beautiful* as

Lupino's attempts to critique instead of replicate negative representation of ambitious women, the films themselves work against such an interpretation. One does not walk away from either film with the sense that Eve's or Milly's fates were unjustified; rather, both women appear to "get what they deserve." Such scenarios remind us of why Lupino's public remaking of her reputation was so essential: Without it, she might appear to be wandering down the same path and into the same pitfalls as her female protagonists. Her representations of these women and their dilemmas suggest, at minimum, Lupino's awareness of her own precarious position. Her films that address the world of women represent versions of female power that seem problematic, at best. However, her male-oriented film suggests the degree to which Lupino understood herself as self-consciously bending the rules of both her profession and her gender.

Male Domains: The Hitch-Hiker *(1953)*
and the Terrain of Direction

Ida Lupino had an affinity for suspense pictures, as can be evidenced in her tense 1953 film, *The Hitch-Hiker*, whose screenplay she co-wrote with Collier Young. Since this was Lupino's only directed film that did not deal explicitly with women's issues—in fact, the film lacks female characters altogether—it is especially noteworthy that the film's first "dialogue" is a woman's scream. Punctuating the film's beginning in this fashion, the scream is at once an acknowledgment of women's cinematic roles—so frequently hysterical, high-pitched, or emotionally frenzied—and a seeming refusal to submit to the traditional representations of women's victimization.

Lupino was determined to make *this* womanless movie in particular, which, given the circumstances, should never have made it to the screen at all. When Lupino first began scripting the project, the Breen office rejected the film under any circumstances, citing Clause 13 of the "Special Regulations re: Crime" of the Production Code, which prohibited "dealing with notorious criminals in recent times."[57] However, Lupino proceeded to get legal clearance from the real-life criminal upon whom the story is based, resulting in a vituperative letter to Breen from James Bennet, Director of the U.S. Department of Justice. Although Breen's office again rejected the story after it was submitted officially on April 18, 1952, Lupino managed to blur the facts of the case enough to eventually receive a hearty endorsement: "Most unusual feature of [*The Hitch-Hiker*] is that it is a red-blooded, virile, rough and ready suspense thriller, and the director is a woman, Ida Lupino, who also wrote the dynamic script."[58] Alongside the all-American rhetoric of the Breen Office lurks yet another suggestion about the novelty of the woman director, particularly in relation to her decidedly male-oriented subject matter. In response to an interviewer who asked Lupino about her consistent attention to women's issues in her films, she responded, "I directed *The Hitch-Hiker*, which was a true story . . . and that certainly was not a woman's story at all."[59] Using the film as evidence of her ability to transcend the limitation of "women's issues," Lupino clearly felt that this picture enabled her to step outside of type once again.

Like its thematically similar noir predecessor, Edgar G. Ulmer's 1945 *Detour*, *The Hitch-Hiker* tells a story about the dark side of the randomness of fate, embodied as it is in both cases by the unfortunate decision to pick up a hitchhiker. Shot entirely on location, the film—which Lupino considered her best—is based on the true story of William Edward Cook Jr., who killed six people in a hitchhiking murder spree in December of 1950. Cook's case was sensationalized and well-documented in the popular press; he became something of a symbol for the psychological dis-ease of the post-war nation. Lauren Rabinovitz points out the significance of Lupino's story choice: "At a time when juvenile delinquency was increasingly popularized as the result of inadequate family attentiveness, and particularly as a loss of maternal nurturing, the events of Cook's life fit neatly into current popular beliefs about the role of the family in developmental psychology, while also serving ideologically to reinforce the family as the structural centre for postwar America."[60] How significant, then, that Lupino's "man's picture" dealt with a scenario that reflected upon the importance of familial and maternal anchoring, especially given Lupino's own repeated assertions about the primacy of her domestic life over her professional life. One might read the film, then, as a parable suggesting the devastating outcome of the abandonment of the family, a reading not at all out of line with Lupino's conflicted allegiances to both work and home.

The Hitch-Hiker tells the story of three men: one, serial killer Emmett Myers (William Talman) who finds his victims by hitchhiking, and the other two, Gilbert Bowen (Frank Lovejoy) and Roy Collins (Edmond O'Brien), who pick him up while en route to a weekend fishing getaway. The film gives Lupino a chance to address a solely masculine world, one in which three men are made to occupy a space that drives each to his behavioral extreme. Rabinovitz interprets the narrative as "a vision of hell that is masculinity fragmented into neurotic components of maladjustment in a world that orders adjustment."[61] Rabinovitz's reference to neurosis seems particularly telling given Lupino's aforementioned invocation of "the neurotic star with no family and no home"; in both cases, "maladjustment" is a symptom of cultural roles that split the individual from his/her "natural" role.

The two traveling men, Collins and Bowen, begin the film on a carefree excursion, directing their own movement en route to a weekend of fishing by altering their destination without telling their wives. Rabinovitz states that the men's plans imply "that they are embarking on a new route for the sheer thrill of defying the women they left behind."[62] Although I think that this is an over-reading of the men's on-screen feelings about their act of "defiance," Rabinovitz is right to point out that this is a decision that suggests something about the men's relationship to the idea of the family. Away from home, they decide to take liberties with their own movement that both physically and symbolically suggest their distance from their homes. Robert Joseph's February 27, 1951, treatment of the film—then called "They Spoke to God"—is even more explicit: Collins and Bowen "had felt smothered by domesticity, and this sudden weekend—they decided to take off at two in the morning—was their way of asserting themselves."[63] In Joseph's treatment, the trip is an act of male rebellion, a reclaiming of that male space Moskin bemoans the loss of. It is also reminiscent of Lupino's declaration that male directors could more easily justify leaving their wives to go off and make a film than a woman director could leave her husband. Like Lupino's figurative male directors, the men in *The Hitch-Hiker* leave their women behind, but the film depicts the near-fatal results of this decision. This is a cautionary tale about men who deceive their wives, since Collins and Bowen end up paying dearly for their disobedient detour.

To return to the plot, Collins thinks of looking up an old female acquaintance while en route to their newly determined Mexican destination. Bowen's past, however, weighs heavily upon him and he comments on the fact that since the war this is his first time away from his wife and kids. World War II looms over this picture, although wives, kids, and homes have replaced it in these men's lives. Joseph's treatment for the film elaborates upon this substitution through a prefatory scene that does not occur in the final film. A week before the men's "declaration of independence," as the treatment refers to it, the men had been "kidding about apron strings, and the jail-like life a man leads after he's been trapped by a wife, kids, a home and time payments."[64] The blame is set squarely here on the shoulders of the "trapping wife," the first in a series of domestic entanglements.

The film constructs a situation in which both war and family linger visibly in at least one of the character's consciousness. But while Bowen's mind may be on his domestic situation, his body remains in the car traveling further away from his home and, it is implied, from safety.

Bowen's wife is invoked both through his comment about her and through crucial traces of her presence that manifest themselves on his body: his watch and his wedding ring. Later in the film, Myers admires the watch, forcing Bowen to give it up momentarily for him to scrutinize and compare it to his own memory of his first purloined timepiece. But the wedding ring is more significant to the narrative, for it provides a crucial clue when Bowen later leaves it for police to find after the trio stops on the road at a filling station. The ring marks Bowen's presence by signifying his distant home and marriage. Bowen's need to part with the ring is a matter of survival, but it is also symbolic of his increasing remoteness from that "other" domestic life that he has temporarily left behind, however ultimately essential that tie to his family proves to be for his own survival.

In a sequence that did not make the film's final cut, Bowen and Collins actually do enter the bar in Mexicali where Collins's "old acquaintance," Florabel, used to work. The January 14, 1952, script synopsis describes the men watching a sultry song-and-dance number followed by a stripper, which makes Forrest [Collins in the final film] uncomfortable to the point that he "insists that they leave."[65] This excursion punctuates the men's "independence" mission with the tease of sexual misconduct unrealized. Although the men avoid committing adultery, their entrance into the bar implies a brief, psychological infidelity. Excised from the final version, the men come off more sympathetically. Lupino's decision to render them in this fashion recalls the degree to which her other films execute similar favors for her male characters. The off-screen women are certainly not "to blame" in *The Hitch-Hiker*; however, neither are the men depicted as doing anything that might cause an audience to turn their sympathies against them. Driving off from the bar without stopping, the film proceeds and eventually ends with their excruciating submission and punishment.

Once trapped by Myers in their own car, which becomes a reconfigured and violated version of the domestic space, Lupino consistently frames the men in tight three-shots in which darkness and light mirror the claustrophobic effects of their entrapment. Bowen, the more family-oriented of the two captives, is a white-collar draftsman who is "used to working to other's specifications (and) endures patiently Talman's [Myers's] sadistic needling."[66] In contrast, Collins, "a mechanic who owns his own garage and controls his own labor, goes almost mad under submission to another's absolute power."[67] Collins, in fact, ultimately has a hysterical breakdown when he begins to cry out of despair over his forced passivity. This feminized breakdown is a reaction to Myers's relentless barking of commands: "do this," "do that," "cook this," "sit down," "stand up," "get out," "move." This primitive form of communication suggests that Myers's gun has become a substitute for the complexities of oral communication; its presence has virtually negated the need for language at all, hence the relative silence of the film. Myers's orders are also decidedly patriarchal in nature; when he barks that the men should "just get the grub ready," we are reminded that this is a nightmare of domestic entrapment. Myers is an overblown patriarch whose comments about the "softness" of the men signify not only in terms of his anxieties about class, but also in terms of his perception of masculine and feminine behavior. Such comments are also reminiscent of Lupino's own ideas regarding the relative hardness and softness of the director's role.

In his excessive commands and orders, Myers is, to some degree, a caricature of a relentless and demanding husband whose power is literalized here by the presence of his gun, which remains visible, appendage-like, throughout the film. When Myers's face is first revealed in the film, an image of his gun precedes it. As Myers's face enters the frame, it appears in a spotlight, further isolating him from his surroundings while continuing to link him to the gun that repeatedly intrudes upon the frame. With the gun always in hand, Myers seems intent on trying to push his captives to the edge as a means of asserting his own (armed) dominance, even instigating a shooting contest that includes a clever point-of-view shot from the gun's perspective. These instances cement the notion of compensatory masculinity linked to the possession of the gun. As Collins says to Myers at one point, "Without it [the gun] you're nothing." In fact, when Myers finally loses his gun, it is suggestively castrating (both visually and symbolically) and results in his having to follow orders for the first time in the film. When Bowen whacks the gun out of Myers's hand in the climactic final scene, it enables a Mexican policeman to give Myers a taste of his own medicine when he commands him to "walk this way," an order reminiscent of the similar dictates placed upon the hostages during the film. Now handcuffed, the loss of the gun literalizes his loss of power as Myers shifts from a position of total dominance to complete submission.

Myers acts not only like a carping husband when he is holding these two seemingly defenseless (by virtue of their lack of weapons) men hostage, he is also a kind of monstrous director ordering his cast about the set of the Mexican desert. Instead of shooting with a movie camera, Myers

FIGURE 25: In *The Hitch-Hiker*, Myers can be understood as monstrous director, using his gun to affirm his absolute power while constantly barking orders. *The Filmakers/RKO, 1953.*

sees (and captures) the world through the lens of his gun. Myers conceives of his position as one of absolute power, telling the men at one point that "you'll die, it's just a matter of time." Myers attempts here and throughout the film to write the script of the men's destiny, directing every scene down to the finest detail. Telling them what to do and when, he is very much like the director who must execute similar demands, demands that Lupino repeatedly associates with maleness in her discussions of filmmaking.

The Hitch-Hiker ends with Myers being taken away by the police as Collins and Bowen walk off together "into the sunset." This near-romantic ending to the film, which reinforces the degree to which this male union is privileged above the invisible domestic scene, was not the original conclusion. In fact, the final screenplay paints quite a different picture of the film's close. In it, Collins and Bowen (referred to in the script as Jim and Forrest) are met by their wives, Vivian and Dorothy, whose plane arrives on the scene:

MED. CLOSE SHOT as Jim Burke, completely unmindful of his injured ankle, half hobbles, half runs to meet Vivian. He sweeps her into his arms.
MED. SHOT—FORREST as he pauses on the last step of the ladder leading to the plane—his eyes resting longingly on the o.s. figure of his wife. He looks—and is an older and wiser man than the husband who went away eight days ago.[68]

With this alternative, unused ending, the film grants its male protagonists a second lease on their domestic lives. Although they originally had sought a temporary escape from the entrapments of home, they enthusiastically return to it here with the anticipation of its safety and security. In this version, theirs would have been a lesson about the value of domestic stability and the danger of the open road. Why Lupino chose to end the film without this closure is uncertain; however, the effect is to even further marginalize the women's presence by eliding them from the film altogether. The film's actual ending manages, through the absence of the wives, to leave open the possibility that the wives in fact needed to be escaped from, that the men's union with each other remains the most valuable relationship.

In the promotional campaign that accompanied the release of *The Hitch-Hiker*, Lupino is still being figured as a novelty woman director. The title of one of the articles in the promotional materials, "Ida Lupino Retains Her Femininity as Director," indicates the gendered nature of the publicity:

I retain every feminine trait. Men prefer it that way. They're more co-operative if they see that fundamentally you are of the weaker sex even though in a position to give orders, which normally is the male's prerogative, or so he likes to think, anyways. While I've encountered no resentment from the male of the species for intruding into their world, I give them no opportunity to think I've strayed where I don't belong. I assume no masculine characteristics, which can often be a fault of career women rubbing shoulders with their male counterparts, who become merely arrogant or authoritative.[69]

This is a highly complex statement that encapsulates many of the questions being addressed in this chapter with regard to Lupino's career-changing ambitions. Its tone is mechanical, reading like a bizarre handbook of 1950s women's professional mantras mixed with a splash of *The Stepford Wives* and a healthy dash of public-relations-speak. First, Lupino attributes her retention of feminine traits to men's preferences, suggesting that she shaped her behavior for a male audience. Without the veil of femininity, Lupino asserts, she would be unable to negotiate the male world of the director. Having to perform herself as "the weaker sex," she calls into question this assumption with a witty aside that men's perception of their own power is an illusion, however much her behavior might reinforce the maintenance of this fiction. Associating masculinity with arrogance is one thing, but with authority is another thing altogether, since without authority—something that Lupino implicitly suggests that she avoids— one can hardly be expected to author, or direct.

Such anxieties about female creative authority are reminiscent of another, much earlier preface—for truly Lupino's statement can be understood as prefatory to the viewing of her film, since theaters were encouraged to use these materials as publicity. More than two hundred years before Lupino's film, the preface to Mary Shelley's 1831 edition of *Frankenstein* struggles with similar fears about her own "hideous progeny."[70] Creating symbolic connections between her novel and Victor Frankenstein's destructive creature, Shelley expresses insecurities regarding her "imperfect animation" that are similar to Lupino's rendering of the uncontrollable Emmett Myers.[71] Myers's nature, the film tells us, is a product of his tragic past: "Nobody ever gave me anything," Myers tells the men in an unusual moment of self-disclosure. Deformed at birth and rejected by his parents, Myers—like Victor Frankenstein's creature—realizes that the only thing that he can create effectively is destruction.

The oft-quoted rhetorical question with which Shelley begins her preface seems little different than the discourse surrounding the novelty of a female director in the 1950s: "I shall thus give a general answer to the question, so very frequently asked me—'How I, then a young girl, came to think of and to dilate upon so very hideous an idea?'"[72] The similarities between this statement and another of *The Hitch-Hiker*'s promotional articles, "*Hitch-Hiker* Is Rugged Drama But Lupino Still Feminine as Director," are striking. Both depict a humility directly tied to the perceived limits of femininity. Lupino's reluctance to assert her own directorial innovation is also reminiscent of Shelley's reticence to do the same. Shelley continues her preface by stating that, "I was a close imitator—rather doing as others had done than putting down the suggestions of my own mind."[73] In this statement, one can hear echoes of Lupino's explanation of her reluctant directorial debut. Both female authors, of radically different periods and texts, figure their roles somewhat derisively; however, both also use this pattern of humility to advance their work in their respective fields.

Although it is ultimately difficult to make claims too grandiose about the autobiographical intent of Lupino's directorial choices, in part because many other collaborators—writers, cinematographers, censors, and more—were involved with their creation, her films, few of them as there are, do frequent the thematic territory of the unsympathetic "director," a role, her comments would indicate, that she saw herself as occupying. Based upon her own self-performance, Lupino represented herself as being potentially as unsympathetic and as out of place as Myers, his one good eye perennially and defensively open. Lupino's actions—although not overtly criminal in nature, unless we are to take Moskin's claims at face value—were also potentially punishable, a fact that she replayed throughout her public utterances and her films' dramatizations of female ambition. Lupino, who was publicly preoccupied with her own cultural position, repeatedly created roles depicting other directing people who were in every way worse than she was; in fact, her films guaranteed that her audiences would judge these controlling characters in a negative fashion. This might be understood as a form of public exorcism, with Lupino recognizing that ambition, particularly of the female variety, was a potentially negative and undesirable quality. Lupino made films about punishable, hyperbolic ambition in part to contrast her own relatively modest participation in a male profession, while she further modeled her publicity to ensure that her reputation did not transgress too greatly a woman's role in 1950s Hollywood and, more generally, in America.

Epilogue

Alternative Systems

CELEBRITY AFTER HOLLYWOOD

Any one gets into the newspapers, either by being in school or by graduating or by playing a game or by going to a party or by going away or coming home, there is practically no one who does not sometime find himself and his name printed in a paper.
—Gertrude Stein[1]

Virtually since its inception and especially since its industrialization, Hollywood changed the stakes of representation and achievement in American culture. The array of individuals who took personal risks of varying degrees in search of their own elusive Hollywood success demonstrate some of the concrete ways in which Hollywood reoriented the dreams of a progressively westward-gazing American culture. As the quote above indicates, Gertrude Stein presciently observed America's somewhat indiscriminate capacity for endowing media attention, anticipating Andy Warhol's oft-cited claim about everyone having their fifteen minutes of fame. Warhol's success was achieved in part by resignifying the concepts of fame and failure, and in part by disrupting the nature of celebrity-making that dominated the first half of the twentieth century.

Invoking Warhol at the end of a book about the consolidation and power of Hollywood is an act of forward gazing: Where our previous chapters have demonstrated the formidable power of the Hollywood industry, Warhol's relationship to the movie industry reveals the degree to which fame was, in the post–Golden age—"after Hollywood"—publicly deconstructed, even parodied, suggesting a mutation of the culture of celebrity that so powerfully controlled the aspirations of previous generations. Warhol's ideas about Hollywood celebrity resulted in the creation of an alternative constellation bearing more resemblance to our current culture of fame than to that encountered by the cast of characters who populate the preceding pages. Our desire to peer into the ordinary, to bear witness to the everyday has now manifested itself full force; our culture's formerly concealed (one might say repressed) voyeuristic desires are no longer latent and our media reflects this state of affairs. More than ever, we have access to an unabashedly voyeuristic media based on a largely fictive, often-humiliating, and typically debased notion of reality that is antithetical to the high-gloss of Hollywood's Golden Age. From the myriad "reality" television programs that have become a broadcast staple, starting in the 1990s, to internet web-cams and blogs, to the ubiquity of twenty-four-hour news with the need for information to fill those twenty-four hours, to the proliferation of video-share and open-source websites, it seems our culture's desires are becoming more and more Warholian, more and more a glimpse into the unrehearsed (or at least the seemingly unreheased), the unevaluated, the unscripted, even the unwatchable. Warhol's films privileged the heroic capacity of the ordinary and the low, a lesson in the arbitrariness of the culture of fame. American culture appears finally to have caught up with Warhol's doctrine.

This study has identified Hollywood as the geographical and psychological epicenter of celebrity-making in the first half of the twentieth century. Warhol, responding to Hollywood's gradual post-1950s degeneration, created his own studio system that was simultaneously a celebration and a mockery of the Hollywood ideal. Designating his own cast of Superstars—many of them literally off the streets of New York—Warhol loomed over his productions, however little he often had to do with the final products. For Warhol, commercial filmmaking was largely an issue of imprimatur: By "giving" his name to Paul Morrissey, films could be made that bore his trademark but not necessarily his labor, a version of the Jack London enterprise pushed to the limits of its authorial relationship. These films existed because of Warhol's reputation; it seems unlikely that they would have ever been granted a commercial release without Warhol's name. David James argues that the Warhol-produced films acknowledge the degradation of that mythic notion of Hollywood to embrace a deromanticized paradigm of production and authorship.[2] However, Warhol's disappearance—"his erasure of authorship"—was only in deed; the films, of course, increased his own celebrity. Warhol's name functioned as a marketing strategy, not unlike the names discussed earlier in this project, like Emmett Dalton or Jack London, which lent value and authenticity (and in Warhol's case, irony, of course: *Andy Warhol's Trash*, for example) to the films with which they were associated.

Andy Warhol's Heat (1972), one of the Warhol films directed by Paul Morrissey, points precisely to the degradation of Hollywood in a fashion that speaks to our current state of celebrity-making affairs. The film opens with a title that locates the narrative in a time decidedly after Hollywood's fall from grace: "In 1971 another film studio, the Fox on Sunset Boulevard, was torn down." With the words still visible on the screen, former child-star Joey (Factory-made Superstar Joe Dallesandro), the film's protagonist, wanders about the rubble of what was once the major studio. From its opening images, the film nods to the passing of the Golden Age, presenting itself as the several-times-removed descendant of post-studio Hollywood. The trashy landlord (with whom Joey eventually will barter sex for rent) at the apartment where Joey plans to live while he tries to reinvigorate his acting career echoes this sentiment to Joey: "This LA's going to the dogs. You used to be on TV, huh? . . . When you was a kid, I sorta' remember . . . yeah . . . it was a Western. I have a lot of show folks stayin' here." These show folks, however, are a different sort than those produced and publicized by the studio system and its big screens; They are the studio era's hideous, cast-off progeny: Joey, who is out of work and will sleep with anything that moves (a recurrent role for Dallesandro in these productions); Jessie, the strange, mentally slow daughter of a desperately lonely aging actress, Sally Todd, who starred on "The Ranch" with Joey when he was a child; and a pair of curly-locked brothers, one a chronic masturbator dressed perpetually in a housedress. The brother's "act," which takes place at a local club, climaxes in their engaging in various sexual acts together. This is the Hollywood underbelly revealed and revolting.

Although frequently inarticulate, always poorly acted, and often downright abrasive, *Heat* toys with the politics of visibility and invisibility upon which Hollywood has always relied. In fact, the film's thematic concerns most closely approximate Warhol's own relationship to the motion picture industry, a relationship predicated upon making the invisible visible, if only for a moment. To this end, David James argues that all of Warhol's "strategies" can be classified as systems of exclusion: "Finally, the films themselves will be made unavailable and all that will remain will be reputation, fame, publicity. Warhol's installation of himself as a device for securing public attention, a device for mediating between a product and the public, begins as a feature of style and ends as a marketing strategy."[3] Although James is right to follow Warhol's lead by reducing the artist to his own holy trinity—reputation, fame, publicity—it is worth also considering Warhol in a somewhat more democratic light. More than a means of catapulting himself into the limelight—which, after all, he already occupied—movies became a way for Warhol to catapult, rescue, and amplify those around him and to ironize the very idea of fame in the process.

In our current, post-Warholian times, Hollywood has receded somewhat from the center of the system of celebrity-making. Hollywood ambitions still exist, of course, but not in the same fashion as they did in the celebrity capital's early years and during the studio's oligopolistic heyday. Images—cinematic, televisual, digital—continue to affect our ever-evolving understanding of celebrity and success, conceptions that have now moved even farther away from reputation in its pre-Hollywood sense. This ongoing redefinition is at least partly a response to the digital age and its promise of media democracy, as it is due to what we might term the de-exceptionalizing of celebrities across the board. The gatekeepers helming what remains of Hollywood may still control certain elements of the celebrity-machine, but the electronic age has guaranteed that theirs is not the only gate.

YouTube.com, whose slogan is "broadcast yourself," is a case in point. Started in early 2005, YouTube is a free portal for sharing and viewing video content, original or recycled, amateur or professional. Anyone can post content on YouTube; no executive decides if your video warrants "broadcasting." In its short existence, YouTube—with its truly democratic conceptualization—has exploded onto the American cultural scene. YouTube's media fact sheet claims that the site is "currently serving 100 million videos per day, with more than 65,000 videos being uploaded daily."[4] According to an October 2006 *New Yorker* profile, by late summer 2006, "there were approximately six million videos archives on the site," helping to make YouTube the "tenth-biggest site on the Internet, drawing more visits than EBay, Amazon, or Wikipedia."[5]

In less than two years, YouTube has become a real alternative to other media experiences—movies, television, newspapers—one whose content and its status are determined by other members, who rank, review, rate, and link to the videos on the site. YouTube already has generated a number of homegrown stars (LonelyGirl15, for example, had her moment) and fleeting sensations (such as the OK Go Treadmill video), leading to some secondary lives in the "legitimate" (remember Jack London's use of this term) media as personalities are invited to appear or videos are rebroadcast on the news, on infotainment programming such as *The Daily Show*, and on the late-night talk-show circuit. Anyone with a video camera, the capability to upload content onto the internet, and an attention-grabbing concept has a shot at YouTube celebrity and its potential rewards (which remain to be seen). This is the Fame and Fortune Contest recast in a virtually unrecognizable form. In some ways, the stakes are seemingly the same: Put yourself out there and see how you are judged. But these are not the relatively well-defined Hollywood ambitions of yesteryear, in nature or in kind. YouTube, and much of the current internet celebrity buzz, raises important questions about where such ambitions might now be located: What are the potential rewards for the "winners" here, and who will bestow them upon this generation of aspirants?

The potential longevity of any YouTube celebrity cannot be determined at this point, although one suspects that, as with so much of contemporary celebrity culture, these personalities will have relatively short shelf lives.[6] Increased access has created a culture of sometimes equally, sometimes considerably less self-aware Warhols—or at least proto-superstars—creating their own modes of publicity, modes that lack the centrality and consolidated power of an earlier age but that promise to reach a potentially unprecedented segment of the world population, remaking the celebrity system—or at least one part of it—once again. Our various media outlets currently cater to and nurture a need to observe the ordinary and to grant celebrity to those who exceed it, however nominally and in whatever, often bizarre fashion. Hollywood still beckons hopefuls and fans alike, but its geographically specific allure; its sense of itself as a concentrated empire of limitless power and potential, and its ability to convince others of the same; its promise to amplify and even to change identity, as well as to dictate the geographical specificity of certain ambitions, have dissipated in the post-studio era of diffusion, indiscriminateness, and immediacy.

Notes

Works frequently cited have been identified by the following abbreviations:

EA	Gertrude Stein, *Everybody's Autobiography*. Originally published 1937. Reprint, Cambridge, Mass.: Exact Change, 1993.
HT	Jack London, *Hearts of Three*. New York: Macmillan, 1920.
JL	Jack London Collection, Huntington Library, San Marino, California.
LGS/CVV	Edward Burns, ed. *The Letters of Gertrude Stein and Carl Van Vechten*, Volumes I and II. New York: Columbia University Press, 1986.
LGS/TW	Edward Burns and Ulla Dydo, eds. *The Letters of Gertrude Stein & Thornton Wilder*. New Haven: Yale University Press, 1996.
SL	Stuart Lake Collection, Huntington Library, San Marino, California.
WSH	William S. Hart Collection, Seaver Center for Western History Research, Los Angeles County Museum of Natural History, Los Angeles, California.

Introduction: Hollywood Ambitions (pages 1–16)

1. James Quirk, "Moral House-Cleaning in Hollywood: An Open Letter to Mr. Will Hays," *Photoplay* (April 1922): 52.

2. Lucy Fischer and Marcia Landy's anthology, *Stars: The Film Reader* (New York: Routledge, 2004), also seeks to "address, augment, and/or modify the range, complexity, and dimension of work on stardom in the extant critical literature," albeit in a different fashion by looking at "European and non-western" cinemas, "'marginalized' audiences," television, the "news star," "performance as industrial labor," opera, and "Asian and African-American performers" (8–9). My ideas about celebrity have been especially informed and influenced by Richard deCordova, *Picture Personalities: The Emergence of the Star System in America* (Chicago: University of Illinois Press, 1990); Richard Dyer, *Stars* (London: British Film Institute, 1979); Christine Gledhill, ed., *Stardom: Industry of Desire* (London: Routledge, 1991); Andrew Britton, *Katharine Hepburn: Star as Feminist* (New York: Columbia University Press, 2003); Joshua Gamson, *Claims to Fame: Celebrity in Contemporary America* (Berkeley: University of California Press, 1994); Gaylyn Studlar, *This Mad Masquerade: Stardom and Masculinity in the Jazz Age* (New York: Columbia University Press, 1996); and P. David Marshall, *Celebrity and Power: Fame in Contemporary Culture* (Minneapolis: University of Minnesota Press, 1997). Leo Braudy, *The Frenzy of Renown* (1986; New York: Random House, 1997), sets the most significant precedent for expanding the study of fame across disciplines.

3. Leo Braudy, *The Frenzy of Renown*, 17.

4. Charles Ponce de Leon, *Self-Exposure: Human-Interest Journalism and the Emergence of Celebrity in America, 1890–1940* (Chapel Hill: University of North Carolina Press, 2002), 4.

5. John Rodden, *The Politics of Literary Reputation* (New York: Oxford University Press, 1989), 54.

6. Gary Alan Fine, *Difficult Reputations: Collective Memories of the Evil, Inept, and Controversial* (Chicago: University of Chicago Press, 2001), 2.

7. Ibid., 7; 2.

8. Britton, *Katharine Hepburn*, 15.

9. Max Horkheimer and Theodor Adorno, *Dialectic of Enlightenment* (New York: Herder and Herder, 1972), 126.

10. For a fascinating study of failure in nineteenth-century America that attends to the American dream and the frustrated aspirations inspired by capitalism, see Scott Sandage, *Born Losers: A History of Failure in America* (Cambridge: Harvard University Press, 2005). Jonathan Auerbach's *The Romance of Failure: First-Person Fictions of Poe, Hawthorne, and James* (New York: Oxford University Press, 1989) also deals with ideas of American self-hood and the frustrated desire for coherence and authenticity. Martha Banta's *Failure and Success in America: A Literary Debate* (Princeton: Princeton University Press, 1978) offers a sweeping survey of success in its myriad guises throughout American literary history.

11. In light of this focus, it is worth considering Fine's somewhat parallel construction with regard to his sociological approach in *Difficult Reputations*: "scholars who have examined the development of reputations and collective memory have generally examined figures who are treated as heroic or as moral exemplars" (10). Where Fine deems that his "eight case studies do not by themselves make for an intellectually coherent argument," my aim is to use the case studies here to present a sense of evolving ideas about reputation, celebrity, and identity that can be brought into focus through these different Hollywood experiences taking place over the course of the first half of the twentieth century.

12. Robert Sklar, *Movie-Made America: A Social History of American Movies* (New York: Random House, 1993), vi.

13. In "Ambiguous Ecologies: Stardom's Domestic Mise-en-Scène," Simon Dixon performs a provocative reading of the "domestic setting of movie stardom," movie star homes, and their figuration in the popular press. *Cinema Journal* 42, no. 3 (Winter 2003): 84. Lupino's own home is pictured on a View-Master reel of star's homes from this era, one of the many commercial products used by Hollywood to publicize its stars and market their lifestyles.

Chapter One: Celebrity in the Movie Age (pages 17–30)

1. See Raymond Williams, "The Romantic Artist," in *Culture and Society: 1780–1950* (New York: Columbia University Press, 1958); and Leo Lowenthal, *Literature*,

Popular Culture, and Society (New Jersey: Prentice Hall, 1961) for more on the evolution of mass culture and its relationship to fame, particularly of the literary variety, in the eighteenth and nineteenth centuries.

2. Lucy Fischer and Marcia Landy's introduction to *Stars: The Film Reader* (New York: Routledge, 2004) begins with a useful overview of the history of film celebrity and star criticism. An earlier assessment of the critical literature appears in Richard Dyer, *Stars* (London: British Film Institute, 1979).

3. Daniel J. Boorstin, *The Image* (1961; New York: Atheneum, 1987).

4. Following Daniel Boorstin's lead, Joy Kasson also defines celebrity along these lines in her *Buffalo Bill's Wild West: Celebrity, Memory, and Popular History* (New York: Hill and Wang, 2000), 123.

5. Richard Ohmann, *Selling Culture: Magazines, Markets, and Class at the Turn of the Century* (New York: Verso, 1996), 239–40.

6. Leo Braudy, *The Frenzy of Renown* (New York: Vintage Boooks, 1997), 493. Kasson also notes that during the 1860s inexpensive photographs "became part of the currency of business, politics, friendship, and show business" (*Buffalo Bill's Wild West*, 18).

7. For more on this see Joshua Gamson, *Claims to Fame: Celebrity in Contemporary America* (Berkeley: University of California Press, 1994), 19–20.

8. Braudy, *Frenzy of Renown*, 498.

9. Gamson briefly discusses Rockefeller's media-driven transformation from greedy capitalist to humanized philanthropist in *Claims to Fame*, 22.

10. See Alan Trachtenberg, *The Incorporation of America* (New York: Hill and Wang, 1982), 126–27, for a useful discussion of early photographs, particularly of the poor. Charles Ponce de Leon, *Self-Exposure: Human Interest Journalism and the Emergence of Celebrity in America, 1890–1940*, also provides a compelling analysis of the rise of celebrity journalism during these years (Chapel Hill: University of North Carolina Pres, 2002).

11. Ponce de Leon, *Self-Exposure*, 30–33.

12. Ibid., 42.

13. Campbell MacCulloch, "What Makes Them Stars?" *Photoplay* (October 1928): 108.

14. See Walter Benjamin's influential article, "The Work of Art in the Age of Mechanical Reproduction," *Illuminations*, ed. Hannah Arendt, trans. Harry Zohn (New York: Schocken Books, 1969), for a discussion of the conceptual shifts inspired by mechanical reproduction.

15. Daniel J. Boorstin, *The Image*, 61.

16. Ibid., 64.

17. An eight-month run of the magazine is available in the Huntington Library rare books collection.

18. *Celebrities Monthly* (April 1895): 1. In "Announcing Wares, Winning Patrons, Voicing Ideals: Thinking about the History and Theory of Film Advertising," Janet Staiger notes that Edison performed a similar promotion over ten years later, in 1909,

by announcing the use of "*real pictorial posters made from actual photographs of scenes in the pictures they advertise.*" *Cinema Journal* 29, no. 3 (1990): 7.

19. As will be noted in chapter three's discussion of Jack London, collecting autographs of famous personages had become a "craze" by the turn of the century.

20. Williams, *Culture and Society*, 32.

21. Leo Lowenthal, *Literature, Popular Culture, and Society* (New Jersey: Prentice Hall, 1961), xvii.

22. Braudy, *Frenzy of Renown*, 417.

23. Ibid., 425.

24. In "Seeing Stars," Janet Staiger notes that the theatrical "star system" began around 1820. *Stardom: Industry of Desire*, ed. Christine Gledhill (New York: Routledge, 1991), 3–16. See Jib Fowles, *Starstruck* (Washington, D.C.: Smithsonian Institution Press, 1992), 18–21, for a brief discussion of the role theater played in relation to the origins of movie stardom.

25. Ohmann, *Selling Culture*, 19.

26. See Eileen Bowser, *The Transformation of Cinema: 1907–1915* (New York: Charles Scribner's, 1990) for a more thorough discussion of Hollywood's formative years in her chapter, "Detours on the Way to Hollywood," 149–65.

27. Kevin Starr, *Inventing The Dream: California through the Progressive Era* (New York: Oxford University Press, 1985), 313.

28. Vachel Lindsay, *The Art of the Moving Picture* (New York: Macmillan, 1915), 218–19; brackets mine.

29. Fox Entertainments advertisement, "An avalanche of entertainment making talent," *Picture-Play Magazine* (November 1919): 9.

30. Starr, *Inventing the Dream*, 320.

31. See Ohmann, *Selling Culture*, especially 77–78, for a discussion of commercial brand names; Eileen Bowser's chapter "Brand Names and Stars," in *The Transformation of Cinema*, 103–21; and Jane Gaines, "From Elephants to Lux Soap: The Programming and 'Flow' of Early Motion Picture Exploitation," *The Velvet Light Trap* 25 (1990), especially her discussion of the Lux Toilet Soap campaign on 40–41.

32. Gertrude Stein, "A Transatlantic Interview 1946," *A Primer for the Gradual Understanding of Gertrude Stein*, ed. Robert Haas (Los Angeles: Black Sparrow Press, 1971), 31.

33. Charles Musser notes this date in "The Changing Status of the Actor," in *Before Hollywood: Turn-of-the-Century Films from American Archives* (New York: American Federation of Arts, 1986).

34. For more on this, see Bowser, *Transformation of Cinema*, 117; and Kathryn Fuller, *At the Picture Show: Small-Town Audiences and the Creation of Movie Fan Culture* (Washington, D.C.: Smithsonian Institution Press, 1996).

35. Richard deCordova, "The Emergence of the Star System in America," in *Stardom: Industry of Desire*, ed. Christine Gledhill (New York: Routledge, 1991), 17.

36. Tom Gunning, "'Now You See It, Now You Don't': The Temporality of the Cinema of Attractions," in *Silent Film*, ed. Richard Abel (New Brunswick: Rutgers University Press, 1996), 73.

37. Ibid.

38. Ibid., 74.

39. "Photographs of Moving Picture Actors: A New Method of Lobby Advertising," *Moving Picture World*, January 5, 1910, 50.

40. "The Actor—Likewise the Actress," *Moving Picture World*, November 12, 1910, 1099.

41. Catherine Kerr illustrates that "in moving from an undifferentiated volume output offered by competitive firms to a highly differentiated consumer product—star personality—offered by vertically integrated corporations, the industry followed the typical course of development for large-scale businesses of this period." "Incorporating the Star: The Intersection of Business and Aesthetic Strategies in Early American Film," *Business History Review* 64, no. 3 (Autumn 1990): 387.

42. MacCulloch, "What Makes Them Stars?" 44.

43. deCordova, "The Emergence of the Star System," 26.

44. Scott Sandage, *Born Losers: A History of Failure in America* (Cambridge: Harvard University Press, 2005), 260.

45. Ibid., 5.

46. Gary Alan Fine, *Difficult Reputations: Collective Memories of the Evil, Inept, and Controversial* (Chicago: University of Chicago Press, 2001), 12–21.

47. In their analysis of artistic reputation, Lang and Lang also point out that select artists "reach the pinnacle of celebrity status, they have arrived—or achieved renown—when their names have become established currency outside the more intimate world of fellow artists and admiring clients." Gladys Engel Lang and Kurt Lang, *Etched in Memory: The Building and Survival of Artistic Reputation* (Chapel Hill: University of North Carolina Press, 1990), 6.

48. Katherine Albert, "Don't Envy the Stars," *Photoplay* (March 1929): 32–33.

Chapter Two: When the West Was Done (pages 31–62)

1. Raoul Walsh, *Each Man in His Time: The Life Story of a Director* (New York: Farrar, Straus and Giroux, 1974), 103.

2. Ibid.

3. While they bear no responsibility for my claim here, I would like to acknowledge my conversations with Peter Blodgett, Don Chaput, and Sue Hodson on this matter. With regard to the recirculation of this story see, for example, Casey Tefertiller, *Wyatt Earp: The Life Behind the Legend* (New York: John Wiley & Sons, 1997); and Allen Barra, *Inventing Wyatt Earp: His Life and Many Legends* (New York: Carroll & Graff, 1998), 341–42. The facts about Wyatt Earp's life are slippery at best. There are few reliable written records that pertain to his actions and as Don Chaput points out in *The Earp Papers: In a Brother's Image* (New York: Affiliated Writers of America, 1994), there is no hard evidence to prove that Earp actually killed anyone during his lifetime despite the fact that he is probably the most famous gunslinger in Western history (xi). Earp was neither a dedicated correspondent nor diarist, so it is difficult to make

claims about the details of his life. Earp in fact calls himself "a poor correspondent" in a May 4, 1928, letter to William S. Hart. [The William S. Hart and Wyatt Earp letters are available at the Seaver Center for Western History Research, Los Angeles County Museum of Natural History, Los Angeles, California. All citations of their correspondence refer to this collection and will be noted as WSH.] On the other hand, Jack London was prolific, as was his wife Charmian, who kept a meticulous diary of his whereabouts and encounters; Russ Kingman, *Jack London: A Definitive Chronology* (Middletown, Calif.: David Rejl, 1992), builds on Charmian's diaries to account for London's day-to-day activities. [Charmian's diaries are part of the extensive Jack London collection at the Huntington Library; the 1913–1915 volumes are relevant here, JL227–229. As with future citations, JL indicates previously unpublished materials in the library's Jack London collection.] There are only a few days in the 1913 to 1915 period—and this is an overly generous window of opportunity—during which such a meeting with Walsh could have taken place. Even if it had transpired during one of these days, it seems unlikely that it would have gone unmentioned in Charmian's diary and in London's prolific correspondence. This is particularly the case because Walsh notes that Charlie Chaplin also chatted with the men during lunch and London was quite an admirer of Chaplin; in fact, Chaplin's films are noted repeatedly in Charmian's diaries, particularly during 1916. My research suggests that the only days London was in Los Angeles during this period were July 20–27, 1913; October 12–14, 1913; December 14–16, 1913; June 26–July 3, 1914; December 11–15, 1914; and July 28–30, 1915. These dates include travel days. More than half of these days are detailed by Charmian to the extent that it would have been impossible for London to meet Earp or Walsh. If this encounter did happen, it was probably on one of the 1914 visits, during which there are some gaps in Charmian's accounting for her husband's movements.

4. See, for example, Paul Andrew Hutton, "Celluloid Lawman: Wyatt Earp goes to Hollywood," *American West* (May/June 1984): 58–65; and "Showdown at the Hollywood Corral: Wyatt Earp and the Movies," *Montana, the Magazine of Western History* (Summer 1995): 2–31.

5. See Steven J. Ross, *Working-Class Hollywood: Silent Film and the Shaping of Class in America* (Princeton: Princeton University Press, 1998) for a useful discussion of cinema's transitional period. See also Charles Musser, *The Emergence of Cinema* (Los Angeles: University of California Press, 1990) and Bowser, *Transformation of Cinema*.

6. Hutton, "Showdown at the Hollywood Corral," 5.

7. John P. Clum, "Wyatt Earp, Frontier Marshall," book review, *Arizona Historical Review* 4, no. 4 (January 1932): 71.

8. Musser, *Emergence of Cinema*, 203; 14.

9. Eileen Bowser, *The Transformation of Cinema* (New York: Charles Scribner's, 1990), 170.

10. Richard Slotkin, *Gunfighter Nation: The Myth of the Frontier in Twentieth-Century America* (New York: Atheneum, 1992).

11. "The Last Stand of the Dalton Boys," advertisement, *Moving Picture World* (July 1912): 277.

12. Jane Tomkins, *West of Everything: The Inner Life of Westerns* (New York: Oxford University Press, 1992), 179.

13. Cody's show actually failed in 1913 but he toured after this failure with a circus and later revived his Wild West show, which continued after his death. Cody referred to it as the "Wild West" and not the "Wild West Show." See Slotkin, *Gunfighter Nation*, for a discussion of Buffalo Bill's Wild West; and Joy Kasson, *Buffalo Bill's Wild West: Celebrity, Memory, and Popular History* (New York: Hill and Wang, 2000), 5; 256–62; and throughout.

14. "Movies Bust Bill Show," *Variety*, August 8, 1913, 14.

15. "Westerns: The Six-Gun Galahad," *Time*, March 30, 1959, 57.

16. Kasson, *Buffalo Bill's Wild West*, 5; 8.

17. Frank Norris, "The Frontier Gone at Last," in *Frank Norris: Novels and Essays*, ed. Donald Pizer (1902; repr., New York: Library of America, 1986), 1185.

18. In *Buffalo Bill's Wild West*, 255–61, Kasson discusses Cody's film involvement in detail.

19. Robert Anderson, "The Role of the Western Film Genre in Industry Competition, 1907–1911," *The Journal of the University Film Association* 11, no. 2 (Spring 1979): 20.

20. Bowser, *Transformation of Cinema*, 192–23; brackets mine. Quite coincidentally, Jack London covered the same fight over the course of eleven days as a *New York Herald* correspondent; Wyatt Earp also had witnessed the famous filming of the Fitzsimmons-Corbett fight over a decade earlier. Based upon one of the dates of Cody's contracts, the probable production date of this picture is 1911. According to Bowser, "Jack Johnson, a 'person of color,' knocked out the white ex-champion, Jim Jeffries" on July 4, 1910. The film was scandalous because reformers and officials feared rioting in response to Johnson's victory and the film was banned in many cities. See Bowser, 201–202.

21. Although I think she overstates her point, Kasson claims that "viewers left his performances believing that they had seen the actual deeds for which he was famous," *Buffalo Bill's Wild West*, 5–6.

22. I want to thank Don Chaput for sharing his insights into and documentation of California and Arizona history. The Los Angeles census of 1910 (Vol. 039, E.D. 0154, No. 0145) lists Earp's occupation as "miner, gold and copper, employer."

23. From the Huntington Library's Stuart Lake Collection, in a letter from Earp to Mr. J. H. Hammond, May 21, 1925. Future references to the Stuart Lake Collection will be noted as SL.

24. See Earp's July 3, 1925, letter to William S. Hart, WSH. No manuscript of Earp's screenplay exists and it is therefore impossible to know if the screenplay was ever written.

25. From the George W. Parsons Diary, September 8, 1900, entry. Arizona Historical Society, courtesy of Don Chaput.

26. Dan Streible, "A Return to the 'Primitive': One Hundred Years of Cinema . . . and Boxing," *Arachne* 2, no. 2 (1995): 308.

27. Musser, *Emergence of Cinema*, 196. The details of the Corbett-Fitzsimmons fight are taken primarily from Musser's account, 194–208.

28. Ibid., 196–97.

29. "Fitzsimmons Now Champion of the World," *The New York World*, March 18, 1897, 1; 2.

30. Ibid., 1.

31. Musser notes that Fitzsimmons "toured with his vaudeville company and gave a sparring exhibition" during the 1897–1898 theatrical season. Musser, *Emergence of Cinema*, 201.

32. Ibid., 197–98. Musser reports that the film had a wide distribution, including showings in Manhattan, Brooklyn, Boston, Chicago, Buffalo, New Haven, Philadelphia, Pittsburgh, San Francisco, Portland, and then overseas (199). In "A Return to the 'Primitive,'" Dan Streible estimates that the Veriscope Company made as much as $750,000 off of the film's exhibition (314).

33. Musser, *Emergence of Cinema*, 201. Lubin provided reenactments of a variety of events, including war-related subjects. Ibid., 257.

34. Ibid., 201.

35. The date is cited in Tefertiller, *Wyatt Earp*, 335.

36. Hutton, "Showdown," 3.

37. Hutton, "Celluloid Lawman," 58; 5.

38. Anderson, "Role of the Western," 22. See Richard Abel's *The Red Rooster Scare: Making Cinema American, 1900–1910* (Berkeley: University of California Press, 1999) for a discussion of the Western film as a distinct American product. Abel also notes developing associations between the American Western and notions of authenticity (for example, 157–58).

39. Anderson, "Role of the Western," 25; 257.

40. Andre Bazin, "The Western: Or the American Film Par Excellence," *What is Cinema?* vol. II, trans. Hugh Gray (Berkeley: University of California Press, 1971), 148.

41. WSH.

42. James McQuade, "Famous Cowboys in Motion Pictures," *The Film Index*, June 25, 1910, 8.

43. Ibid.

44. In 1894, Thomas Edison discussed not the cowboy but the opera when coming to similar conclusions about motion pictures, commenting on the medium's ability to record the living in order to later project the dead in his preface to Antonia and W. K. L. Dickson, "Edison's Invention of the Kineto-Phonograph," *Century* 48 (May 1894–October 1894): 206–14.

45. For more on the cowboy environment in early Hollywood, see Tefertiller, *Wyatt Earp*, 317; Ben E. Pingenot, *Siringo* (College Station: Texas A&M University Press, 1989); and Diana Serra Cary's *The Hollywood Posse: The Story of a Gallant Band of Horsemen Who Made Movie History* (Norman: University of Oklahoma Press, 1996).

46. Kasson notes an analogous kind of rupture in cinematic believability that

might have resulted had Earp played himself at this point in his life: for the one-reel film, *The Life of Buffalo Bill* (1912), the sixty-seven-year-old Cody was re-enacting "deeds he had done at the age of thirty." *Buffalo Bill's Wild West*, 257. The film "was not popular and disappeared from view" (257).

47. *Moving Picture World*, March 27, 1920, 2102.

48. Ibid.

49. The advertisement appeared in *Moving Picture World*, July 1912, 277. Courtesy of Don Chaput. The advertisement infers that the term "actuality" means that the film represents "actual" (and therefore real) events. I also use the term "reality" here in the same way that Musser uses the term "realism" in his discussion of *The Great Train Robbery* to connote the ways in which that film uses cinematic techniques to best approximate reality. Musser, *Emergence of Cinema*, 355.

50. *Moving Picture World*, November 30, 1918, 914.

51. *Moving Picture World*, September 14, 1918, 1584.

52. *Los Angeles Times*, February 15, 1920, unpaged, courtesy of Don Chaput. This kind of Western movie exploitation had been done before: Al Jennings toured the country with Thanhouser's *Beating Back* (1913) and marshal William Tilghman toured with *The Passing of the Oklahoma Outlaw* (1915). See Suzanne Schrems, "Al Jennings: The Image of an Outlaw," *Journal of Popular Culture* 22, no. 4 (Summer 1989): 113–14. Kasson reports that Buffalo Bill made an appearance at a Denver screening of one of his films to enhance "the film's claims to realism. After the segments that featured his exploits, Buffalo Bill appeared onstage, riding his horse Isham." *Buffalo Bill's Wild West*, 262.

53. Unpaged, unsourced, undated advertisement courtesy of Don Chaput.

54. *Moving Picture World*, November 30, 1918, 914.

55. According to Pingenot, Siringo moved to California in 1922 and to the "heart of Hollywood" in 1924; he was born in 1855 and was sixty-six when he expressed interest in going to Hollywood to act in films. *Siringo*, 101–104.

56. WSH, February 14, 1927.

57. Pingenot, *Siringo*, 105; 109.

58. "Jennings Outlaw Film Winning Praise," *Moving Picture World*, January 4, 1919, 51.

59. *Motion Picture Studio Directory* (n.p., 1921), 181. The Natural History Museum of Los Angeles has a run of this publication.

60. Reprinted in Jack London, *Jack London Reports,* ed. King Hendricks and Irving Shepard (New York: Doubleday, 1970), 265.

61. WSH, September 6, 1926.

62. "With Bill Hart on Location," *Pictures and Picturegoer*, September 4, 1920, 295.

63. William S. Hart, "Bill Hart Introduces a Real—not Reel—Hero," *Morning Telegraph* 98, section five (October 9, 1921): 2. The quotations from this article that follow are all from this page.

64. WSH, November 16, 1928.

65. WSH, February 22, 1926.

66. Ibid.

67. WSH, Earp to Hart, April 11, 1925.

68. WSH, October 21, 1925.

69. *Los Angeles Times*, January 15, 1929, unpaged; courtesy of Don Chaput.

70. WSH, December 18, 1928.

71. WSH. The letter is dated June 3, but the year is only legible as 192(?).

72. WSH.

73. WSH, April 11, 1925.

74. WSH, Earp to Hart, July 3, 1925.

75. Kevin Brownlow, *The War, The West, and the Wilderness* (New York: Alfred A. Knopf, 1979), 280.

76. SL.

77. See William Luhr, "Reception, Representation, and the OK Corral: Shifting Images of Wyatt Earp," in *Authority and Transgression in Literature and Film*, ed. Bonnie Braendlin and Hans Braendlin (Gainesville: University of Florida Press, 1996) for a discussion of the ways that Earp has been used by filmmakers over the course of the twentieth century to reflect upon shifting notions of masculinity.

78. Quoted in John Richard Stephens, *Wyatt Earp Speaks!* (Cambria, Calif.: Fern Canyon Press, 1998), 264.

79. J. M. Scanland, "Lurid Trials are Left by Olden-Day Bandits," *Los Angeles Times*, Part II, March 12, 1922, 2.

80. In a November 18, 1924, letter to Hart, Earp recounts his visit with Scanland, who "expressed regret over the incident and offered apologies and amends, and gave me a type-written retraction of the story which he very willingly signed" (WSH).

81. WSH, November 18, 1924.

82. WSH, October 21, 1925.

83. WSH.

84. For more on these issues, see David Bordwell, Janet Staiger, and Kristin Thompson, *The Classical Hollywood Cinema: Film Style and Mode of Production to 1960* (New York: Columbia University Press, 1985), 131–32.

85. Letter from Earp to Doubleday, June 25, 1927, Walter Noble Burns Collection, University of Arizona Library, Special Collections. Courtesy of Don Chaput.

86. Walter Noble Burns Collection. Telegram dated June 15, 1927.

87. Tefertiller, *Wyatt Earp*, 324.

88. SL, William S. Hart correspondence folder, January 28, 1929.

89. SL.

90. SL, November 6, 1928; brackets indicate illegible writing in handwritten letters.

91. SL, November 14, 1928.

92. Earp handed over legal rights to Lake on this matter, writing from Los Angeles on November 16, 1928, that "This will authorize you to act for me in any settlement of my claim against the publishers or author of the book 'Helldorado' for publishing

my photograph with a copyright ownership ascribed to one, Newton, it being understood that there is to be no expense to me whatsoever resulting from any action you may take." SL.

93. SL.

94. Adela Rogers St. Johns, "I Knew Wyatt Earp," *The American Weekly*, May 22, 1960, 10.

95. Charles Ponce de Leon, *Self-Exposure: Human-Interest Journalism and the Emergence of Celebrity in America, 1890–1940* (Chapel Hill: University of North Carolina Press, 2002), 42.

96. One such autograph request can be found in the Ellsworth Collection, Arizona Historical Society. In the same collection is a 1928 letter from someone else who sought out Earp's pictures: Fran Wilstach of the Motion Picture Producers and Distributors of America, who sought to pass the autograph on to the New York Public Library.

Chapter Three: Rethinking Authorship in Jack London's Hollywood (pages 63–98)

1. The film does not appear to survive, nor is it listed in Tony Williams, *Jack London: The Movies* (Los Angeles: David Rejl, 1992), though Williams mentions it elsewhere in his book. The New York press, however, covered its arrival and run and the Jack London scrapbooks at the Huntington Library (Box 17, microfilm reel #8, Vol. 12) document the event with extensive clippings. All primary press citations are from the scrapbook and page numbers are rarely identified. As in chapter two, all previously unpublished Jack London material will be noted with JL.

2. Many incorrect press reports claimed that London would star in these films. For example, an excerpt from the Long Beach California *Citizen* (April 28, 1913), "Jack London's Various Works Will Be Shown in Films Made by Local Company," asserts that "Mr. London will play the part of the leading character himself in some of his stories, and his photograph, as that of the author, will be sown [*sic*] on the films." JL Box 517, Scrapbook (microfilm) Vol. 12. More accurate was the Los Angeles *Tribune*'s April 26, 1913, account: "'I am not an actor,' he said last night, 'and I never plan to be. My connection with the motion pictures will be solely as author and advisor for their production, although I may pose at my desk.'" Ibid.

3. JL Box 517, Scrapbook (microfilm) Vol. 15 contains this detailed synopsis from an advertisement for the film in which London is described only in the context of the film's first image. While it is appropriate that the famous author should open the film, his absence during the remainder is surprising given the film's marketing and reception.

4. JL Box 517, Ephemera: Scrapbooks (microfilm) Vol. 12.

5. Ibid.

6. Martin Johnson, *Through the South Seas with Jack London* (New York: Dodd, Mead and Company, 1913), ix. The cruise was recycled in many forms: it was heavily

covered in the newspapers; London published *The Cruise of the Snark* in 1911 (New York: Macmillan); Charmian followed with *The Log of the Snark* in 1915 (New York: Macmillan). It is worth noting that Johnson's book, which advertises itself as possessing "numerous illustrations" (thirty-three to be exact), contains only one photograph of the Londons.

7. JL Box 517, Ephemera: Scrapbooks (microfilm) Vol. 12.

8. Jack London, "When Jack London Was Amazed," *The Motion Picture News*, December 6, 1913, 17.

9. Williams, *Jack London*, 223–24.

10. Robert S. Birchard, "Jack London and the Movies," *Film History* 1 (1987): 15–37.

11. Jonathan Auerbach, *Male Call: Becoming Jack London* (Durham: Duke University Press, 1996), 2–3.

12. Ibid., 24.

13. Loren Glass, "Nobody's Renown: Plagiarism and Publicity in the Career of Jack London," *American Literature* 71, no. 3 (1999): 531.

14. Birchard, "Jack London," 16.

15. London, "When Jack London Was Amazed," 18.

16. Jack London, "The Message of Motion Pictures," orig. pub. February 1915; reprinted in *Authors on Film*, ed. Harry Geduld (Bloomington: Indiana University Press, 1972), 106.

17. Ibid., 106–107.

18. Vachel Lindsay, *The Art of the Motion Picture* (New York: Macmillan, 1915), 289.

19. W. Stephen Bush, "Jack London—'Picture Writer'," *Moving Picture World*, June 31, 1914, 547.

20. Ibid., 548.

21. Ibid., 547. Throughout *Martin Eden*, Martin is subject to vivid visions of his past and future (New York: Macmillan, 1909); reprinted in *Jack London: Novels and Social Writing*, ed. Donald Pizer (New York: Library of America, 1982). The use of such intense visual ruptures prefigures London's reliance on this device in the novel that I will explore later in the chapter, *Hearts of Three* (1920, first American edition).

22. Bush, "Jack London," 547; emphasis mine.

23. JL11033; emphasis mine.

24. According to Hensley Woodbridge, John London, and George Tweney in *Jack London: A Bibliography* (Georgetown: Talisman Press, 1966), "London is known to have personally written the majority of the text in this sketch of his life" (263).

25. Henry Meade Bland, "Jack London," *Overland Monthly* (May 1904): 374.

26. Glass, "Nobody's Renown," 531.

27. The ephemera collection is arranged by subject in JL Boxes 518–590. JL Box 522 contains the autograph requests.

28. See Eileen Bowser, *The Transformation of Cinema: 1907–1915* (New York: Charles Scribner's, 1990), particularly 42–44, for a further discussion of this era.

29. For more on the use of literary sources for early films, see William Uricchio and Roberta Pearson, "The Film Industry's Drive for Respectability" in *Reframing Culture: The Case of the Vitagraph Quality Films* (Princeton: Princeton University Press, 1993), 41–65.

30. See JL Box 517, reel 8. Writers such as Rex Beach, Ida Tarbell, and Booth Tarkington had also been dabbling in this "no-man's land" of cinematic production.

31. JL Box 517, Scrapbook Vol. 14.

32. JL Box 517, Scrapbook Vol. 12.

33. From the Hobart Bosworth Collection at the Margaret Herrick Library, Academy of Motion Pictures, Los Angeles, CA. #U-375, Scrapbook No. 4. *Herald Times* dated August 6, 1913.

34. Auerbach, *Male Call*, 30.

35. Hobart Bosworth Collection, Scrapbook #4, *Fresno Republican*, "Jack London's Many Adventures Reviewed at the Kinema Today," March 9, 1914.

36. April 29, 1913. JL Box 517, Scrapbook Vol. 12.

37. JL21042.

38. Hobart Bosworth Collection, Scrapbook #4, Gardiner Bradford, "'Sea Wolf' Picture War Holds Center of Stage," *Los Angeles Times*, December 8, 1913.

39. Quoted in Bush, "Jack London," 547.

40. Hobart Bosworth Collection, Scrapbook #4; the only other marking on the page reveals that it is from "Page Nine" of whatever unsourced periodical it was torn from.

41. *New York Dramatic Mirror*, October 22, 1913, 26.

42. London refers to the Balboa Amusement Company's version of *The Sea Wolf*, which was released concurrently with Bosworth's film and resulted in a lawsuit over copyright infringement, which London and Bosworth eventually won. In a November 1, 1913, *Picture Player* magazine, however, the following text concerning *The Sea Wolf* appeared in an advertisement from Balboa entitled, "Injunction Still Denied against The Balboa Amusement Producing Co.": "Mr. Exhibitor: Watch for our release. Be sure and demand the three-reel production. Do not take the seven-reel pattern production." Hobart Bosworth Collection, Scrapbook #4.

43. "Bosworth Incorporated," *Moving Picture World*, August 23, 1913, 848.

44. Reels one, two, and five, FGF 0664-0665.

45. Auerbach, *Male Call*, 26.

46. Williams, *Jack London*, 36.

47. Hobart Bosworth Collection, notebook #II, "A Word from Jack London," undated.

48. Bowser, *Transformation of Cinema*, 136–37.

49. JL11771.

50. November 19, 1913. JL Box 517, Scrapbook Vol. 14.

51. October 7, 1913. JL13781.

52. Jack London, *Hearts of Three* (New York: Macmillan, 1920), vi. Hereafter cited as *HT*.

53. September 6, 1913. JL11032.

54. Cited in Birchard, "Jack London and the Movies," 15–16; Frank A. Garbutt to Jack London, December 10, 1913, JL 6489.

55. October 15, 1913, Amended Complaint for Injunction. JL21112, p. 11.

56. JL11812.

57. May 18, 1915. JL11816.

58. September 11, 1914. JL6524.

59. May 4, 1915. JL11817.

60. Bush, "Jack London," 547.

61. Ibid., 548.

62. See Woodbridge et al., *Jack London: A Bibliography*, 133–34.

63. Alex Kershaw, *Jack London: A Life* (New York: St. Martin's Press, 1998), 279.

64. Bowser, *Transformation of Cinema*, 206.

65. JL13544.

66. JL13551.

67. While I am referring to the novel as "London's" and while London is the sole person credited with authorship when it was published, it is worth reminding the reader that it originated with Goddard's scenarios, which themselves are labeled "'Hearts of Three' by Jack London & Charles W. Goddard," JL752. Only scenarios 6–11 and 13–15 (the last) are extant in the Huntington Library's Jack London collection.

68. Almost all sources indicate that the film was never made, except for an unusual reference made by London to Sisson in a letter dated August 5, 1916: "What has happened to the screening of HEARTS OF THREE? I noticed that the Vitagraph had started to screen it, then I read clippings about a law-suit against me for violation of contract, and then I have heard no further in the matter" (JL13551). This was much to London's dismay, and he inquired about the film's status several times; as he put it in the first staunch telegram to Sisson on November 6, 1916: "WHY HAS HEARTS OF THREE DIED DEAD" (JL13562).

69. *HT*, 2.

70. Ibid., viii.

71. Ibid., v.

72. Ibid., vii.

73. The exception to this is London's collaboration with Anna Strunsky on *The Kempson-Wace Letters* (New York: Macmillan, 1903).

74. *HT*, ix. It is unclear what London means by "We have never had a word," since Goddard in fact spent time with London at his ranch writing the scenarios in October 1915. See Charmian's diaries for that year (JL229); and Russ Kingman, *Jack London: A Definitive Chronology* (Middletown, Calif.: David Rejl, 1992).

75. Ibid., 26.

76. Ibid., 355.

77. JL753.

78. See, for example, the end of Episodes #6 and #7.

79. Bowser, *Transformation of Cinema*, 59.

80. *HT*, 28–29.

81. Unfortunately Goddard's photoplay model for this scene would have been contained in one of the scenarios missing from the Huntington Library's collection. Although it would have been interesting to note if London was following Goddard's lead with regard to this visual rendering, it ultimately matters little since I am interested in the greater source: the visual language of cinema.

82. Jack London, *The Call of the Wild* (1903; repr., New York: Macmillan, 1915), 56.

83. Ibid., 101–104.

84. Jack London, *The Sea-Wolf* (1904; repr., New York: Macmillan, 1919), 101.

85. London, *Martin Eden*, 560.

86. For example, London, *The Sea-Wolf*, 250.

87. JL752, Episode #13, Scene 10.

88. *HT*, 302.

89. JL18415.

90. September 23, 1914. JL13513.

91. Christopher Wilson, *The Labor of Words* (Athens: University of Georgia Press, 1985), 201.

Chapter Four: Making It *in Hollywood (pages 99–135)*

1. Harry Lang, "Roughing It with Clara," *Photoplay* (September 1931): 104.

2. David Stenn, *Clara Bow: Runnin' Wild* (New York: Doubleday, 1988), provides a biographical account of Bow's life.

3. Robert Sklar, *Movie-Made America: A Social History of American Movies* (New York: Random House, 1993), 81.

4. Charles Ponce de Leon, *Self-Exposure: Human-Interest Journalism and the Emergence of Celebrity in America, 1890–1940* (Chapel Hill: University of North Carolina Press, 2002), 33.

5. Louis E. Bisch, "Why Hollywood Scandal Fascinates Us," *Photoplay* (January 1930): 73.

6. Bisch, "What Does Acting Do to the Actor?" *Photoplay* (January 1928): 68.

7. T. Gallant, "Can She Ever Come Back?" *Movie Classic* (September 1931): 20.

8. Bow kept a selection of fan letters, which are available in the Clara Bow collection at the Margaret Herrick Library of the Academy of Motion Pictures. The letters deposited at the Margaret Herrick Library are those that Bow chose to save, making them a biased sampling of what she actually received. The volume of fan mail—"more than double any star's in movie history"—is cited in David Stenn's biography, *Clara Bow* (159); a June 27, 1928, *Variety* advertisement also reports the Los Angeles postmaster's declaration that Bow had set fan mail records by receiving 33,727 a month. Adela Rogers St. Johns' memoir, *Love, Laughter and Tears* (New York: Doubleday, 1978), includes the henna statistic (233).

9. The exception to this was Bow's 1928 film, *Red Hair*, one of the many Bow films

that has been lost (in 2003, UCLA Film and Television Archive preserved around two minutes of footage from the film that was found at Clarence Badger's Lone Pine Ranch; however, the color was faded from the opening of the film). The film uses a two-strip Technicolor process so that audiences might see the color of Bow's hair, as reported in Stenn, *Clara Bow*, 128. Virtually every article on Bow discusses her hair color. In three selections from contemporary fan magazines, one begins by noting "her shock of dashing red hair," a second begins with "Clara Bow's hair is red and so are her fingernails," and still another claims parenthetically that "(You've never seen such hair. It's red. Just red red)." Alma Whitaker, "How They Manage Their Homes," *Photoplay* (September 1929): 64; Michael Woodward, "That Awful 'IT'!" *Photoplay* (July 1930): 39; Lois Shirley, "Empty Hearted," *Photoplay* (October 1929): 29. It is worth noting that the fan magazine contest that Bow entered and eventually won had only two choices for hair color: "blonde or brunette."

10. Kathryn Fuller discusses the evolution of the magazine from a "story" publication, to its inclusion of a "photo portrait gallery of film actors and actresses" (April 1911), to its emergence, by 1912, as an "interactive colloquium for the sharing of movie fans' knowledge and creative interests" in *At the Picture Show: Small-Town Audiences and the Creation of Movie Fan Culture* (Washington, D.C.: Smithsonian Institution Press, 1996), 137.

11. An interesting example of this shaping can be found in one of Dorothy Blum's scrapbooks on deposit at the Library of Congress Motion Picture Sound Division. In her meticulously constructed two-volume homage to Joan Crawford—filled with autographed pictures, 8×10s, and fan magazines articles—Blum typed up a list of Joan Crawford's "stats": height, weight, hair color, etc. Although she first had typed that Crawford had brown eyes, she later crossed out this typewritten note and wrote a hand-scrawled amendment of "blue." Did Blum get her original information from a fan magazine and later correct this when she met Crawford, who often arranged to meet her fans when she traveled? Or did she speculate on Crawford's eye color based on the movies she had seen and later learn the correct "blue eyes" information from a fan magazine? Either way, Blum's scrapbooks nicely demonstrate the way that some fans collected information about the stars as a means of developing a tangible relationship with them.

12. Charles Eckert, "The Carole Lombard in Macy's Window," in *Fabrications: Costumes and the Female Body*, ed. Jane Gaines and Charlotte Herzog (New York: AFI, 1990), 103; 107. In "Announcing Wares, Winning Patrons, Voicing Ideals," *Cinema Journal* 29, no. 3 (1990), Janet Staiger claims that by 1916 department stores were already starting to create tie-ins to star fashions (11).

13. For more on Bow's moral lapses, see Jane Gaines, *Contested Culture: The Image, the Voice, and the Law* (Chapel Hill: University of North Carolina Press, 1991), 37. Gaines discusses a gambling incident involving Clara Bow; if the publicity department tried to cover up the incident as a "publicity stunt," as Gaines asserts, they failed. Bow's Tahoe gambling episode made the usual press rounds and inspired numerous speculations about the state of the star.

14. Stenn, *Clara Bow*, 70–72.

15. Ponce de Leon, *Self-Exposure*, 115; 33.

16. *Motion Picture* (January 1921): 122.

17. Joli Jenson, "Fandom as Pathology: The Consequences of Characterization," in *The Adoring Audience: Fan Culture and Popular Media*, ed. Lisa Lewis (New York: Routledge, 1992), 10.

18. From the Clara Bow Collection, Margaret Herrick Library, Fan Mail 1926 folder, letter dated August 28, 1926.

19. Fuller, *At the Picture Show*, 151.

20. Ibid., 160. Lynn Kirby affirms this characterization, arguing that "both advertising and American cinema sought in the teens and twenties increasingly to address and influence, and in a sense produce, a middle-class female consumer." "Gender and Advertising in American Silent Film: From Early Cinema to the Crowd," *Discourse* 13, no. 2 (1991): 5. Mary Ryan suggests that "the rate of female employment skyrocketed in the teens and increased at only a moderate rate, if at all, between 1920 and 1930 when over ten million women were at work outside the home." "The Projection of a New Womanhood: The Movie Moderns in the 1920's," in *Our American Sisters: Women in American Life and Thought*, ed. Jean E. Friedman and William Shade (Lexington, Mass.: D.C. Heath and Company, 1982), 508. Married women were also perceived as the primary family shopper, even when they were not earning wages.

21. Cecilia Radnovich to Clara Bow, Tuesday, June 9, 1931. Clara Bow collection, Margaret Herrick Library, Fan Mail 1931 folder.

22. Such assumptions led to a spate of examinations of films' effects upon spectators, such as the twelve-part Payne Fund Studies. Books such as Herbert Blumer's *Movies and Conduct* (New York: Macmillan, 1933) focused on the moral consequences of cinema for modern society, and their existence attests to the perception (and the anxiety) that cinema had a transformative effect upon its spectators.

23. Staiger, "Announcing Wares," 3.

24. Richard Ohmann discusses the origins of the term "New Woman" in late-nineteenth-century discourse, suggesting that Sarah Grand first used the term in an 1894 issue of the *North American Review*. The term gets applied, however, to women throughout the twentieth century who appear to disrupt the contemporary standards for gendered behavior; as Ohmann puts it, "a woman was unsettlingly 'new' if she disrupted old understandings of the feminine." *Selling Culture: Magazines, Markets, and Class at the Turn of the Century* (New York: Verso, 1996), 270. This was as much the case at the turn of the century, the subject of Ohmann's study, as it was during the 1920s.

25. Jeanine Basinger, *Silent Stars* (New York: Alfred A. Knopf, 1999).

26. Shelley Stamp, *Movie-Struck Girls* (Princeton: Princeton University Press, 2000), provides a fascinating account of the ways that women were courted as audiences in the post-Nickelodeon era. Stamp notes the significant ways that theaters had to elevate their status in the culture in order to accommodate women's perceived needs and tastes.

27. There are endless examples of this genre. Marquis Busby's March 1931 *Silver*

Screen piece, "The Price They Pay for Fame," calls fame "the consolation prize which is given when everything else has been sacrificed" (30).

28. Carolyn Van Wyck, "Friendly Advice on Girls' Problems: Should a Wife Work?" *Photoplay* (March 1927): 88.

29. Ibid.

30. Dorothy Manners, "What do Men Want?" *Motion Picture* (August 1927): 24.

31. Undated letter from Connie Romero, Los Angeles, California, to Clara Bow. Clara Bow Collection, Margaret Herrick Library, Fan Mail 1926 folder.

32. Nicholas Daly, *Literature, Technology, and Modernity, 1860–2000* (Cambridge: Cambridge University Press, 2004), 79.

33. In relation to the post–World War II era, Elaine May points out that "the movie industry was perhaps the only place in which women could achieve status and income equal to men." Elaine Tyler May, *Homeward Bound: American Families in the Cold War Era* (New York: Basic Books, 1988), 41.

34. The circulation statistic is provided by Tino Balio in *Grand Design: Hollywood as a Modern Business Enterprise, 1930–1939* (Los Angeles: University of California Press, 1993), 170.

35. Elinor Glyn, "What's the Matter with *You* American *Women?*" *Cosmopolitan* (November 1921): 26.

36. Ibid., 25–26.

37. Undated letter from Connie Romero, Los Angeles, California, to Clara Bow. Clara Bow Collection, Margaret Herrick Library, Fan Mail 1926 folder.

38. Richard deCordova, *Picture Personalities: The Emergence of the Star System in America* (Chicago: University of Illinois Press, 1990), 113.

39. Instances of this intended influence include such articles as Marguerite Henry's "Use Picture Ideas to Beautify Your Home at Very Small Cost," *Photoplay* (April 1925): 48. Gustav Kobbe, *Famous Actors and Actresses and Their Homes* (Boston: Little, Brown, 1903), sets the stage for much of this kind of discourse in its descriptions of the lives and homes of theatrical players.

40. Blumer, *Movies and Conduct*, 43.

41. Beth Brown, "Making Movies for Women," *Moving Picture World*, March 26, 1927, 34.

42. Paramount, directed by Clarence Badger. Josef von Sternberg shot several unidentified scenes in the film when Badger became ill; however, von Sternberg is not credited as a co-director.

43. Dorothy Spensley, "What Is It?" *Photoplay* (February 1926): 30.

44. Basinger, *Silent Stars*, 435–36. Space does not permit an extensive analysis of Glyn's influence in Hollywood or of her cameo in the film *It*. Interested readers are encouraged to see Lori Landay's study of the female trickster for a discussion of Glyn's celebrity and its role in the making and marketing of *It*. In *Madcaps, Screwballs, and Con Women: The Female Trickster in American Culture* (Philadelphia: University of Pennsylvania Press, 1998), Landay writes that "Glyn first used the term ["It"]

in a 1915 novel and then bandied about in popular magazines like *Photoplay* in order to strengthen her celebrity status as arbiter of sexiness and romance" (76).

45. Elaine May points out that "the plots of the most popular films in the 1920s centered on the romance between two young moderns leading to marriage, or on stagnant marriages that were revitalized through recreation, sensuality, and excitement." May, *Homeward Bound*, 42. While on the surface many of these films may have appeared to advocate a new wildness of behavior, particularly for women, for the most part these films end conservatively.

46. In an early version of this chapter published in *Cinema Journal* 42, no. 4 (Summer 2003): 76–97, I incorrectly identified these camera movements as dollies. I have since encountered Barry Salt's discussion of Paramount's pioneering use of zoom shots starting in 1926, including the zooms used in these opening shots from *It*. See Barry Salt, *Film Style and Technology: History and Analysis* (London: Starward, 1992), 185–86.

47. Miriam Hansen, *Babel and Babylon: Spectatorship in American Silent Film* (Cambridge: Harvard University Press, 1991), 85.

48. Where Nicholas Daly reads this moment as establishing Bow's sexual aggression from the outset, I think it's equally important to emphasize that Bow is more flirtatious than predatory. Daly, *Literature, Technology, Modernity*, 98. This moment also recalls the connections among fashion, promotion, and entertainment in feature films discussed by Charlotte Herzog in "'Powder Puff' Promotion: The Fashion Show-in-the-Film," in *Fabrications*, 100–21.

49. Daly, *Literature, Technology, Modernity*, 97.

50. Laura Mulvey, "Visual Pleasure and Narrative Cinema," in *Feminism and Film Theory*, ed. Constance Penley (New York: Routledge, 1998), 57–68.

51. Library of Congress Motion Picture Sound Division, Box E5.

52. Mary Ryan notices a similar trend across films of the 1920s, arguing that "once the essential features of woman's work had been established, the thrust of the heroine's dream was obvious—escape." "The Projection of the New Womanhood," 510. The film thus represents the failure of the 1920s modern idea of the happily married, working girl that Bow espoused (as discussed in the previous section).

53. Lori Landay also discusses the film's relationship women's consumer culture: "*It* participated in the construction of a public femininity that depended on women's active satisfaction of their desires, an idea that encouraged women to participate in the public sphere as consumer as well as commodities." Landay, *Madcaps*, 76.

54. Paula S. Fass, *The Damned and the Beautiful: American Youth in the 1920s* (New York: Oxford University Press, 1977), 260.

55. William Leach, "Transformations in a Culture of Consumption: Women and Department Stores, 1890–1925," *Journal of American History* 71, no. 2 (September 1984): 320.

56. Daly, *Literature, Technology, and Modernity*, 105.

57. This is an invocation of the World War I campaign enacted by the minute

men, a reminder of the historical roots of the New Woman's economic and behavioral liberation.

58. As Landay puts it, "It is clear that she is not insulted by but pleased by his advance, but it is also clear that her sexual favor is not easily purchased and that she will hold out for marriage." Landay, *Madcaps*, 82.

59. Alexander Walker, "Elinor Glyn and Clara Bow," *The Stars Appear*, ed. Richard Dyer MacCann (Metuchen, N.J.: Scarecrow Press, 1992), 201.

60. Alice Tildesley, "She Wants to Succeed," *Motion Picture Classic* (June 1926): 90.

61. Cal York, "Gossip of All the Studios," *Photoplay* (October 1929): 46.

62. I am referring to the most visible of these scandals involving Mary Pickford and Douglas Fairbanks, Fatty Arbuckle, William Desmond Taylor, and Wallace Reid, which brought unwanted attention—including governmental—to the alleged moral dangers being fostered in Hollywood.

63. As previously noted, what circulated in the fan magazines is questionable, at best, in terms of its historical accuracy. In the Clara Bow collection at the Margaret Herrick Library, the Louella Parsons Serial clippings folder includes the May 25, 1931, *Los Angeles Examiner* Chapter XIII of Bow's story, in which Parsons addresses Bow's reported engagement with director Victor Fleming: "I don't like to tell tales out of school, but her engagement to Victor Fleming was largely the result of a press agent story . . . It was a bright idea of a member of the "Wings" company to get world-wide publicity on the air picture" (unpaged).

64. Stenn, *Clara Bow*, 227. The editor and publisher of the *Coast Reporter* eventually received an eight-year prison sentence for publishing such slanderous and obscene material.

65. Adrienne McLean and David Cook, eds., *Headline Hollywood* (New Brunswick, N.J.: Rutgers University Press, 2001), 5.

66. Anne Morey notes that "Hollywood had to be sold as a concatenation of appealing individuals with touching stories, but fan magazines could not seem to be condoning immorality. Presenting stars as essentially normal or as victims of their own talent often required considerable powers of sympathy." Morey, "'So Real as to Seem Like Life Itself': The *Photoplay* Fiction of Adela Rogers St. Johns," in *A Feminist Reader in Early Cinema*, ed. Jennifer Bean and Diane Negra (Durham: Duke University Press, 2002), 336.

67. Harrison Ford quoted in Dorothy Woolridge, "What the Screen Idols Think of the Flapper," *Motion Picture Classic* (August 1927): 21 and 79. Brackets mine.

68. Clara Bow quoted in Manners, "What Do Men Want?" 24.

69. Gaylyn Studlar, "The Perils of Pleasure? Fan Magazine Discourse as Women's Commodified Culture in the 1920s," in *Silent Cinema*, ed. Richard Abel (New Brunswick, N.J.: Rutgers University Press, 1996). As Studlar notes, "in the 1920s, women's sexual desire, dismissed a few short years before as 'mainly a pretense,' was quickly becoming *the* national preoccupation, as the politically focused, prewar feminism appeared to be superceded by a 'new feminism' grounded in sexual expression" (276).

70. The studios and the fan magazines were creative inventors, so it is impossible to discern if an interview with a star represents the star's responses or those fabricated for him or her by the studio's public relations department. However, it is unlikely that the responses attributed to Bow would have emanated from any studio publicity department. One *Photoplay* article about the end of Bow's career from 1931 claimed that "Paramount did everything to keep her going, save buy our way into the theaters to see her pictures. They gave Bow every break and every chance." Leonard Hall, "Where Now, Clara?" *Photoplay* (August 1931): 55. As always, it is difficult to ascertain the source of such information or the motivations for preserving or sacrificing a star of Bow's status. One must naturally start with economics and go from there.

71. Ruth Biery, "Interview with Clara Bow," *Motion Picture* (November 1928): 44.

72. Stenn, *Clara Bow*, 116.

73. Basinger, *Silent Stars*, 448. The following quotations are from the Clara Bow fan mail collection, organized by year at the Margaret Herrick library.

74. Leonard Hall, "What About Clara Bow?" *Photoplay* (October 1930): 60.

75. I would like to thank David Stenn for making this point during a phone conversation. Stenn contends that fan magazine readers were not so innocent as to think that these were literal engagements, but rather understood that "engagement" referred to sexual intercourse, particularly when used in reference to Bow.

76. Shirley, "Empty Hearted," 29.

77. Ruth Biery, "Misinformation," *Photoplay* (June 1928): 40.

78. Ibid., 41.

79. Mildred Spain, "Those Awful Reporters!" *Photoplay* (May 1931): 40.

80. Carl Vonnel, "Clara Bow—Housewife of Rancho Clarito," *Photoplay* (July 1932): 28.

81. As Anne Morey writes, such conflicted results were not out of the ordinary, for the fan magazines themselves frequently "traded on a notion of the female reader as ready to disbelieve familiar hype or the clichés of agents and fan magazine writers themselves." Morey, "'So Real'," 335.

82. Cedric Belfrage, "Classic Holds Open Court: Clara Bow Defends Sex Appeal," *Motion Picture Classic* (September 1930): 37.

83. Ibid., 36.

84. Ibid., 89.

85. September 20, 1926, letter from Mac Smith of Knoxville, Tennessee, to Clara Bow, Margaret Herrick Library's Clara Bow Collection, 1926 fan mail folder.

86. Letter from Marion Clarke of Middletown, Connecticut, to Clara Bow dated June 24, 1931, Margaret Herrick Library's Clara Bow Collection, 1931 fan mail folder.

87. For useful discussions of Fatty Arbuckle and Wallace Reid, see Sam Stoloff, "Fatty Arbuckle and the Black Sox: The Paranoid Style of American Popular Culture, 1919–1922"; and Mark Lynn Anderson, "Shooting Star: Understanding Wallace Reid and His Public," both in *Headline Hollywood*.

88. Paul Jarvis, "Quit Pickin' On Me!" *Photoplay* (April 1931): 32.

89. Lang, "Roughing It," 102.

90. The letter is dated June 3, 1931. Quoted in Rudy Behlmer, ed., *Memo from David O. Selznick* (New York: Viking Press, 1972), 35.

91. The letter is reprinted in full in Stenn, *Clara Bow*, 229–30.

92. Ibid., 32.

93. Undated letter from Marjorie Derr, from Sacramento, California, to Clara Bow, Clara Bow Collection, Margaret Herrick Library, Fan Mail 1931 folder.

94. Burial Instructions, Clara Bow Collection, Margaret Herrick Library, 2.

Chapter Five: "If We Are Ever to Be in Hollywood" (pages 136–69)

1. W. G. Rogers, *When This You See Remember Me* (New York: Rinehart & Co., 1948), 142. Gertrude Stein used the phrase that is this chapter's title in a letter to Samuel Steward postmarked May 1, 1940, from Samuel Steward, ed., *Dear Sammy: Letters from Gertrude Stein and Alice B. Toklas* (Boston: Houghton Mifflin, 1977), 149–50.

2. "Stein's Way," *Time*, September 11, 1933, 57.

3. Anne Friedberg, "Introduction: Reading *Close-Up*," in *Close Up: 1927–1933: Cinema and Modernism*, ed. Donald James, Ann Friedberg, and Laura Marcus (Princeton: Princeton University Press, 1998), 14. The editors describe *Close Up* as decidedly "anti mainstream," vii.

4. Susan McCabe, *Cinematic Modernism: Modernist Poetry and Film* (Cambridge: Cambridge University Press, 2005), 2. See also Laura Marcus, "How Newness Enters the World: The Birth of Cinema and the Origins of Man," in *Literature and Visual Technologies: Writing after Cinema* ed. Julian Murphet and Lydia Rainford (New York: Palgrave Macmillan, 2003), and P. Adams Sitney, *Modernist Montage: The Obscurity of Vision in Cinema and Literature* (New York: Columbia, 1990).

5. An important exception to this tendency to ignore the mainstream is Katherine Hopewell, "'The Leaven, Regarding the Lump': Gender and Elitism in H.D.'s Writing on the Cinema," *Feminist Media Studies* 5, no. 2 (2005), which argues against the "presumption . . . that literary modernism occupies a position diametrically opposed to that of popular culture" (163).

6. Edward Burns and Ulla Dydo, eds., *The Letters of Gertrude Stein and Thornton Wilder* (New Haven: Yale University Press, 1996), 114; brackets mine (hereafter cited as *LGS/TW*).

7. Ibid.

8. For press coverage of her return, see "Gertrude Stein Arrives and Baffles Reporters by Making Herself Clear," *New York Times*, October 25, 1934, 25.

9. See also P. Adams Sitney, *Modernist Montage*, 146–47.

10. From Stein's November 12, 1934, radio interview with William Lundell, reprinted as Stephen Meyer, ed., "Gertrude Stein: A Radio Interview," *Paris Review* 116 (1990): 92.

11. James Mellow, *Charmed Circle: Gertrude Stein and Company* (Boston: Houghton Mifflin, 1974), 354.

12. Ibid., 127.

13. Ibid., 5.

14. Bob Perelman, *The Trouble with Genius: Reading Pound, Joyce, Stein, and Zukofsky* (Berkeley: University of California Press, 1994), 22.

15. Richard Bridgman, *Gertrude Stein in Pieces* (New York: Oxford University Press, 1970), 276–77.

16. Stein enacts a similarly self-serving alignment of her literary style with Picasso's cubist style in her book-length study, *Picasso* (1938; repr., New York: Dover, 1984).

17. The quotation in the section heading is from Gertrude Stein, *Everybody's Autobiography* (1937; repr., Cambridge, Mass.: Exact Change, 1993), 239 (hereafter cited as *EA*). See the useful Appendix I in *LGS/TW* for a day-by-day account of Stein's lecture tour, 333–55.

18. *EA*, 288.

19. Ibid.

20. Edward Burns, ed., *The Letters of Gertrude Stein and Carl Van Vechten*, Volumes I and II (New York: Columbia University Press, 1986), 422–23 (hereafter cited as *LGS/CVV*).

21. Society editor's column, "Society in Filmland," *Hollywood Citizen-News*, April 10, 1935, 10.

22. *EA*, 2.

23. Ibid., 3.

24. Rogers, *When This You See*, 129.

25. *EA*, 41; brackets mine.

26. Ibid.

27. Ibid., 44.

28. "Stein's Way," *Time*, 57. "The Cult of Unintelligibility" is a phrase coined by *The Masses* editor Max Eastman.

29. Kevin Starr, *Inventing the Dream: California through the Progressive Era* (New York: Oxford University Press, 1985), 245.

30. Leonard Leff notes that "advances in photojournalism in the second and third decades of the new century conspired with the movies and the accent Hollywood placed on renown and success not only to produce one famous persona after another, on the screen and off, but—more important—to equate celebrity and success." Leff, *Hemingway and His Conspirators: Hollywood, Scribners, and the Making of Celebrity Culture* (New York: Rowman & Littlefield, 1997), xiii.

31. Barbara Will has also framed Stein's authorial dilemma in the context of genius and celebrity: "the manufacturing of 'celebrityhood' by America's publicity machine is far removed from the idea of 'genius' as unique and innate, as original and self-originating." Will, *Gertrude Stein, Modernism, and the Problem of "Genius"* (Edinburgh: Edinburgh University Press, 2000), 14.

32. In *The Trouble with Genius*, Bob Perelman makes the related argument that

"Stein often seems quite aware of the relation of her impenetrability to her fame" (152).

33. Donald Gallup, ed., *The Flowers of Friendship: Letters Written to Gertrude Stein* (New York: Octagon Books, 1979), 269.

34. *LGS/CVV*, 277.

35. Ibid., 649.

36. Gallup, *Flowers*, 279.

37. Ray Lewis White, ed., *Sherwood Anderson/Gertrude Stein* (Chapel Hill: University of North Carolina Press, 1972), 102.

38. Gertrude Stein, "American Crimes and How They Matter," *The New York Herald Tribune*, March 30, 1935, 13; emphasis mine.

39. "Gertrude Stein Home After Thirty-One Years," *Literary Digest*, November 3, 1934, 34; emphasis mine.

40. "Stein's Way," *Time*, 57.

41. *EA*, 2.

42. See *LGS/CVV* letters postmarked 15 September 1935 (444) and 23 October 1935 (452).

43. Stein names William S. Hart in one of her homecoming interviews by Kenneth O'Hara, bearing the typically parodic title, "Oh Gertrude Oh Stein Here to Here to Talk," *Los Angeles Times*, Morning Edition, March 30, 1935, 1–2. Stein's interest in Hart may also indicate her contemporary disengagement with the movies, since his last film was released a full decade prior in 1925.

44. *EA*, 180.

45. Meyer, "Gertrude Stein," 87.

46. P. David Marshall, *Celebrity and Power: Fame in Contemporary Culture* (Minneapolis: University of Minnesota Press, 1997), 83.

47. Rogers, *When This You See*, 151.

48. Steward, *Dear Sammy*, 150.

49. The "he" is Ford Hicks, whom Steward describes as "a second-rate 'agent' who had wanted to handle their lectures for tremendous fees during their first American tour," ibid., 82. The block quote is from ibid., 146–47.

50. Gertrude Stein, "Yes is For a Very Young Man," in *Last Operas and Plays*, ed. Carl Van Vechten (New York: Vintage, 1975), 3.

51. See, for example, the letter from Stein received by Thornton Wilder, September 10, 1936, *LGS/TW*, 111.

52. Stein, "A Transatlantic Interview 1946," *A Primer for the Gradual Understanding of Gertrude Stein*, ed. Robert Haas (Los Angeles: Black Sparrow Press, 1971), 18.

53. This thinking mirrors the central ideas in Virginia Woolf's 1926 essay, "The Cinema," which dismisses mainstream film as derivative and primitive. Woolf muses about what will happen when film moves away from its parasitic relationship to literature and finds its own implicitly avant-garde and abstract language. Reprinted in Virginia Woolf, *The Captain's Death Bed and Other Essays* (New York: Harcourt, Brace and Company, 1950).

54. T. S. Matthews, "Gertrude Stein Comes Home," *The New Republic*, December 5, 1934, 100.

55. Ibid., 100–101.

56. Stein, "Transatlantic Interview," 22; brackets mine.

57. *EA*, 48.

58. Bernard Fay, "A Rose is a Rose," *The Saturday Review of Literature*, September 2, 1933, 77.

59. Edmund Wilson, "27 Rue de Fleurus," review of *The Autobiography of Alice B. Toklas*, *The New Republic*, October 11, 1933, 247.

60. *EA*, 6.

61. Ibid., 6.

62. Ibid., 22. For a discussion of Einstein's visit, see Harry Lang, "Einstein in Hollywood," *Photoplay* (April 1931): 36+.

63. *EA*, 28.

64. Stein, "A Transatlantic Interview," 22.

65. Gertrude Stein, "A Movie," written 1920; originally published 1932. Reprinted in *Operas and Plays*, ed. James Mellow (New York: Staton Hill Press, 1987), 395.

66. Gertrude Stein, "Photograph," in *Last Operas and Plays*, 152.

67. Alan Knight, "Masterpieces, Manifestoes and the Business of Living: Gertrude Stein Lecturing," in *Gertrude Stein and the Making of Literature*, ed. Shirley Neuman and Ira Nadel (Boston: Northeastern University Press, 1988), 151.

68. With a few important exceptions, American films and American movie stars have held a domineering place in international movie-going and perceptions of celebrity culture. Stein's correspondence, especially with Van Vechten, attests to the fact that most popular American films eventually made their way to France.

69. Mellow, *Charmed Circle*, 384.

70. Gertrude Stein, *Lectures in America* (1935; repr., New York: Vintage Books, 1975), 176–77.

71. According to David Cook in *A History of Narrative Film*, "weekly attendance shot up from sixty million in 1927 to ninety million in 1930," largely as a result of the conversion to sound filmmaking (New York: Norton, 1996), 250. Tino Balio points out in *Grand Design: Hollywood as a Modern Business Enterprise, 1930–1939*, that motion pictures were "the last business to feel the pinch of the Depression" (Los Angeles: University of California Press, 1993), 30; however, all of the studios were financially challenged by the Depression years, which resulted in significant attendance drop-offs and a lowering of ticket prices. Theaters had to go to extra lengths—dish giveaways, raffles, etc.—to convince the American public that movie theaters were worthy places to spend money. While it took a world war for the industry to fully recover and exceed its prior financial gains, attendance figures were back in the fifty to eighty million range (depending upon which sources you trust) by the mid- to late 1930s (Balio, 30–31).

72. Stein, "Transatlantic Interview," 31.

73. Charles Caramello, *Henry James, Gertrude Stein, and the Biographical Act* (Chapel Hill: University of North Carolina Press, 1996), 159.

74. *LGS/CVV*, 667.
75. *EA*, 288.
76. Ibid.
77. Kenneth O'Hara, "Oh Gertrude," 2.
78. Ibid.
79. Stein, *Lectures in America*, 176.
80. Ibid., 177.
81. Ibid., 179. Julian Murphet argues that Stein does not capture the "intensity of movement" she claimed, but rather that *Making of Americans* is decidedly "bereft of momentum." Murphet, "Gertrude Stein's Machinery of Perception," in *Literature and Visual Technologies: Writing after Cinema*, ed. Julian Murphet and Lydia Rainford (New York: Palgrave Macmillan, 2003), 77.
82. O'Hara, "Oh Gertrude," *Los Angeles Times*, 2.
83. Ibid.
84. Stein, "Transatlantic Interview," 35.
85. *LGS/CVV*, 437. The quotation in the section heading is from Stein to Van Vechten in a letter postmarked April 1940 (*LGS/CVV*, 675) regarding plans to have the *Autobiography* made into a Hollywood film.
86. Ibid., 440.
87. Ibid., 446. Searches through the Ivan Kahn papers at the Academy of Motion Pictures' Herrick Library reveal no documentation of a business relationship, if it existed in any formal capacity, between Kahn and Stein.
88. Ibid., 450.
89. From the Margaret Herrick Library of the Academy of Motion Picture Arts and Sciences' Miscellaneous S correspondence file.
90. *LGS/TW*, 106; brackets mine.
91. *LGS/CVV*, 670.
92. "Stein's Way," *Time*, 59.
93. *LGS/TW*, 240.
94. Ibid., 112.
95. *LGS/CVV*, 667–68.
96. Ibid., 671.
97. Ibid., 674.
98. Ibid., 573.
99. "Names Make News," *Time*, June 6, 1938, 36. I have not encountered any other references along these lines.
100. See Bridgman, *Gertrude Stein in Pieces*, 203, for a discussion of the screenplay.
101. *LGS/TW*, 116. According to the editors of *LGS/TW*, Edward Burns and Ulla Dydo, the parenthetical insertion in this sentence is "Wilder's interpolation into his transcription of Stein's letter" (email correspondence with Ulla Dydo, July 26, 2003). Stein was responding to Wilder's letter of September 27, 1936, in which he informs her that legendary MGM producer Irving Thalberg had died, perhaps taking hopes of a Hollywood deal for Stein (brokered through Wilder) with him.

Chapter Six: Redirecting Reputation (pages 170–203)

1. See William Donati, *Ida Lupino: A Biography* (Lexington: University Press of Kentucky, 1996) for an account of Lupino's career. Donati contends that Lupino was devastated to realize that she could be forced by the studios to play demeaning roles in substandard films. He also notes that Lupino refused to sign a long-term contract with Warner Bros. in 1940, preferring a non-exclusive, one-year contract that allowed her to make films outside of the studio.

2. Annette Kuhn, "Introduction: Intestinal Fortitude," in *Queen of the 'B's: Ida Lupino Behind the Camera* (Westport, Conn.: Praeger, 1995), 2.

3. Wheeler Winston Dixon, "Ida Lupino: Director," *Classic Images* (February 1996): 15. Lupino explains: "For about eighteen months back in the mid forties I could not get a job in pictures as an actress . . . I was on suspension. It seems we were always on suspension, because we wouldn't do some of the shows we were asked to do." Ida Lupino, "Me, Mother Directress," *Action* (May/June 1967): 15.

4. Gladwin Hill, "Hollywood's Beautiful Bulldozer," *Colliers* (May 12, 1951): 77.

5. Cited in Annette Kuhn and Susannah Radstone, eds., "Ida Lupino," in *Women in Film: An International Guide* (New York: Fawcett, 1990), 248. Lupino discusses her selectivity and suspensions in a May 25, 1965, draft of Hedda Hopper's "Ida Lupino," which is part of the Hedda Hopper collection at the Margaret Herrick Library. Because of a loophole in her contract at Warner Bros., she was able to survive by doing radio gigs during the year and a half she did not work on screen.

6. Although Lupino directed only seven films, she successfully transitioned into television and directed over one hundred television shows. This chapter focuses on her film direction because Lupino was the most visible and most vocal about her status during this era.

7. For a useful discussion of this phenomenon, see Alison McMahan, *Alice Guy Blaché: Lost Visionary of the Cinema* (New York: Continuum, 2003).

8. "Why Are There No Women Directors?" *Motion Picture Magazine* 30, no. 4 (November 1925): 5. Thanks to Anne Morey for sharing this article with me.

9. Ibid.

10. See Judith Mayne, *The Woman at the Keyhole: Feminism and Women's Cinema* (Bloomington: University of Indiana Press, 1990), for a useful chapter about Arzner titled "Female Authorship Reconsidered."

11. Quoted in Debra Weiner, "Interview with Ida Lupino," in *Women and the Cinema: A Critical Anthology*, ed. Karen Kay and Gerald Perry (New York: E.P. Dutton, 1977), 177.

12. Barbara Quart notes that Dorothy Arzner elicited similar discourse, as a reporter indicates in a 1936 newspaper article entitled "Hollywood's Only Woman Director Never Bellows Orders Herself": "Practically all successful directors are dominant people who know when to do a bit of outright bullying, and how. Players might not take kindly to bullying from a woman; they'd call it nagging. And so there's only

one woman director in Hollywood." Quoted in Barbara Koenig Quart, *Women Directors: The Emergence of a New Cinema* (New York: Praeger, 1988), 23.

13. Lupino, "Me, Mother Directress," 14.

14. J. Robert Moskin, "Why Do Women Dominate Him?" in *The Decline of the American Male* (New York: Random House, 1958), 3–4. Philip Wylie's *Generation of Vipers* (New York: Farrar & Rinehart, 1942), while ranting about the decline of almost everything and everyone, seems to take special pleasure in accusing women and mothers for the downfall of American men.

15. Moskin, "Why Do Women Dominate Him?" 23.

16. "Lady Director," *Hollywood Citizen-News*, March 8, 1950, 1.

17. Joanne Meyerowitz, "Beyond the Feminine Mystique: A Reassessment of Postwar Mass Culture, 1946–1958," *Journal of American History* 79, no. 2 (March 1993): 1475.

18. Ibid., 1460.

19. Ibid.

20. Cited in Peter Bart, "Lupino the Dynamo," *New York Times*, late edition, Section 2, March 7, 1965, 7. Donati notes that the deterioration of Lupino's first marriage to Louis Hayward was linked to personal difficulties generated by her success: "She wanted to be recognized as a fine dramatic actress, but she also wanted to be a good wife; she was aware that her sudden fame denied her husband a solid identity." Donati, *Ida Lupino*, 72.

21. Hedda Hopper collection, Margaret Herrick Library, 3.

22. Lupino's productive use of her "time-off" due to suspensions is discussed in the July 14, 1962, *TV Guide* article on actors-turned-directors, "They Work Both Sides of the Camera," 19–20.

23. The Filmakers, as the final iteration of the company would come to be known, was formed officially on the heels of the success of *Not Wanted* by Lupino, Young, and writer Malvin Wald. See Donati, *Ida Lupino*, 147–56, for more on the permutations of Lupino's independent productions. The Filmakers attempted to challenge studio moviemaking by turning out low-budget films with new talent on serious subjects such as rape, bigamy, polio, and illegitimate children. As in her producing career, in her directing career Lupino tackled taboo social issues during an era in which such subjects were difficult to breach because of Hollywood's in-house regime of self-censorship outlined in the Production Code, as well the pervasive sense that controversial material might incur the attention of those seeking to purge subversive (specifically Communist) elements in Hollywood.

24. Lucy Ann Liggett Stewart claims that this heart attack occurred three days into shooting *Not Wanted*, while William Donati states that the heart attack took place "a few days before the cameras were to roll." Donati, *Ida Lupino*, 150.

25. Weiner, "Interview," 171.

26. Hedda Hopper collection, Margaret Herrick Library, "Ida Lupino," 4. As Wheeler Winston Dixon points out, Lupino "was obviously driven by a very real need to direct. Otherwise, it seems unlikely that she would have relinquished a secure career as a leading lady to do so." Dixon, "Ida Lupino," 14.

27. Weiner, "Interview," 174.

28. As will be noted in relation to Lupino's *The Hitch-Hiker*, this notion is particularly telling in relation to the two male protagonists and the reason for their journey. Weiner, "Interview," 178.

29. Ibid., 170.

30. Donati, *Ida Lupino*, 267.

31. In an article on *The Bigamist*, Ellen Seiter asserts that, "The dangers of women overpowering men was a discourse acute in 1945 when GIs were returning home from war. It had continued relevance throughout the 1950s when many women continued to work, often because two incomes were needed to maintain the level of consumerism the family desired." Ellen Seiter, "*The Bigamist*," in *Queen of the 'B's*, 110.

32. From the Filmakers Releasing Organization report for Breen, available at the Margaret Herrick Library for Motion Picture Arts and Sciences.

33. From a Breen letter dated June 19, 1953, to Collier Young, Margaret Herrick Library file on *The Bigamist*.

34. It is worth noting that Lupino played a number of roles, both before and after making *The Bigamist*, that define a woman's problem in terms of her ambition and her frigidity. This is not unusual for the genre of the woman's film, as Jeanine Basinger observes in *A Woman's View: How Hollywood Spoke to Women, 1930–1960* (New York: Alfred A. Knopf, 1993). Basinger points out that in *The Hard Way* (1942), Lupino's character "is accused of coldness, the most common male form of insult to women in films" (438). Basinger also notes that in 1955 Lupino played a prison warden in *Women's Prison*, which makes the point that "If women are loved, given sex and children, perhaps they would not need . . . excessive power" (226). Another obvious iteration of this would be Michael Curtiz's *Mildred Pierce* (1945), in which Joan Crawford's business ambitions blind her to the misdeeds taking place under her own roof. This is all to say that these associations were circulating in the culture at large and found expression in numerous of films of the period.

35. Gladys Hall Collection, Margaret Herrick Library, 9. "Mad Idesy" appeared in *Silver Screen* on August 15, 1940.

36. Ibid., 10.

37. Seiter, "*The Bigamist*," 106.

38. For more on this contrast, see ibid., 107; 113.

39. Ibid., 105.

40. Wendy Dozoretz, "The Mother's Lost Voice in *Hard, Fast and Beautiful*," *Wide Angle* 6, no. 3 (1984): 56.

41. Mandy Merck, "*Hard, Fast and Beautiful*," in *Queen of the 'B's*, 81.

42. Lupino played a somewhat analogous role to Milly's in Vincent Shermans' *The Hard Way* (1942). Jeanine Basinger describes that film, about two women's ambitions to escape a coal town, in *A Woman's View*; see especially 437–38.

43. Merck, "*Hard*," 76.

44. Dozoretz argues that, "Mr. Farley is so 'feminine' in character that he develops hysterical symptoms that land him in a hospital when Florence stays away too

long." Dozoretz, "Mother's Lost Voice," 56. Sickness historically has been the curse of female characters, particularly those illnesses that seem the consequence of "bad nerves." Mr. Farley's doctor has to feel his pulse while he listens to Florence play a match on the radio, making it fair to conclude that his problem is of this "feminine" variety. Mr. Farley can thus be understood as one of those men described by Moskin who has fallen victim to the domineering modern woman and whose manhood has suffered.

45. Merck, "Hard," 77.

46. Dozoretz, "Mother's Lost Voice," 53.

47. As Merck puts it, "Florence is exploited, not by herself, but by her mother. The taint of prostitute is displaced onto Milly, who conducts the film's financial transaction and keeps as much information as she can from her daughter." Merck, "Hard," 82.

48. This comment to the reporter is also a reminder of the degree to which we should question what the media is told by public personalities.

49. Dozoretz, "Mother's Lost Voice," 52.

50. Ibid.

51. Dixon, "Ida Lupino," 16.

52. RKO Radio Pictures Studio Collection (Collection 3), Arts Library Special Collection, Research Library, University of California, Los Angeles. RKO S1592, 115.

53. Ibid. Martha Wilkerson's revisions, 104.

54. Lupino, "Me, Mother Directress," 14.

55. Dwight Whitney, "Follow Mother, Here We Go Kiddies!" *TV Guide*, October 8, 1966, 15.

56. Francine Parker, "Discovering Ida Lupino," *Action* (July/August 1973): 23. Parker also observes that "Lupino's women are feisty, strong, wrestling with their problems, driving hard—but not driving too hard, since this receives inevitable punishment from the outside world—rejection. To avoid rejection, the ambition and drive must be given up voluntarily, as in the case of the young tennis champion in *Hard, Fast and Beautiful*. Otherwise one suffers the fate of the champion's mother" (22).

57. From the Production Code file on *The Hitch-Hiker* at the Margaret Herrick Library, file memo dated February 2, 1951.

58. From the final Production Code studio handbook of publicity data for "The Difference" (an early name for *The Hitch-Hiker*), October 24, 1952.

59. Weiner, "Interview," 174.

60. Lauren Rabinovitz, "The Hitch-Hiker," in *Queen of the 'B's*, 94.

61. Ibid., 92. Richard Koszarski also observes that "Lupino was able to reduce the male to the same sort of dangerous, irrational force that women represented in most male-directed examples of Hollywood film noir," 371. Richard Koszarski, ed., *Hollywood Directors 1941–1976* (New York: Oxford University Press, 1977).

62. Rabinovitz, "Hitch-Hiker," 95.

63. RKO Radio Pictures Studio Collection (Collection 3), Arts Library Special Collection, Research Library, University of California, Los Angeles. RKO S-1595. "They Spoke to God," 2.

64. Ibid.

65. Ibid., Richard Bluel synopsis, 3.

66. Ronnie Scheib, "Ida Lupino," in *American Directors, Volume I*, ed. Jean-Pierre Coursodon with Pierre Sauvage (New York: McGraw Hill, 1983), 225.

67. Ibid.

68. RKO Radio Pictures Studio Collection (Collection 3), Arts Library Special Collection, Research Library, University of California, Los Angeles. RKO S-1595. Final Screenplay, *The Hitch-Hiker*, 92.

69. The Roan Group released a facsimile of this document with their 1997 laser disc version of *The Hitch-Hiker*.

70. Mary Shelley, *Frankenstein* (1831; repr., New York: Dover, 1994), ix.

71. Ibid.

72. Ibid., v.

73. Ibid.

Epilogue: Alternative Systems (pages 204–8)

1. Gertrude Stein, "American Crimes and How They Matter," *New York Herald Tribune*, March 30, 1935, 13.

2. David James, "The Producer as Author," in *Andy Warhol: Film Factory*, ed. Michael O'Pray (London: BFI, 1989), 138.

3. Ibid., 144.

4. http://www.youtube.com/t/fact_sheet.

5. Ben McGrath, "It Should Happen to You," *The New Yorker*, October 16, 2006, 88.

6. Ben McGrath claims that "the first real YouTube star" might be Brooke Brodack—"a skinny, gap-toothed, twenty-year-old receptionist from western Massachusetts" who was hired by Carson Daily as a result of her YouTube videos. Ibid.

Bibliography

Archives

Margaret Herrick Library, Academy of Motion Picture Arts and Sciences, Los Angeles, California.
Motion Picture, Broadcasting and Recorded Sound Division, Library of Congress, Washington, D.C.
Seaver Center for Western History Research, Los Angeles County Museum of Natural History, Los Angeles, California.
University of California at Los Angeles Film and Television archive, Los Angeles, California.

Print Sources

Abel, Richard. *The Red Rooster Scare: Making Cinema American, 1900–1910*. Berkeley: University of California Press, 1999.
"The Actor—Likewise the Actress." *Moving Picture World*, November 12, 1910, 1099.
Albert, Katherine. "Don't Envy the Stars." *Photoplay* (March 1929): 32–33.
Anderson, Mark Lynn. "Shooting Star: Understanding Wallace Reid and His Public." In *Headline Hollywood*. ed. Adrienne McLean and David Cook, 83–106. New Jersey: Rutgers, 2001.
Anderson, Robert. "The Role of the Western Film Genre in Industry Competition, 1907–1911." *The Journal of the University Film Association* 11, no. 2 (Spring 1979): 19–26.
Auerbach, Jonathan. *Male Call: Becoming Jack London*. Durham: Duke University Press, 1996.
———. *The Romance of Failure: First-Person Fictions of Poe, Hawthorne, and James*. New York: Oxford University Press, 1989.
Balio, Tino. *Grand Design: Hollywood as a Modern Business Enterprise, 1930–1939*. Los Angeles: University of California Press, 1993.
Banta, Martha. *Failure and Success in America: A Literary Debate*. Princeton: Princeton University Press, 1978.
Barra, Alan. *Inventing Wyatt Earp: His Life and Many Legends*. New York: Carroll & Graff, 1998.
Bart, Peter. "Lupino the Dynamo." *New York Times*, March 7, 1965, late edition, section 2, 7.

Bibliography

Basinger, Jeanine. *A Woman's View: How Hollywood Spoke to Women, 1930–1960.* New York: Alfred A. Knopf, 1993.

———. *Silent Stars.* New York: Alfred A. Knopf, 1999.

Bazin, Andre. "The Western: Or the American Film Par Excellance." In *What is Cinema?* vol. II, trans. Hugh Gray. Berkeley: University of California Press, 1971.

Behlmer, Rudy, ed. *Memo from David. O. Selznick.* New York: Viking Press, 1972.

Belfrage, Cedric. "Classic Holds Open Court: Clara Bow Defends Sex Appeal." *Motion Picture Classic* (September 1930): 36+.

Benjamin, Walter. "The Work of Art in the Age of Mechanical Reproduction." In *Illuminations*, ed. Hannah Arendt, trans. Harry Zohn, 219–53. New York: Schocken Books, 1969.

"*Beyond the Law*" advertisement. *Los Angeles Times*, February 15, 1920. Unpaged, courtesy of Don Chaput.

———. *Moving Picture World*, March 27, 1920, 2102.

———. *Moving Picture World*, September 14, 1918, 1584.

———. *Moving Picture World*, November 30, 1918, 914.

Biery, Ruth. "Interview with Clara Bow." *Motion Picture* (November 1928): 44+.

———. "Misinformation." *Photoplay* (June 1928): 40+.

Birchard, Robert S. "Jack London and the Movies." *Film History* 1 (1987): 15–37.

Bisch, Louis E. "What Does Acting Do to the Actor?" *Photoplay* (January 1928): 68+.

———. "Why Hollywood Scandal Fascinates Us." *Photoplay* (January 1930): 73+.

Bland, Henry Meade. "Jack London." *Overland Monthly* (May 1904): 370–75.

Blumer, Herbert. *Movies and Conduct.* New York: Macmillan, 1933.

Boorstin, Daniel J. *The Image.* 1961. New York: Atheneum, 1987.

Bordwell, David, Janet Staiger, and Kristin Thompson. *The Classical Hollywood Cinema: Film Style and Mode of Production to 1960.* New York: Columbia University Press, 1985.

"Bosworth Incorporated." *Moving Picture World*, August 23, 1913, 828.

Bow, Clara. "My Life Story." As told to Adela Rogers St. Johns. *Photoplay* (February through April 1928).

Bowser, Eileen. *The Transformation of Cinema: 1907–1915.* New York: Charles Scribner's Sons, 1990.

Braudy, Leo. *The Frenzy of Renown.* 1986. New York: Random House, 1997.

Breakenridge, William. *Helldorado: Bringing the Law to Mesquite.* New York: Houghton Mifflin, 1928.

Bridgman, Richard. *Gertrude Stein in Pieces.* New York: Oxford University Press, 1970.

Britton, Andrew. *Katharine Hepburn: Star as Feminist.* 1984. Reprint, New York: Columbia University Press: 2003.

Brown, Beth. "Making Movies for Women." *Moving Picture World*, March 26, 1927, 34+.

Brownlow, Kevin. *The War, the West, and the Wilderness.* New York: Alfred A. Knopf, 1979.

Burns, Edward, ed. *The Letters of Gertrude Stein and Carl Van Vechten*. Volumes I and II. New York: Columbia University Press, 1986.

Burns, Edward, and Ulla Dydo, eds. *The Letters of Gertrude Stein and Thornton Wilder*. New Haven: Yale University Press, 1996.

Busby, Marquis. "The Price They Pay for Fame." *Silver Screen* (March 1931): 30+.

Bush, W. Stephen. "Jack London—'Picture Writer'." *Moving Picture World*, June 31, 1914, 547–78.

Caramello, Charles. *Henry James, Gertrude Stein, and the Biographical Act*. Chapel Hill: University of North Carolina Press, 1996.

Cary, Diana Serra. *The Hollywood Posse: The Story of a Gallant Band of Horsemen Who Made Movie History*. Norman: University of Oklahoma Press, 1996.

Chaput, Don. *The Earp Papers: In a Brother's Image*. New York: Affiliated Writers of America, 1994.

Clum, John P. "Wyatt Earp, Frontier Marshall." Book review. *Arizona Historical Review* 4, no. 4 (January 1932): 71.

Cook, David. *A History of Narrative Film*. New York: Norton, 1996.

Daly, Nicholas. *Literature, Technology, and Modernity, 1860–2000*. Cambridge: Cambridge University Press, 2004.

deCordova, Richard. "The Emergence of the Star System in America." In *Stardom: Industry of Desire*, ed. Christine Gledhill, 17–30. New York: Routledge, 1991.

———. *Picture Personalities: The Emergence of the Star System in America*. Chicago: University of Illinois Press, 1990.

Dickson, W. K. L., and Antonia Dickson. "Edison's Invention of the Kineto-Phonograph." *Century* 48 (May 1894-October 1894): 206–14.

Dixon, Simon. "Ambiguous Ecologies: Stardom's Domestic Mise-en-Scène." *Cinema Journal* 42, no. 3 (Winter 2003): 81–100.

Dixon, Wheeler Winston. "Ida Lupino: Director." *Classic Images* (February 1996): 14–22.

Donati, William. *Ida Lupino: A Biography*. Lexington: University Press of Kentucky, 1996.

Dozoretz, Wendy. "The Mother's Lost Voice in *Hard Fast and Beautiful*." *Wide Angle* 6, no. 3 (1984): 50–57.

"A Dream Come True." *Motion Picture Classic* (January 1922): 63+.

Dyer, Richard. *Stars*. London: British Film Institute, 1979.

Eckert, Charles. "The Carole Lombard in Macy's Window." In *Fabrications: Costumes and the Female Body*, ed. Jane Gaines and Charlotte Herzog, 100–21. New York: AFI, 1990.

"The Fame and Fortune Contest of 1921." *Motion Picture* (January 1921): 122.

Fass, Paula S. *The Damned and the Beautiful: American Youth in the 1920s*. New York: Oxford University Press, 1977.

Fay, Bernard. "A Rose is a Rose." *The Saturday Review of Literature*, September 2, 1933, 77+.

Fine, Gary Alan. *Difficult Reputations: Collective Memories of the Evil, Inept, and Controversial.* Chicago: University of Chicago Press, 2001.

Fischer, Lucy, and Marcia Landy. *Stars: The Film Reader.* New York: Routledge, 2004.

"Fitzsimmons Now Champion of the World." *The New York World*, March 18, 1897, 1+.

Fowles, Jib. *Starstruck.* Washington, D.C.: Smithsonian Institution Press, 1992.

Fox Entertainments advertisement. "An avalanche of entertainment making talent." *Picture-Play Magazine* (November 1919): 9.

Friedberg, Anne. "Introduction: Reading *Close-Up*." In *Close Up 1924–1933: Cinema and Modernism*, ed. Donald James, Anne Friedberg, and Laura Marcus, 1–26. Princeton: Princeton University Press, 1998.

Fuller, Kathryn. *At the Picture Show: Small-Town Audiences and the Creation of Movie Fan Culture.* Washington, D.C.: Smithsonian Institution Press, 1996.

Gaines, Jane. *Contested Culture: The Image, the Voice, and the Law.* Chapel Hill: University of North Carolina Press, 1991.

———. "From Elephants to Lux Soap: The Programming and 'Flow' of Early Motion Picture Exploitation." *The Velvet Light Trap* 25 (1990): 29–43.

Gallant, T. "Can She Ever Come Back?" *Movie Classic* (September 1931): 20+.

Gallup, Donald, ed. *The Flowers of Friendship: Letters Written to Gertrude Stein.* New York: Octagon Books, 1979.

Gamson, Joshua. *Claims to Fame: Celebrity in Contemporary America.* Berkeley: University of California Press, 1994.

"Gertrude Stein Arrives and Baffles Reporters by Making Herself Clear." *New York Times*, October 25, 1934, 25.

"Gertrude Stein Home after Thirty-One Years." *Literary Digest*, November 3, 1934, 34.

Glass, Loren. "Nobody's Renown: Plagiarism and Publicity in the Career of Jack London." *American Literature* 71, no. 3 (1999): 529–49.

Gledhill, Christine, ed. *Stardom: Industry of Desire.* London: Routledge, 1991.

Glyn, Elinor. "What's the Matter with *You* American *Women*?" *Cosmopolitan* (November 1921): 25+.

Gunning, Tom. "'Now You See It, Now You Don't': The Temporality of the Cinema of Attractions." In *Silent Film*, ed. Richard Abel, 71–85. New Brunswick: Rutgers University Press, 1996.

Hall, Gladys. "Mad Idesy." *Silver Screen*, August 15, 1940. Gladys Hall Collection, Margaret Herrick Library.

Hall, Leonard. "What About Clara Bow?" *Photoplay* (October 1930): 60+.

———. "Where Now, Clara?" *Photoplay* (August 1931): 55+.

Hansen, Miriam. *Babel and Babylon: Spectatorship in American Silent Film.* Cambridge: Harvard University Press, 1991.

Hart, William S. "Bill Hart Introduces a Real—Not Reel—Hero." *The Morning Telegraph* 98, October 9, 1921, section 5, 2.

Henry, Marguerite. "Use Picture Ideas to Beautify Your Home at Very Small Cost." *Photoplay* (April 1925): 48+.

Herzog, Charlotte. "'Powder Puff' Promotion: The Fashion Show-in-the-Film." In

Fabrications: Costume and the Female Body, ed. Jane Gaines and Charlotte Herzog, 100–121. New York: AFI, 1990.

Hill, Gladwin. "Hollywood's Beautiful Bulldozer." *Colliers*, May 12, 1951, 18+.

Hopewell, Katherine. "'The Leaven, Regarding the Lump': Gender and Elitism in H.D.'s writing on the Cinema." *Feminist Media Studies* 5, no. 2 (2005): 163–76.

Hopper, Hedda. "Ida Lupino." May 25, 1965. Hedda Hopper Collection, Margaret Herrick Library.

Horkheimer, Max, and Theodor Adorno. *Dialectic of Enlightenment*. Trans. John Cumming. New York: Herder and Herder, 1972.

Hutton, Paul Andrew. "Celluloid Lawman: Wyatt Earp Goes to Hollywood." *American West* (May/June 1984): 58–65.

———. "Showdown at the Hollywood Corral: Wyatt Earp and the Movies." *Montana, the Magazine of Western History* (Summer 1995): 2–31.

Jack London: A Sketch of His Life and Work With Portrait. New York: Macmillan, 1905.

James, David. "The Producer as Author." In *Andy Warhol: Film Factory*, ed. Michael O'Pray, 136–146. London: BFI, 1989.

James, Donald, Anne Friedberg, and Laura Marcus, eds. *Close Up 1927–1933: Cinema and Modernism*. Princeton: Princeton University Press, 1998.

Jarvis, Paul. "Quit Pickin' on Me!" *Photoplay* (January 1931): 32–3.

Jenson, Joli. "Fandom as Pathology: The Consequences of Characterization." In *The Adoring Audience: Fan Culture and Popular Media*, ed. Lisa Lewis, 9–30. New York: Routledge, 1992.

Johnson, Martin. *Through the Seas with Jack London*. New York: Dodd, Mead and Company, 1913.

Kasson, Joy. *Buffalo Bill's Wild West: Celebrity, Memory, and Popular History*. New York: Hill and Wang, 2000.

Kerr, Catherine. "Incorporating the Star: The Intersection of Business and Aesthetic Strategies in Early American Film." *Business History Review* 64, no. 3 (Autumn 1990): 383–410.

Kershaw, Alex. *Jack London: A Life*. New York: St. Martin's Press, 1998.

Kingman, Russ. *Jack London: A Definitive Chronology*. Middletown, Calif.: David Rejl, 1992.

Kirby, Lynn. "Gender and Advertising in American Silent Film: From Early Cinema to the Crowd." *Discourse* 13, no. 2 (1991): 3–20.

Knight, Alan. "Masterpieces, Manifestoes and the Business of Living: Gertrude Stein Lecturing." In *Gertrude Stein and the Making of Literature*, ed. Shirley Neuman and Ira B. Nadel, 150–68. Boston: Northeastern University Press, 1988.

Kobbe, Gustav. *Famous Actors and Actresses and Their Homes*. Boston: Little, Brown, 1903.

Koszarski, Richard, ed. *Hollywood Directors 1941–1976*. New York: Oxford University Press, 1977.

Kuhn, Annette. "Introduction: Intestinal Fortitude." In *Queen of the 'B's: Ida Lupino Behind the Camera*, ed. Annette Kuhn, 1–13. Westport, Conn.: Praeger, 1995.

Kuhn, Annette, and Susannah Radstone, eds. "Ida Lupino." In *Women in Film: An International Guide*, 248–250. New York: Fawcett, 1990.
"Lady Director." *Hollywood Citizen-News* (March 8, 1950): 1.
Landay, Lori. "The Flapper Film: Comedy, Dance, and Jazz Age Kinaesthetics." In *A Feminist Reader in Early Cinema*, ed. Jennifer Bean and Diane Negra, 221–50. (Durham: Duke University Press, 2002).
———. *Madcaps, Screwballs, and Con Women: The Female Trickster in American Culture*. Philadelphia: University of Pennsylvania Press, 1998.
Lang, Gladys Engel, and Kurt Lang. *Etched in Memory: The Building and Survival of Artistic Reputation*. Chapel Hill: University of North Carolina Press, 1990.
Lang, Harry. "Einstein in Hollywood." *Photoplay* (April 1931): 36+.
———. "Roughing It with Clara." *Photoplay* (September 1931): 30+.
Larkin, Mark. "What Happens to Fan Mail?" *Photoplay* (August 1928): 38+.
"The Last Stand of the Dalton Boys." *Moving Picture World* (July 1912): 277. [Advertisement]
Leach, William. "Transformations in a Culture of Consumption: Women and Department Stores, 1890–1925." *Journal of American History* 71, no. 2 (September 1984): 319–42.
Leff, Leonard. *Hemingway and His Conspirators: Hollywood, Scribners, and the Making of Celebrity Culture*. New York: Rowman & Littlefield, 1997.
Lindsay, Vachel. *The Art of the Moving Picture*. New York: Macmillan, 1915.
London, Charmian. *The Log of the Snark*. New York: Macmillan, 1915.
London, Jack. *The Call of the Wild*. 1903. Reprint, New York: Macmillan, 1919.
———. *The Cruise of the Snark*. New York: Macmillan, 1911.
———. *Hearts of Three*. New York: Macmillan, 1920.
———. *Jack London Reports*. Edited by King Hendricks and Irving Shepard. New York: Doubleday, 1970.
———. *Martin Eden*. New York: Macmillan, 1909. Reprinted in *Jack London: Novels and Social Writing*, ed. Donald Pizer. New York: Library of America, 1982.
———. "The Message of Motion Pictures." February 1915. Reprinted in *Authors on Film*, ed. Harry Geduld, 104–105. Bloomington: Indiana University Press, 1972.
———. *The Sea-Wolf*. 1904. Reprint, New York: Macmillan, 1919.
———. "When Jack London Was Amazed." *Motion Picture News*, December 6, 1913, 17–18.
London, Jack, and Anna Strunsky. *The Kempton-Wace Letters*. New York: Macmillan, 1903.
Lowenthal, Leo. *Literature, Popular Culture, and Society*. New Jersey: Prentice Hall, 1961.
Luhr, William. "Reception, Representation, and the OK Corral: Shifting Images of Wyatt Earp." In *Authority and Transgression in Literature and Film*, ed. Bonnie Braendlin and Hans Braendlin. Gainesville: University of Florida Press, 1996.
Lupino, Ida. "Me, Mother Directress." *Action* (May/June 1967): 14–15.

MacCulloch, Campbell. "What Makes Them Stars?" *Photoplay* (October 1928): 43+.
Manners, Dorothy. "What Do Men Want?" *Motion Picture* (August 1927): 24+.
Marcus, Laura. "How Newness Enters the World: The Birth of Cinema and the Origins of Man." In *Literature and Visual Technologies: Writing after Cinema*, ed. Julian Murphet and Lydia Rainford. New York: Palgrave Macmillan, 2003.
Marshall, P. David. *Celebrity and Power: Fame in Contemporary Culture*. Minneapolis: University of Minnesota Press, 1997.
Matthews, T. S. "Gertrude Stein Comes Home." *The New Republic*, December 5, 1934, 100+.
May, Elaine Tyler. *Homeward Bound: American Families in the Cold War Era*. New York: Basic Books, 1988.
Mayne, Judith. *The Woman at the Keyhole: Feminism and Women's Cinema*. Bloomington: Indiana University Press, 1990.
McCabe, Susan. *Cinematic Modernism: Modernist Poetry and Film*. Cambridge: Cambridge University Press, 2005.
McDonald, Paul. *The Star System: Hollywood's Production of Popular Identities*. London: Wallflower, 2000.
McGrath, Ben. "It Should Happen to You." *The New Yorker*, October 16, 2006, 88+.
McLean, Adrienne, and David Cook, eds. *Headline Hollywood*. New Brunswick, N.J.: Rutgers University Press, 2001.
McMahan, Alison. *Alice Guy Blaché: Lost Visionary of the Cinema*. New York: Continuum, 2003.
McQuade, James. "Famous Cowboys in Motion Pictures." *The Film Index*, June 25, 1910, 8+.
Mellow, James. *Charmed Circle: Gertrude Stein and Company*. Boston: Houghton Mifflin, 1974.
Merck, Mandy. "*Hard, Fast and Beautiful*." In *Queen of the 'B's: Ida Lupino Behind the Camera*, ed. Annette Kuhn, 73–90. Westport, Conn.: Praeger, 1995.
Meyer, Stephen, ed. "Gertrude Stein: A Radio Interview." Interviewed by William Lundell, November 12, 1934. *Paris Review* 116 (1990): 85–97.
Meyerowitz, Joanne. "Beyond the Feminine Mystique: A Reassessment of Postwar Mass Culture, 1946–1958." *Journal of American History* 79, no. 2 (March 1993): 1455–82.
Morey, Anne. "'So Real as to Seem Like Life Itself': The *Photoplay* Fiction of Adela Rogers St. Johns." In *A Feminist Reader in Early Cinema*, ed. Jennifer Bean and Diane Negra, 333–48. Durham: Duke University Press, 2002.
Moskin, J. Robert. "Why Do Women Dominate Him?" In *The Decline of the American Male*, ed. Editors of *Look*, 3–25. New York: Random House, 1958.
Motion Picture Studio Directory. n.p., 1921.
"Movies Bust Bill Show." *Variety*, August 8, 1913, 14.
Mulvey, Laura. "Visual Pleasure and Narrative Cinema." In *Feminism and Film Theory*, ed. Constance Penley, 57–68. New York: Routledge, 1988.

Murphet, Julian. "Gertrude Stein's Machinery of Perception." In *Literature and Visual Technologies: Writing After Cinema*, ed. Julian Murphet and Lydia Rainford, 61–81. New York: Palgrave Macmillan, 2003.

Musser, Charles. *The Emergence of Cinema*. Los Angeles: University of California, 1990.

———. "The Changing Status of the Actor." In *Before Hollywood: Turn-of-the-Century Film from American Archives*. With Jay Leyda. New York: American Federation of Arts, 1986.

Norris, Frank. "The Frontier Gone at Last." 1902. Reprinted in *Frank Norris: Novels and Essays*, ed. Donald Pizer, 1183–90. New York: Library of America, 1986.

O'Hara, Kenneth. "Oh Gertrude Oh Stein Here to Here to Talk." *Los Angeles Times*, March 30, 1935, Morning Edition, 1–2.

Ohmann, Richard. *Selling Culture: Magazines, Markets, and Class at the Turn of the Century*. New York: Verso, 1996.

Parker, Francine. "Discovering Ida Lupino." *Action* (July/August 1973): 19–23.

Perelman, Bob. *The Trouble with Genius: Reading Pound, Joyce, Stein, and Zukofsky*. Berkeley: University of California Press, 1994.

"Photographs of Moving Picture Actors. A New Method of Lobby Advertising." *Moving Picture World*, January 5, 1910, 50.

"Picturing Horse Race." *Variety*, August 8, 1913, 14.

Pingenot, Ben E. *Siringo*. College Station: Texas A & M University Press, 1989.

Ponce de Leon, Charles. *Self-Exposure: Human-Interest Journalism and the Emergence of Celebrity in America, 1890–1940*. Chapel Hill: University of North Carolina Press, 2002.

Quart, Barbara Koenig. *Women Directors: The Emergence of a New Cinema*. New York: Praeger, 1988.

Quirk, James. "Moral House-Cleaning in Hollywood: An Open Letter to Mr. Will Hays." *Photoplay* (April 1922): 52+.

Rabinovitz, Lauren. "The Hitch-Hiker." In *Queen of the 'B's: Ida Lupino Behind the Camera*, ed. Annette Kuhn, 90–102. Westport, Conn.: Praeger, 1995.

Rodden, John. *The Politics of Literary Reputation*. New York: Oxford University Press, 1989.

Rogers, W. G. *When This You See Remember Me*. New York: Rinehart & Co., 1948.

Ross, Steven J. *Working-Class Hollywood: Silent Film and the Shaping of Class in America*. Princeton: Princeton University Press, 1998.

Ryan, Mary. "The Projection of a New Womanhood: The Movie Moderns in the 1920's." In *Our American Sisters: Women in American Life and Thought*, ed. Jean E. Friedman and William G. Shade, 500–18. Lexington, Mass.: D.C. Heath and Company, 1982.

Salt, Barry. *Film Style and Technology: History and Analysis*. London: Starward, 1992.

Sandage, Scott. *Born Losers: A History of Failure in America*. Cambridge: Harvard University Press, 2005.

Scanland, J. M. "Lurid Trials Are Left by Olden-Day Bandits." *Los Angeles Times*, March 12, 1922, Part II, 2.

Scheib, Ronnie. "Ida Lupino." In *American Directors, Volume I*, ed. Jean-Pierre Coursodon with Pierre Sauvage, 216–28. New York: McGraw Hill, 1983.
———. "Ida Lupino." *Film Comment* 16, no. 1 (1980): 54–64.
Schrems, Suzanne. "Al Jennings: The Image of an Outlaw." *Journal of Popular Culture* 22, no. 4 (Summer 1989): 109–18.
Seiter, Ellen. "The Bigamist." In *Queen of the 'B's: Ida Lupino Behind the Camera*, ed. Annette Kuhn, 90–103. Westport, Conn.: Praeger, 1995.
Shelley, Mary. *Frankenstein*. 1831. Reprint, New York: Dover, 1994.
Shirley, Lois. "Empty Hearted." *Photoplay* (October 1929): 29+.
Siringo, Charles A. *A Texas Cowboy, or, Fifteen Years on the Hurricane Deck of a Spanish Pony*. 1885. Chicago: Siringo & Dobson, 1886.
Sitney, P. Adams. *Modernist Montage: The Obscurity of Vision in Cinema and Literature*. New York: Columbia University Press, 1990.
Sklar, Robert. *Movie-Made America: A Social History of American Movies*. New York: Random House, 1993.
Slotkin, Richard. *Gunfighter Nation: The Myth of the Frontier in Twentieth-Century America*. New York: Atheneum, 1992.
Society editor's column. "Society in Filmland." *Hollywood Citizen-News*, April 10, 1935, 10.
Spain, Mildred. "Those Awful Reporters!" *Photoplay* (May 1931): 40.
Spensley, Dorothy. "What Is It?" *Photoplay* (February 1926): 30+.
Staiger, Janet. "Announcing Wares, Winning Patrons, Voicing Ideals." *Cinema Journal* 29, no. 3 (1990): 3–31.
———. "Seeing Stars." In *Stardom: Industry of Desire*, ed. Christine Gledhill, 3–16. New York: Routledge, 1991.
Stamp, Shelley. *Movie-Struck Girls*. Princeton: Princeton University Press, 2000.
Starr, Kevin. *Inventing the Dream: California through the Progressive Era*. New York: Oxford University Press, 1985.
Stein, Gertrude. "American Crimes and How They Matter." *The New York Herald Tribune*, March 30, 1935, 13.
———. *The Autobiography of Alice B. Toklas*. 1933. Reprint, New York: Vintage, 1990.
———. "Film Deux Soeurs Qui Ne Sont Pas Soeurs." Written 1929; originally published 1932. Reprinted in *Operas and Plays*, ed. James Mellow, 399. New York: Staton Hill Press, 1987.
———. *Everybody's Autobiography*. 1937. Reprint, Cambridge, Mass.: Exact Change, 1993.
———. *Lectures in America*. 1935. Reprint, New York: Vintage Books, 1975.
———. *The Making of Americans*. 1925. Reprint, Normal, Ill.: Dalkey Archive Press, 1995.
———. "A Movie." Written 1920; originally published 1932. Reprinted in *Operas and Plays*, ed. James Mellow, 395–98. New York: Staton Hill Press, 1987.
———. "Photograph." In *Last Operas and Plays*, ed. Carl Van Vechten, 152–54. New York: Vintage, 1975.

——. *Picasso*. 1938. Reprint, New York: Dover, 1984.
——. "A Transatlantic Interview 1946." In *A Primer for the Gradual Understanding of Gertrude Stein*, ed. Robert Haas, 11–35. Los Angeles: Black Sparrow Press, 1971.
——. *Three Lives*. New York: The Grafton Press, 1909.
——. *The World is Round*. New York: William R. Scott, Inc., 1939.
——. "Yes Is For A Very Young Man." In *Last Operas and Plays*, ed. Carl Van Vechten, 3–51. New York: Vintage, 1975.
"Stein's Way." *Time*. Cover story, September 11, 1933, 57+.
Stenn, David. *Clara Bow: Runnin' Wild*. New York: Doubleday, 1988.
Stephens, John Richard. *Wyatt Earp Speaks!* Cambria, Calif.: Fern Canyon Press, 1998.
Steward, Samuel, ed. *Dear Sammy: Letters from Gertrude Stein and Alice B. Toklas*. Boston: Houghton Mifflin, 1977.
Stewart, Lucy Ann Liggett. *Ida Lupino as a Film Director, 1949–1953: An Auteur Approach*. New York: Arno Press, 1980.
St. Johns, Adela Rogers. "I Knew Wyatt Earp." *The American Weekly*, May 22, 1960, 10.
——. *Love, Laughter and Tears: My Hollywood Story*. New York: Doubleday, 1978.
Stoloff, Sam. "Fatty Arbuckle and the Black Sox: The Paranoid Style of American Popular Culture, 1919–1922." In *Headline Hollywood*, ed. Adrienne McLean and David Cook, 52–82. New Jersey: Rutgers University Press, 2001.
Streible, Dan. "A Return to the 'Primitive': One Hundred Years of Cinema . . . and Boxing." *Arachne* 2, no. 2 (1995): 297–323.
Studlar, Gaylyn. *This Mad Masquerade: Stardom and Masculinity in the Jazz Age*. New York: Columbia University Press, 1996.
——. "The Perils of Pleasure? Fan Magazine Discourse as Women's Commodified Culture in the 1920s." In *Silent Cinema*, ed. Richard Abel, 263–99. New Brunswick: Rutgers University Press, 1996.
Tefertiller, Casey. *Wyatt Earp: The Life Behind the Legend*. New York: John Wiley & Sons, 1997.
"They Work Both Sides of the Camera." *TV Guide*, July 14, 1962, 19–20.
Tildesley, Alice. "She Wants to Succeed." *Motion Picture Classic* (June 1926): 36+.
Tomkins, Jane. *West of Everything: The Inner Life of Westerns*. New York: Oxford University Press, 1992.
Trachtenberg, Alan. *The Incorporation of America*. New York: Hill and Wang, 1982.
Uricchio, William, and Roberta Pearson. *Reframing Culture: The Case of the Vitagraph Quality Films*. Princeton: Princeton University Press, 1993.
Van Wyck, Carolyn. "Friendly Advice on Girls' Problems: Should a Wife Work?" *Photoplay* (March 1927): 88+.
Vonnel, Carl. "Clara Bow—Housewife of Rancho Clarito." *Photoplay* (July 1932): 28+.
Walker, Alexander. "Elinor Glyn and Clara Bow." In *The Stars Appear*, ed. Richard Dyer MacCann, 199–258. Metuchen, N.J.: Scarecrow Press, 1992.

Walsh, Raoul. *Each Man in His Time: The Life Story of a Director.* New York: Farrar, Straus and Giroux, 1974.
Weiner, Debra. "Interview with Ida Lupino." In *Women and the Cinema: A Critical Anthology*, ed. Karen Kay and Gerald Perry, 169–78. New York: E.P. Dutton, 1977.
"Westerns: The Six Gun Galahad." *Time*, March 30, 1959, 52+.
"Which of 'Em Looks Most Dangerous? Outlaws, Real and Mimic, in Films." *Oklahoma City News*, October 20, 1919. Unpaged, courtesy of Don Chaput.
Whitaker, Alma. "How They Manage Their Homes." *Photoplay* (September 1929): 64+.
White, Ray Lewis, ed. *Sherwood Anderson/Gertrude Stein.* Chapel Hill: University of North Carolina Press, 1972.
Whitney, Dwight. "'Follow Mother, Here We Go Kiddies!'" *TV Guide*, October 8, 1966, 15–18.
"Why Are There No Women Directors?" *Motion Picture Magazine* 30, no. 4 (November 1925): 5.
"Wild Bill Hickok." Review. *Seattle Daily Times*, December 16, 1923.
Will, Barbara. *Gertrude Stein, Modernism, and the Problem of "Genius."* Edinburgh: Edinburgh University Press, 2000.
Williams, Raymond. "The Romantic Artist." In *Culture and Society: 1780–1950.* New York: Columbia University Press, 1958: 30–48.
Williams, Tony. *Jack London: The Movies.* Los Angeles: David Rejl, 1992.
Wilson, Christopher. *The Labor of Words.* Athens: University of Georgia Press, 1985.
Wilson, Edmund. "27 rue de Fleurus." Review of *The Autobiography of Alice B. Toklas*, by Gertrude Stein. *The New Republic*, October 11, 1933, 246–47.
"With Bill Hart on Location." *Pictures and Picturegoer*, September 4, 1920, 295.
Woodbridge, Hensley, John London, and George Tweney. *Jack London: A Bibliography.* Georgetown: Talisman Press, 1966.
Woodward, Michael. "That Awful 'IT'!" *Photoplay* (July 1930): 39+.
Wooldridge, Dorothy. "What the Screen Idols Think of the Flapper." *Motion Picture Classic* (August 1927): 20+.
Woolf, Virginia. "The Cinema." 1926. Reprinted in *The Captain's Death Bed and other Essays.* New York: Harcourt, Brace and Company, 1950.
Wylie, Philip. *Generation of Vipers.* New York: Farrar & Rinehart, 1942.
York, Cal. "Gossip of All the Studios." *Photoplay* (October 1929): 46.
Young, Collier, and Ida Lupino. "Why We Made 'The Hitch-Hiker.'" Reprinted by the Roan Group. Included with *The Hitch-Hiker* laser disc, 1997.

Filmography

The Battle of Gettysburg. Charles Giblyn and Thomas Ince, directors. New York Motion Picture Co., 1913.
Beating Back. Caryl S. Fleming, director. Thanhouser, 1913.

Bibliography

The Beloved Cheater. Christy Cabanne, director. Lew Cody Films, 1919.
Beyond the Law. Theodor Marston, director. Emmett Dalton, performer. Southern Feature Film, 1918.
The Bigamist. Ida Lupino, director. Filmakers, 1953.
The Big Knife. Robert Aldrich, director. United Artists, 1951.
Billy the Kid. King Vidor, director. MGM, 1930.
Double Indemnity. Billy Wilder, director. Paramount, 1944.
Get Your Man. Dorothy Arzner, director. Clara Bow, performer. Paramount, 1927. Only an incomplete print survives at the Library of Congress.
The Great Train Robbery. Edwin S. Porter, director. Edison Manufacturing Company, 1903.
Hard, Fast and Beautiful. Ida Lupino, director. Filmakers/RKO, 1951.
The Hard Way. Vincent Sherman, director. Warner Bros., 1942.
Heat (a.k.a. *Andy Warhol's Heat*). Paul Morrissey, director. Filmfactory, 1972.
The Hitch-Hiker. Ida Lupino, director. Filmakers/RKO, 1953.
Hula. Victor Fleming, director. Clara Bow, performer. Paramount, 1927.
It. Clarence Badger, director. Clara Bow, performer. Paramount, 1927.
Jack London's Adventures in the South Sea Islands. A. H. Woods, presenter. Martin Johnson, camera. 1913.
The Lady of the Dugout. W.S. Van Dyke, director. Al Jennings Production, Co., 1918.
The Last Stand of the Dalton Boys. Jack Kenyon, director. Atlas Manufacturing Co., 1912.
The Life of Buffalo Bill. Paul Panzer, director. Pawnee Bill Film Co., 1912.
The Life of General Villa. Raoul Walsh, director. Mutual Film Corporation, 1914.
Martin Eden. Hobart Bosworth, director. Bosworth, Inc., 1917.
Mildred Pierce. Michael Curtiz, director. Warner Bros., 1945.
Never Fear. Ida Lupino, director. Filmakers, 1950.
Not Wanted. Ida Lupino, director. Elmer Clifton, credited director. Emerald, 1949.
The Passing of the Oklahoma Outlaw. Eagle Film Company, 1915.
The Plastic Age. Wesley Ruggles, director. Clara Bow, performer. Preferred Pictures, 1925.
Queen Christina. Rouben Mamoulian, director. Greta Garbo, performer. MGM, 1933.
Quo Vadis? Enrico Guazzoni, director. Cines, 1913.
Red Hair. Clarence Badger, director. Clara Bow, performer. Paramount, 1928. No complete print survives.
The Sea Wolf. Hobart Bosworth, director. Bosworth Inc., 1913.
Top Hat. Mark Sandrich, director. RKO, 1935.
Trash (a.k.a. *Andy Warhol's Trash*). Paul Morrissey, director. Filmfactory, 1970.
Tumbleweeds. King Baggot, director. William S. Hart, performer. William S. Hart Productions, 1925.
Whatever Happened to Baby Jane? Robert Aldrich, director. Warner Bros., 1962.

Wild Bill Hickok. Clifford Smith, director. William S. Hart, performer. Famous Players–Lasky, 1923.
Wings. William Wellman, director. Clara Bow, performer. Paramount, 1927.

Index

Page numbers in *italics* represent illustrations.

actuality, 45, 65, 217n
adaptation: and Gertrude Stein, 14, 138, 148–50, 160–69; and Jack London, 74–98
Adorno, Theodor, 10, 135
advertisements: and celebrity, 21–22, *24*, *76*, 76–79; and copyright infringement, 85; fan magazines, *105*, 105–9, 125; and film spectatorship, 113–15; and Gertrude Stein, 151, 165; and *It*, 120–21; and Westerns, 45–46
Aldrich, Robert, 176
Anderson, Robert, 42
Anderson, Sherwood, 138, 145
Arbuckle, Roscoe "Fatty," 103, 132
Arzner, Dorothy, 123, 172, 235–36n
Astaire, Fred, 147
Atlantic Monthly, 139
Auerbach, Jonathan, 66–67, 72–73, 83
authenticity: and authors, 65, 78–83; and boxing films, 41; and filmmaking, 13, 34; and the West, 38, 43–45, 47–49, 53
Author's League of America, 60, 84–85
authorship: and audience, 136–37, 164–65; and celebrity, 25, 70–71, 78–84, 137–40, 144–48, 150–53, 163–64; and the marketplace, 22, 66–67, 72–77, 86–88, 139–40, 142–43; and the motion picture industry, 88–98, 137–38, 143; and photography, 63. See also literary marketplace
autobiography: cinematic, 13, 62, 73; literary, 58
Autobiography of Alice B. Toklas, The (Stein), 55, 138–39, 142–43, 145, 149–51, 154–55, 161–62, 164–68
autographs, 27, *59*, 72, 75, 77–80, *80*, 219n
Ayres, Sidney, 63

Badger, Clarence, 101, 224n
Balboa Amusement Company, 63, 74–75, 84–85, 221n
Balio, Tino, 233n
Bancroft, George, 134
Banky, Vilma, 112
Barker, Donald, 86
Basinger, Jeanine, 108, 112, 128, 237n
Bazin, Andre, 42–43
Belfrage, Cedric, 129
Bell, Rex, 99
Benjamin, Walter: aura, 77; mechanical reproduction, 18, 21, 46
Beyond the Law, 44–46
Biery, Ruth, 127, 129
Big Knife, The, 176
Bigamist, The (Lupino), 15, 173, 179–91, 194, 237n
Biograph, 89
Birchard, Robert, 66
Bisch, Louis E., 102, 111
Blumer, Herbert, 111, 225n
Boorstin, Daniel, 17, 20, 100
Bosworth, Hobart, 67, 68–70, 74–88
Bow, Clara: background, 127; *Call Her Savage*, 135; and the downside of fame, 99, 117, 134–35; and fan magazines, 104–6, 118, 125–33, 175; and fans, 109–11, 128, 130, 223n; *Get Your Man*, 123; going to Hollywood, 1, 4, 14–15, 170; as Hollywood "insider," 5–6; *Hoopla*, 102, 135; *Hula*, 123, 132; images of, *103*, *107*; *The Plastic Age*, 130–31; *Red Hair*, 223–24n; and scandal, 126–35, 224n; sexuality, 129–30; as a star, 30, 102–35, 163; *Wings*, 133. See also *It*
Bowser, Eileen, 35, 38, 93
boxing, 35, 39–42, 45, 49–50
Braudy, Leo, 4, 17–18, 23, 62

Breakenridge, William, 58
Breen Office, 182, 195–96
Brewster Publications, 14, 100, 104
Bridgman, Richard, 140
Britton, Andrew, 9
Brown, Beth, 111–12
Brownlow, Kevin, 55
Buffalo Bill's Wild West, 36–39, 55. *See also* Cody, Buffalo Bill
Burns, Walter Noble, 57
Bush, W. Stephen, 68–69

Caramello, Charles, 157
Celebrities Monthly, 20–22, 101
celebrity: culture, 3, 5, 7, 204, 207–8; Hollywood's impact on, 8, 12, 15, 18, 29–30, 144, 231n; literary, 14, 25, 70–88, 137–40, 144–48, 150–53, 163–64, 231n; in the 1920s, 14; in relation to "hero," 20; and reputation, 9, 29, 131; and scandal, 126–35, 224n; studies, 3, 5–6
Cerf, Bennett, 162
Chaplin, Charlie, 1, 141, 214n
Chaput, Don, 213n
Clarke, Robert, 189
Clifton, Elmer, 177
Close-Up, 137
Clum, John P., 35
Cody, Buffalo Bill (William F.), 34–39, 42, 47, 55, 215n, 217n. *See also* Buffalo Bill's Wild West
Cohn, Harry, 177
Colliers, 171
Columbia Studios, 177
consumer culture: and Hollywood, 14, 102, 104–11, 225n; and image, 22; and *It*, 113–17; 119–21, 124–26
Cook, David, 233n
copyright, 54, 57, 60–61, 78–88
Corbett-Fitzsimmons fight, 39–41, 45, 50
Cosmopolitan, 88, 110, 112, 118, 123
Crawford, Joan, 224n, 237n
Curtiz, Michael, 237n

Dallesandro, Joe, 206
Dalton, Emmett, 34, 40, 44–46, 50, 58, 83, 205
Daly, Nicholas, 109, 114–15, 121
Davidson, Jo, 163

Davis, Bette, 171
deCordova, Richard, 26–28, 111
Detour, 196
Dixon, Wheeler Winston, 193
Donati, William, 171, 179, 235–36n
Double Indemnity, 181
Dozoretz, Wendy, 188, 190, 193, 237–38n
Dreiser, Theodore, 19–20
Dwan, Allan, 55
Dyer, Richard, 126

Earp, Josephine, 54, 60
Earp, Wyatt: and autographs, 59, 219n; and biography, 33; as boxing referee, 35, 39; and copyright, 57–58, 60, 86, 218–19n; and failure, 36; and film ideas, 42–43, 47, 58, 61, 73; and the Fitzsimmons-Corbett fight, 40–41; going to Hollywood, 1, 4, 11, 13, 33–39, 99, 163, 170; and historical inaccuracy, 37, 39, 55–57, 213–14n; as Hollywood "outsider," 5–6, 30; and Jack London, 31–34; as movie consultant, 35; and O.K. Corral, 31–35, 39–40, 42, 47, 215n; and William S. Hart, 33, 39, 42, 44, 47–52, 54–59, 59, 147
Eckert, Charles, 102
Edison, Thomas, 21, 37, 216n
Ehrman, Lillian, 141–42, 160–61
Einstein, Albert, 152
Emerson, John, 141
Essanay, 35, 72
Everybody's Autobiography (Stein), 14, 142, 147, 151–53, 158, 164
Ewing, Max, 144

fame: Hollywood's impact on, 4, 8, 14, 205; and technology, 22–23, 140–41. *See also* celebrity
fan magazines: and consumer culture, 109–11, 121; contests, 100, 104–6, 108, 118, 207; discourse of, 107; and Hollywood lifestyle, 50, 108, 148; nature of, 100–101, 111–12, 124–25, 228–29n; and stars, 14, 22, 26, 128–35
fan mail, 30, 106, 109–11, 128, 130, 134, 223n
Fass, Paula, 119
Faulkner, William, 163
Fay, Bernard, 151

Filmakers, The, 177–79, 236n
Fine, Gary Alan, 9, 29, 101, 210n
Fitzgerald, F. Scott, 163
Fitzsimmons-Sharkey, 35
flashback, 93–95
Fleming, Victor, 123, 132, 228n
Flood, John, 42, 53
Fontaine, Joan, 180–81
Ford, Harrison, 127
Ford, John, 194
Forrest, Sally, 188
Fox Studios, *24*, 24–25, 206
Frankenstein (Mary Shelley), 202
Friedan, Betty, 174
Friedberg, Anne, 137, 139
Fuller, Kathryn, 106, 224n

Gaines, Jane, 224n
Garbo, Greta, 144–45, 162–63, 168
Garbutt, Frank, 74–75, 84–87
Gish, Lillian, 162
Glass, Loren, 67, 72
Glyn, Elinor, 110, 112, 123, 126, 226n
Goddard, Charles, 88–96, 222n
Great Train Robbery, The, 37, 83
Gunning, Tom, 27, 46, 93
Gwenn, Edmund, 181

Hall, Gladys, 183
Hall, Leonard, 128
Hammett, Dashiell, 141–42
Hammond, John Hays, 55
Hansen, Miriam, 113
Hard, Fast and Beautiful (Lupino), 179, 188–195
Hart, William S.: and authenticity, 49–50, *51*; correspondence with Earp, 39; and Earp's Hollywood plans, 42, 48–51, *51*, 54, 61; friendship with Earp, 33, 44, 47–48, 58, *59*; and Gertrude Stein, 147, 232n
Hays Office, 156, 189
H.D., 137
Hearst, William Randolph, 97
Hearts of Three (London), 14, 47, 85–86, 88–97, 222n
Heat, Andy Warhol's, 206–7
Hemingway, Ernest, 138, 155
Hepburn, Katharine, 9

Hickok, Wild Bill, 34, 54
Hitchcock, Alfred, 194
Hitch-Hiker, The (Lupino), 179, 195–203
Hollywood: and American culture, 12; and authors, 90–91, 137, 221n; as celebrity capital, 2–3, 8, 15, 25, 29–30, 134, 145, 149; and consumer culture, 13–14, 110, 148; decline of, 16, 204–5; as destination, 4–5, 9; and distribution, 23; history, 4, 6, 14, 25, 34, 69–70, 84, 100, 126, 140, 156, 176, 208, 233n; impact on America, 11–12, 163, 170, 208; and literature, 25, 88–98; and mythology, 3, 11, 34; and publicity, 15, 23, 26; and scandal, 126, 130, 132; and star system, 14, 143; and success, 2, 12, 148, 170; and Western figures, 35–36, 44–48, 217n; and women, 109–10, 170–75, *175*, 179, 180
Hollywood Citizen-News, 173
Hopper, Hedda, 176–77
Horkheimer, H. M., 63, 86
Horkheimer, Max, 9–10, 135
Hutton, Paul, 34, 42

identification, 110–111
It (Badger): Adela Van Norman, 120; and class, 117–18, 120–23; and consumer culture, 101, *114*, *121*; and the gaze, 116–23, 133; Molly, 123–24; Monty, 118–20, 122; press kit, 116–17, *117*; and spectatorship, 119–21; as star vehicle, 14; 111–25; Waltham *113*, 113–25

James, David, 205–6
James, Jesse, 34
Jarvis, Paul, 133
Jennings, Al, 40, 44, 48, 50, 52, 217n
Jenson, Joli, 104
Johnson, Martin, 63–65, 83, 219–20n

Kahn, Ivan, 160–61, 234n
Kalem, 72, 89
Kasson, Joy, 36–37, 217n
Kerr, Catherine, 213n
Kershaw, Alex, 88
Kingman, Russ, 222n
Kirby, Lynn, 225n
Knight, Alan, 154
Koszarski, Richard, 238n

Ladies Home Journal, 110
Lake, Stuart, 39, 42, 58–60, 218n
Landay, Lori, 226–27n
Lang, Gladys, and Kurt, 29
Lang, Harry, 133
Last Stand of the Dalton Boys, 45–46
Latimer, George Horace, 52–53
Leach, William, 120–21
Leff, Leonard, 231
Lindsay, Vachel, 25, 68
Literary Digest, 147
literary marketplace 13, 25, 67, 88–98, 138, 163–64, 221n
London, Charmian, 64, 214n, 220n, 222n
London, Jack: and authenticity, 44, 65; and boxing, 49, 215n; *The Call of the Wild*, 32, 94; as a celebrity, 64, 70–72, 75–79, 143; and copyright, 54, 57, 60, 84–88; correspondence, 61, 214n; on film, 75, *80, 82, 83*; going to Hollywood, 4, 33, 168, 170, 219n; as Hollywood "outsider," 5–6; images of, *71, 76, 79–84*; *Jack London: A Sketch of His Life and Work with Portrait*, 70–71; *Jack London's Adventures in the South Sea Islands*, 63–66; *John Barleycorn*, 76, 78, 88; and the literary marketplace, 66–67, 72, 86–88, 97–98, 138, 167, 205; *Little Lady of the Big House*, 97; *Martin Eden*, 78–84, 95–96, 220n; "The Message of Motion Pictures," 68; and the motion picture industry, 13, 30, 45–46, 62–67, 73–88, 149; movie contracts, 1, 63; on movies, 25, 68–69; *A Piece of Steak*, 85; *The Sea Wolf* (motion picture), 74–75, 78–79, 86–87, 221n; *The Sea-Wolf* (novel), 94–95; and the *Snark*, 63–65, 219–20n; on writing, 68; writing for the screen, 88–97; and Wyatt Earp, 31–34. See also *Hearts of Three*
Loos, Anita, 141
Los Angeles Times, 53–54, 75, 158–59
Lovejoy, Frank, 196
Lubin, Sigmund, 41
Luhr, William, 218n
Lundell, William, 147–48
Lupino, Ida: and directing, 15, 30, 170, *175*, 177–79, 189, 193, 196, 199–203, 238n; and family, 178–79, 182–83, 192; and gender roles, 177–81, 184–88, 191, 194, 195, 201–3; going to Hollywood, 1, 4, 15; as Hollywood "insider," 5–6; *Never Fear*, 177; *Not Wanted*, 177, 194; and Production Code, 182, 195–96; and reputation, 8; as a star, 170–71, 176–78, 180, 235n, 237n. See also *The Bigamist*; *Hard, Fast and Beautiful*; *The Hitch-Hiker*

McBride, Henry, 145, 150
McLean, Adrienne, 126
McQuade, James, 43–44, 52
Mamoulian, Rouben, 144
masculinity, 31, 36, 56, 173–74, 218n
mass media, 17
Masterson, Bat, 49, 52
Matisse, Henri, 138, 155, 159
Matthews, T. S., 150
May, Elaine, 227n
Mellow, James, 139, 155
Merck, Mandy, 189–90, 238n
Meyerowitz, Joanne, 174
Mildred Pierce, 237
Mix, Tom, 33, 44–45
modernism, 30, 137–38, 143, 159
Morey, Anne, 228n
Morrissey, Paul, 205–6
Moskin, J. Robert, 173–74, 180, 182, 197, 203
Motion Picture, 104, 109, 127, 171
Motion Picture Classic, *51*, 129–30
Motion Picture Patents Company, 84
Motion Picture Story, 102
Motion Picture World, 44
Movie Classic, 102
Moving Picture Story Magazine, 26
Moving Picture World, 27, 45–46, 48, 68–69, 79, 85
Mulvey, Laura, 115
Murphet, Julian, 234n
Musser, Charles, 35, 41, 93
myth: and Hollywood, 5, 13, 34; and the West, 36, 53

New Movie Magazine, 135
New Republic, The, 150
New Women, 106, 108–12, 115–17, 119, 123–24, 126–27
New York Herald Tribune, 145

Index 259

New York Telegraph, 26
New York World, 40
newsreels, 23, 158
Norris, Frank, 37–38, 47

O'Brien, Edmond, 180, 196
O'Hara, Kenneth, 158
Ohmann, Richard, 17, 23, 119, 225n

Palance, Jack, 176
Paramount, 100, 103, 125, 134–135, *135*, 171
Park, Ida May, 171
Parker, Francine, 194, 238n
Parsons, George, 38
Parsons, Louella, 228n
Patterson, Kenneth, 188
Payne Fund, 156, 225n
Perelman, Bob, 139
photography: and autographs, *59*; and copyright, 54, 58–61; and famous authors, 63, *71*; and a new image culture, 18, 20–23
Photoplay, 28, 99, *103*, 109, 128–29, 131, 133
Picabia, Francis, 163
Picasso, Pablo, 138, 155, 159–60, 163
Pickford, Mary, 1, 151–52
Picturegoer, 171
Pingenot, Ben, 217n
Ponce de Leon, Charles, 4, 18, 61, 104
Production Code, 156, 195, 236n
publicity: and America, 148; emergence of, 18, 23; and Hollywood, 15, 26–27, 100; and literature, 150; and theater, 19, 23

Quart, Barbara, 235n
Queen Christina, 144
Quirk, James, 2, 106

Rabinowitz, Lauren, 196–97
realism, 44, 48–55, 74, 217n
renown, *See* fame
reputation: in America, 8–9; and celebrity, 9, 29–30, 99–100, 126–35; and fan magazines, 108; in Hollywood, 28, 157; and the motion picture industry, 12, 14, 81–88, 179; revising, 16, 170–71; and success, 10, 210n; value of, 19, 29, 97; and Western figures, 46
Richman, Harry, 129

Rockefeller, John, 18
Rodden, John, 8
Rogers, Ginger, 147
Rogers, W. G., 136, 142, 148, 168
Ryan, Mary, 225n, 227n

St. Johns, Adela Rogers, 61, 223n
Salt, Barry, 227n
Sandage, Scott, 28
Saturday Evening Post, 52
Scanland, J. M., 56–57
Schulberg, B. P., 134
Seiter, Ellen, 184, 237n
Selig, 35, 93
Selznick, David O., 134
serials, 89
sexuality: and the Breen Office, 182; and Clara Bow, 129–35; in *It*, 115–25
Shelley, Mary, 202
simulation: filmmakers and, 34; and the West, 38, 52–53
Siringo, Charles, 34, 44, 47, 217n
Sister Carrie, 19–20
Sisson, Edward Grant, 88, 97
Sklar, Robert, 12, 101
Slotkin, Richard
Spain, Mildred, 129
Staiger, Janet, 107
Stamp, Shelley, 225n
Starr, Kevin, 25, 143
star studies, 3, 5–6
stars: circulation of, 2, 14, 26, 99–136; history of, 17, 27–29, 233n; logic of, 118, 124–25; press representation of, 128
Steiger, Rod, 176
Stein, Gertrude: in America, 138, 140, 145–46, *146*, 151–61, 165–66; on being in the movies, 55, 158; and celebrity, 16, 137, 138–40, 143–48, 149, 151, 166; and *Close-Up*, 137; correspondence, 61; "Deux Soeurs Qui Ne Sont Pas Soeurs," 168; failure in Hollywood, 34, 136; *Four Saints in Three Acts*, 136; going to Hollywood, 1, 4, 11, 14, 159–70; as Hollywood "outsider," 5–6, 30; interest in Hollywood, 138, 151, 153, 161–62, 165–69; *Lectures in America*, 14, 153–56, 164; *The Making of Americans*, 139, 156; on motion pictures, 140–41, 154–56,

Stein, Gertrude *(continued)* 159–60, 168, 232n; "A Movie," 153–54; "Photograph," 154; "Pigeons on the Grass," 158; and publicity, 150; self-promotion, 157, 167; success, 138–39, 142–43, 150–51, 165, 169; *Three Lives*, 139, 160, 165, 167; *The World is Round*, 149, 167; as a writer, 145, 147, 160, 234n; "Yes Is For a Very Young Man," 149. See also *The Autobiography of Alice B. Toklas*; *Everybody's Autobiography*
Stenn, David, 126–27, 223n
Steward, Samuel, 148–49
Studlar, Gaylyn, 228n
success: and Hollywood, 2, 10, 12, 14, 28, 141, 144, 231n; and literature, 66, 70–72, 139–40, 142–43
Swanson, Gloria, 112

Talman, William, 196
Tefertiller, Casey, 58
television, 205
theater: relation to motion picture industry, 17, 23, 44, 69–70, 72; and *Sister Carrie*, 19
Tilghman, William, 217n
Time, 136, 143, 147, 163, 168
Toklas, Alice B., 138–39, 141, 145–46, *146*, 148, 160, 164, 166
Tomkins, Jane, 36
Top Hat, 147
Trevor, Claire, 188

Van Vechten, Carl, 141, 144, 157–58, 160–67
Variety, 35, 93
vaudeville, 17
Villa, Pancho, 31–32
Vonnel, Carl, 129

Walker, Alexander, 124–25
Walsh, Raoul, 31–33, 214n
Warhol, Andy, 16, 204–7
Warner, Jack, 171
Warner Bros.: and Gertrude Stein, 1, 141; and Ida Lupino, 171, 176–77
Weber, Louis, 171
Wellman, William, 133
Westerns, 30, 36–38, 42–55, 65, 75
Whatever Happened to Baby Jane?, 176
Wild West, 12, 16, 33
Wilder, Thornton, 138, 144, 161–65, 169
Will, Barbara, 231
Williams, Raymond, 22
Williams, Tony, 66, 84, 219n
Wilson, Christopher, 97
Wilson, Edmund, 151
Wilson, Mary Jane, 171
Woolf, Virginia, 232n
Wylie, Philip, 173, 180, 236n

Young, Carleton, 188
Young, Collier, 177, 181, 194–95
YouTube.com, 207

Zanuck, Daryl, 177